CATHOLIC BIBLE IN 52 WEEKS FOR WOMEN

Daily Scripture Studies to Grow your Faith

Kristi k. Miller

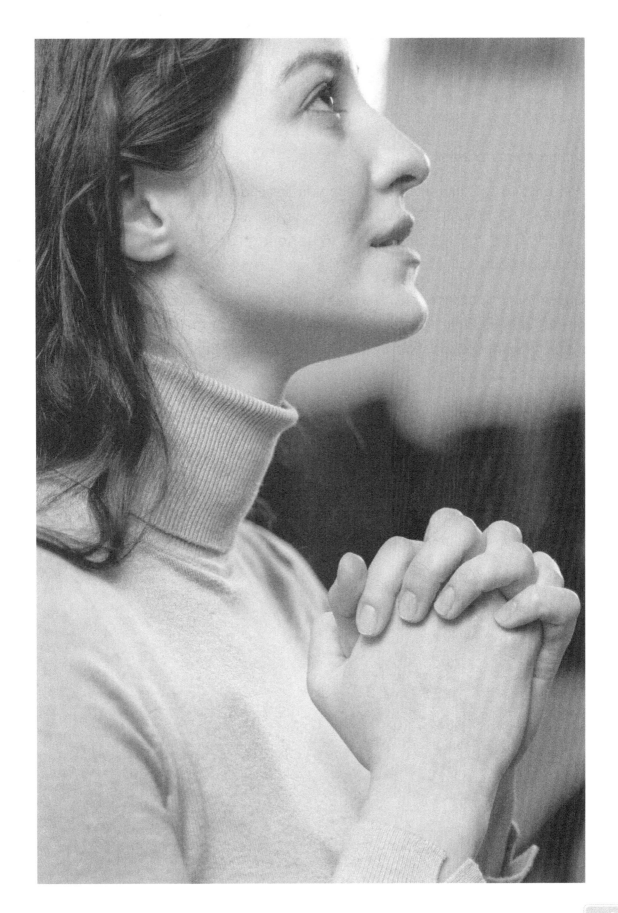

THANK YOU

Dear Sisters in Christ,

Welcome to this journey! And thank you for choosing this book, "**CATHOLIC BIBLE IN 52 WEEKS FOR WOMEN**," signifying a bold step in deepening your Catholic faith. You've entrusted me, to be your guide, and I'm honored to walk alongside you.

This isn't just another book; it's a bridge. It's designed to lead you (as a member of the Catholic Church) to a deeper understanding of the Catholic Bible and a more fulfilling participation in the Catholic Church. Imagine it as a year-long exploration of scripture, crafted specifically for women like you.

As it finds a place on your nightstand or graces your family table, knowing this book is part of your spiritual journey brings me immense joy. Witnessing your growth in faith is a privilege I cherish.

Prepare to be challenged, inspired, and strengthened. May "**CATHOLIC BIBLE IN 52 WEEKS FOR WOMEN**" become a source of unwavering faith, knowledge, peace, and inspiration as you walk closer to Christ.

With warmest regards,

Kristi k. Miller

ABOUT THE AUTHOUR

Kristi k. Miller is a passionate advocate for empowering men and women to explore and deepen their Catholic faith. Driven by a desire to make scripture accessible and engaging, she crafted "**CATHOLIC BIBLE IN 52 WEEKS FOR WOMEN**" as a bridge between women and a richer understanding of the Church and its teachings.

Her dedication extends beyond mere words. She has poured her experience and knowledge into creating a practical, year-long guide specifically tailored to the lives and interests of Catholic women.

When Maria isn't engrossed in the world of scripture, she finds inspiration in spending time with family, or volunteering in the community. Her faith is a cornerstone of her life, and she is excited to share its transformative power with readers through this book.

CONTENT

BONUS FEATURES: DEEPEN YOUR FAITH JOURNEY **349**

INTRODUCTION: Faithfully Fierce

Welcome, Sisters in Christ! Have you ever felt the call to be more than ordinary? To embrace your faith with a strength and passion that sets you ablaze? This book, **"CATHOLIC BIBLE IN 52 WEEKS FOR WOMEN,"** is your invitation to embark on a transformative journey of exploration, reflection, and growth.

Faithful and Fierce: A Woman Defined

The world often portrays women as one-dimensional figures. We're the nurturing mothers, the supportive wives, the gentle caregivers. But within the pages of Scripture and throughout history, Catholic women have shattered these limitations. We are the fierce protectors of our faith, the courageous leaders who changed the Book of history, the scholars and mystics who deepened our understanding of God.

Faithful and Fierce embodies this powerful duality. It's about clinging resolutely to the teachings of Christ while simultaneously embracing the strength, courage, and fire that reside within each of us. It's about being a woman who doesn't shy away from her faith, who uses her voice to defend what she believes in, and who lives her life as a radiant testament to God's love.

The Power of Women in the Bible: Our Ancestral Legacy

The Bible isn't silent on the incredible women who walked alongside Jesus, challenged societal norms, and left an indelible mark on the faith. From the unwavering loyalty of Ruth to the courageous leadership of Esther, from the insightful wisdom of Proverbs 31 to the unwavering faith of Mary Magdalene, scripture is brimming with stories that showcase the power and diversity of Catholic women.

This book delves into these inspiring narratives, drawing parallels between the challenges faced by these women and the realities of our own lives. We'll discover how their unwavering faith, unwavering courage, and unwavering love for God can serve as a source of strength and inspiration for us today.

How to Use This Book: Cultivating a Personal and Communal Journey

Whether you're a seasoned Bible scholar or just embarking on your faith journey, **"CATHOLIC BIBLE IN 52 WEEKS FOR WOMEN"** is designed to be an enriching experience for all. This Inspiring Bible Study guide combines a daily Bible reading plan and reflection with weekly lesson, discussion, and activity that will help strengthen your catholic faith and apply scriptural wisdom in your daily life.

Individual Exploration:

- **Weekly lessons:** Each week consist of activities, journaling prompts and action steps to help you internalize the week's lessons and integrate them into your daily life.

- **Deeper Dives:** We'll provide suggestions for further exploration, including relevant scripture passages, recommended reading materials, and online resources.

> **Group Discussion:**
>
> This book is also a fantastic resource for group Bible studies. The discussion starters and challenges at the end of each week lesson provide a springboard for lively and enriching conversations with fellow Catholic women.

Creating a Faith-Filled Space: Your Sacred Corner

Imagine a haven within your home, a space dedicated to fostering your connection with God. This could be a quiet corner bathed in natural light, a cozy nook adorned with religious imagery, or a simple table adorned with a crucifix and your favorite Bible.

Here are some tips for creating your faith-filled space:

- **Curate the Atmosphere:** Surround yourself with inspiring elements - a crucifix, religious artwork, candles, or a rosary.

- **Personalize it:** Add objects that hold special meaning for you, such as a family heirloom, a meaningful quote, or a journal filled with prayers.

- **Invite Comfort:** Ensure the space is comfortable and inviting, with a chair or cushion for reflection and prayer.

- **Banish Distractions:** Choose a quiet location away from the hustle and bustle of everyday life.

This sacred space will become your personal sanctuary, a place to connect with God through prayer, reflection, and Bible study.

We invite you, dear sisters, to embark on this 52-week journey with open hearts and curious minds. Let's explore the rich Journey of scripture, celebrate the legacy of powerful Catholic women, and ignite the faithful and fierce spirit within each of us.

Part 1: Rooted in Faith

(Weeks 1-13)

Theme: Building a Strong Foundation in Scripture

WEEK 1: Creation and the Dignity of Woman

Welcome, Faithful and Fierce Women!

We begin our exploration of the Bible with the very foundation of our faith: the story of Creation. As we delve into Genesis 1-2, we encounter a powerful message about God's love, purpose, and the inherent dignity bestowed upon all creation, especially women.

God, the Master Creator:

The opening verses of Genesis paint a majestic picture. God, the divine architect, speaks creation into existence. Each day, order emerges from chaos as light separates from darkness, land rises from water, and the heavens are filled with celestial bodies. This creation narrative isn't merely a scientific account; it's a theological statement about God's power, wisdom, and artistry.

The Creation of Humanity - A Shared Calling:

On the sixth day, God declares, "Let us make man in our image, after our likeness" (Genesis 1:26). This verse is significant. God doesn't create humanity in isolation. He uses the plural pronoun "us," hinting at a divine council or the multifaceted nature of God Himself. Furthermore, humanity is created "in God's image and likeness." This doesn't imply a physical resemblance but a reflection of God's characteristics - love, creativity, reason, and dominion.

The Arrival of Woman - Completing the Picture:

Genesis 1:27 emphasizes the equal creation of man and woman: "So God created man in his own image, in the image of God he created him; male and female he created them." Woman isn't an afterthought; she's an integral part of God's plan. Together, man and woman are entrusted with dominion over creation, tasked with cultivating, caring for, and stewarding the wonders God has brought forth.

Genesis 2: A Deeper Look at Woman's Creation:

Chapter 2 offers additional details about woman's creation. Here, God fashions woman from the rib of man, not as a lesser being, but as a companion and equal helper (Genesis 2:18). The Hebrew word for "helper" (ezer) carries connotations of strength, support, and partnership. Woman isn't created to be subordinate; she's created to walk alongside man, complementing him and fulfilling God's purposes together.

The Action Step: Reflecting Your God-Given Gifts

This week's creation story highlights the inherent dignity and worth of women. We are created in God's image, entrusted with a vital role in the world, and called to be partners in God's unfolding plan.

Now it's your turn to reflect!

1. **Journaling Prompt:** Reread Genesis 1:26-28 and Genesis 2:18. What aspects of these passages speak to you about the dignity and purpose of women?

2. **Identifying Your Gifts:** Take some time to reflect on your unique talents and skills. These can be artistic talents, leadership abilities, intellectual strengths, or acts of service.

3. **Connecting Your Gifts:** How do your God-given gifts contribute to the world around you? Do you use them to nurture your family, inspire others, solve problems, or create beauty?

4. **Sharing Your Gifts:** Consider ways you can further utilize your gifts to make a positive impact. Perhaps you can volunteer your skills, mentor younger women, or use your talents to glorify God.

Discussion Starter (For Group Bible Study):

- Share with the group one of your talents or gifts. How do you see this gift as a reflection of God's creativity in your life?

- How can we, as Catholic women, support and empower each other to utilize our unique gifts in service to God and our communities?

Remember, dear sisters, you are fearfully and wonderfully made (Psalm 139:14). Embrace your God-given gifts and let them shine brightly in the world. You are an essential part of God's creation story, and He has a unique purpose for you.

With our weekly lesson completed, get ready to begin an incredible adventure! We'll be spending the next 52 weeks delving into the entire Catholic Bible, one day at a time. Starting from week one, we'll explore and reflect on each passage, gaining a deeper understanding of the Catholic faith.

BIBLE READING: Week 1

To get the most out of our study and enhance our shared reflection, consider bringing a pen and notebook to jot down key points, thoughts, questions and lessons that resonate with you for further reflection during our study of the Catholic Bible.

Day 1: 1 John 1:1-3:10 Psalm 1 Matthew 1:1-17

1 John 1:1-3:10

Reflection: In these verses, John emphasizes the importance of fellowship with God and walking in the light. Reflect on a moment when you felt closest to God. What were the circumstances? How did that experience shape your understanding of your relationship with Him?

Psalm 1

Reflection: Psalm 1 contrasts the ways of the righteous and the wicked. Consider the influences in your life. Are they guiding you towards righteousness or leading you astray? How can you ensure that you're rooted in God's Word, like a tree planted by streams of water?

Matthew 1:1-17

Reflection: The genealogy of Jesus in Matthew 1 highlights God's faithfulness throughout history. Reflect on your own family history. How do you see God's hand at work in the generations that came before you? How might your family's story shape your understanding of God's plans and purposes for your life?

Day 2: 1 Jn 3:11-5:21 Ps 2 Mt 1:18-25

1 John 3:11-5:21

Reflection: John emphasizes love for one another as a sign of being born of God. Reflect on a time when you experienced the transformative power of love, either in giving or receiving it. How did that experience deepen your understanding of God's love for you and others?

Psalm 2

Reflection: Psalm 2 speaks of the sovereignty of God amidst earthly powers. Reflect on a time when you felt overwhelmed by the chaos or challenges of the world. How did meditating on God's sovereignty bring you peace or perspective in that situation?

Matthew 1:18-25

Reflection: The birth of Jesus fulfills Old Testament prophecy and demonstrates God's faithfulness to His promises. Reflect on a promise of God that you're holding onto in your life right now. How does the story of Jesus' birth encourage you to trust in God's faithfulness to fulfill His promises?

Day 3: Genesis 1-3 Ps 3 Mt 2:1-12

Genesis 1-3

Reflection: The creation story in Genesis reveals God's power, wisdom, and intentionality in forming the world and humanity. Reflect on the beauty and complexity of nature around you. How does observing God's creation inspire awe and deepen your appreciation for His character?

Psalm 3

Reflection: Psalm 3 expresses trust in God's protection amidst adversity. Reflect on a time when you faced a challenge or trial. How did relying on God's strength and promises sustain you through that difficult season?

Matthew 2:1-12

Reflection: The visit of the Magi to Jesus highlights the universal significance of Christ's birth. Reflect on the different responses to Jesus in this passage, from Herod's fear to the Magi's worship. How does this story challenge you to respond to Jesus in your own life?

Day 4: Gn 4-5 Ps 4 Mt 2:13-23

Genesis 4-5

Reflection: The stories of Cain and Abel, as well as the genealogy of Adam, highlight the consequences of sin and the frailty of human life. Reflect on a time when you witnessed the destructive power of sin in your own life or in the world around you. How did that experience deepen your awareness of the need for redemption and restoration?

Psalm 4

Reflection: Psalm 4 is a prayer for God's deliverance and guidance. Reflect on a situation in your life where you need God's intervention or direction. How does this psalm inspire you to bring your concerns before God in prayer with trust and confidence?

Matthew 2:13-23

Reflection: The flight to Egypt and Herod's massacre of the infants fulfill Old Testament prophecies about the Messiah. Reflect on the theme of refuge and God's protection in this passage. How does the story of Jesus' escape to Egypt resonate with your own experiences of seeking refuge and safety in God?

Day 5: Gn 6-8 Ps 5 Mt 3

Genesis 6-8

Reflection: The story of Noah's ark and the flood highlights God's judgment on sin and His faithfulness to those who trust in Him. Reflect on a time when you faced a "flood" of challenges or difficulties in your life. How did God sustain you through that season, and what did you learn about His faithfulness?

Psalm 5

Reflection: Psalm 5 is a prayer for God's guidance and protection against enemies. Reflect on the theme of morning prayer and seeking God's direction at the start of each day. How can you incorporate intentional prayer and dependence on God into your daily routine?

Matthew 3

Reflection: John the Baptist prepares the way for Jesus by preaching repentance and baptism. Reflect on the significance of repentance in your own spiritual journey. How does the call to repentance challenge you to examine your heart and turn towards God in areas where you may be drifting away from Him?

Day 6: Gn 9:1-11:26 Ps 6 Mt 4:1-17

Genesis 9:1-11:26

Reflection: The passages cover the covenant God makes with Noah and the story of the Tower of Babel. Reflect on God's faithfulness in keeping His promises despite humanity's propensity for sin. How does the story of Noah and the Tower of Babel illustrate the consequences of human rebellion and the importance of obedience to God's commands?

Psalm 6

Reflection: Psalm 6 is a prayer for mercy and healing in times of distress. Reflect on a season of trial or suffering in your life. How did you experience God's comfort and presence during that time? How does the psalmist's cry for mercy resonate with your own prayers during difficult seasons?

Matthew 4:1-17

Reflection: Jesus' temptation in the wilderness and the beginning of His ministry illustrate His victory over temptation and the fulfillment of Old Testament prophecies. Reflect on a time when you faced temptation or spiritual warfare. How did Jesus' example of reliance on Scripture inspire you to resist temptation and remain faithful to God?

Day 7: Gn 11:27-13:18 Ps 7 Mt 4:18-25

Genesis 11:27-13:18

Reflection: The passages cover the genealogy of Terah, the Tower of Babel, and Abram's journey to Canaan. Reflect on Abram's obedience to God's call to leave his country and family. How does Abram's journey of faith challenge you to trust and obey God's leading in your own life, even when it requires leaving behind the familiar and comfortable?

Psalm 7

Reflection: Psalm 7 is a prayer for deliverance from enemies and vindication from God. Reflect on a time when you felt unjustly accused or persecuted. How did you seek God's justice and vindication in that situation? How does this psalm inspire you to trust in God's righteousness and timing for deliverance?

Matthew 4:18-25

Reflection: Jesus calls His first disciples and begins His ministry of teaching, preaching, and healing. Reflect on the response of Simon Peter, Andrew, James, and John to Jesus' call. How does their immediate obedience challenge you to respond wholeheartedly to Jesus' call to follow Him? What steps can you take to follow Jesus more closely in your own life?

WEEK 2: Women of Strength in the Early Church

Welcome back, Faithful and Fierce women! This week, we turn the pages of the New Testament and delve into the Acts of the Apostles, a thrilling account of the burgeoning Christian Church. While the spotlight often falls on male figures like Peter and Paul, the early Church wouldn't have flourished without the dedication, leadership, and courage of remarkable women.

Beyond the Kitchen: Women on the Move

The prevailing culture of the time relegated women to domestic roles. Yet, the Acts of the Apostles paints a refreshingly different picture. We encounter women actively participating in the life of the early Church, defying societal expectations and leaving an indelible mark on its growth.

Meet the Powerhouse Duo: Priscilla and Aquila

First up, let's explore the dynamic couple of Priscilla and Aquila (Acts 18:1-3). They're introduced as tentmakers, a skilled trade that likely provided financial support for both themselves and the fledgling Church. They also partnered with Paul in spreading the Gospel, even taking the bold step of correcting his understanding of Scripture (Acts 18:26).

Discussion Prompt 1:

Consider the significance of a married couple working together in ministry. How does their partnership challenge traditional gender roles within the Church?

Lydia: From Businesswoman to Pillar of the Church

Next, we meet Lydia, a merchant from Thyatira (Acts 16:11-15). Lydia wasn't just any businesswoman; she was a successful one, likely dealing in expensive fabrics like purple dye. Lydia's open heart and eagerness to learn led her to embrace the Gospel message. She became the first Christian convert in Philippi and generously opened her home to Paul and his companions, establishing the first church in the entire region of Macedonia.

Discussion Prompt 2:

Lydia's story highlights the role of women in hospitality and establishing Christian communities. How can we, as women today, continue this tradition of welcoming others into our homes and faith communities?

Phoebe: A Woman of Service and Leadership

Phoebe, another inspiring woman from Cenchreae, receives a glowing recommendation from Paul in his letter to the Romans (Romans 16:1-2). She's identified as a "deacon" (diakonos) in the Greek, suggesting a leadership role within the Church. Paul entrusts her with delivering his letter to the Roman church, a significant task requiring trust, competence, and courage.

Discussion Prompt 3:

The role of deacon is often debated. How does Phoebe's story challenge traditional understandings of women's leadership roles in the Church?

Beyond These Three: A Journey of Women

These are just a few of the many women who played crucial roles in the early Church. Acts also mentions women like Dorcas, known for her acts of charity (Acts 9:36-42), Mary, the mother of John Mark (Acts 12:12), and the four women who prophesied in the Church at Corinth (Acts 21:9). These women weren't simply passive bystanders; they were active participants, leaders, teachers, and patrons.

Remember:

The stories of these women in Acts are a testament to the power of the Holy Spirit working through all believers, regardless of gender. Their courage, faith, and leadership paved the way for future generations of women to play vital roles in the life of the Church.

Challenge:

Take some time this week to research other women who have made significant contributions to the Church throughout history. Share your findings with the group and discuss the legacy of these women of faith.

With our weekly lesson completed, let's continue our Catholic Bible study and reflection, one passage at a time.

BIBLE READING: Week 2

Day 8: Gn 14-15 Ps 8 Mt 5:1-12

Genesis 14-15

Reflection: These chapters recount Abram's encounter with Melchizedek and God's covenant with Abram. Reflect on God's faithfulness in fulfilling His promises to Abram. How does Abram's trust in God's provision and protection inspire you to trust God's promises in your own life?

Psalm 8

Reflection: Psalm 8 celebrates the majesty and sovereignty of God as displayed in creation. Reflect on a moment when you felt in awe of God's creation. How does contemplating the vastness and intricacy of the universe deepen your appreciation for God's greatness and care for humanity?

Matthew 5:1-12

Reflection: The Beatitudes outline the characteristics of those who are blessed in God's kingdom. Reflect on which of the Beatitudes resonates with you the most at this moment in your life. How can you embody that attitude or virtue more fully as you seek to follow Jesus?

Day 9: Gn 16-17 Ps 9 Mt 5:13-26

Genesis 16-17

Reflection: These chapters detail the birth of Ishmael and God's covenant with Abram, including the institution of circumcision. Reflect on the theme of waiting on God's timing in these passages. How do Abram and Sarai's attempts to fulfill God's promise on their own reflect patterns of impatience or distrust in your own life?

Psalm 9

Reflection: Psalm 9 is a song of praise and thanksgiving for God's justice and protection. Reflect on a time when you experienced God's deliverance or answered prayer. How did that experience deepen your trust in God's faithfulness and righteousness?

Matthew 5:13-26

Reflection: In these verses, Jesus teaches about the importance of salt and light, reconciliation, and the seriousness of anger and lust. Reflect on how you can be a "salt" and "light" in your community, workplace, or family. How can you pursue reconciliation and guard your heart against anger and lust in your relationships?

Day 10: Gn 18-19 Ps 10 Mt 5:27-37

Genesis 18-19

Reflection: These chapters contain the visit of the three visitors to Abraham and the destruction of Sodom and Gomorrah. Reflect on the themes of hospitality, intercession, and judgment in these passages. How do Abraham's actions and intercession for Sodom challenge you to advocate for justice and righteousness in your own community?

Psalm 10

Reflection: Psalm 10 is a lament and prayer for God's justice against the wicked. Reflect on the psalmist's cries for help and deliverance. How does this psalm give voice to your own struggles and questions in the face of injustice or suffering?

Matthew 5:27-37

Reflection: Jesus addresses issues of lust, divorce, and honesty in these verses. Reflect on the high standards of righteousness that Jesus sets for His followers. How can you cultivate purity of heart, faithfulness in relationships, and integrity in your words and actions?

Day 11: Gn 20-21 Ps 11 Mt 5:38-48

Genesis 20-21

Reflection: These chapters recount Abraham's interactions with Abimelech and the birth of Isaac. Reflect on the themes of deception, trust, and God's faithfulness in these passages. How does Abraham's journey of faith include both moments of obedience and failure, yet ultimately reveal God's sovereignty and provision?

Psalm 11

Reflection: Psalm 11 expresses trust in God's righteousness and sovereignty in times of trouble. Reflect on a situation in your life where you faced adversity or opposition. How does the psalmist's confidence in God's protection and justice encourage you to trust in God's provision and guidance?

Matthew 5:38-48

Reflection: Jesus teaches about non-retaliation, love for enemies, and perfection in these verses. Reflect on the radical nature of Jesus' commands to love and forgive those who mistreat us. How can you demonstrate God's love and grace towards others, even when it's challenging or goes against cultural norms?

Day 12: Gn 22 Ps 12 Mt 6:1-18

Genesis 22

Reflection: Genesis 22 records the testing of Abraham's faith through the sacrifice of Isaac. Reflect on the profound obedience and trust demonstrated by Abraham in this passage. How does Abraham's willingness to surrender his most precious possession challenge you to trust God completely, even in the face of uncertainty or sacrifice?

Psalm 12

Reflection: Psalm 12 is a prayer for God's protection and deliverance from deceitful and wicked people. Reflect on the psalmist's plea for God's intervention in the face of injustice and falsehood. How does this psalm resonate with your own prayers for integrity and righteousness in a world filled with deception?

Matthew 6:1-18

Reflection: Jesus teaches about giving, prayer, and fasting in these verses, emphasizing sincerity and humility. Reflect on your own practices of giving, prayer, and fasting. How can you cultivate a deeper intimacy with God and a genuine desire to honor Him in these spiritual disciplines?

Day 13: Gn 23:1-25:18 Ps 13 Mt 6:19-34

Genesis 23:1-25:18

Reflection: These chapters detail Sarah's death, Abraham's purchase of a burial site, and the genealogy of Ishmael and Isaac. Reflect on the theme of legacy and inheritance in these passages. How do the lives of Sarah, Abraham, and their descendants illustrate God's faithfulness in fulfilling His promises across generations?

Psalm 13

Reflection: Psalm 13 expresses lament and trust in God's steadfast love and salvation. Reflect on a time when you felt abandoned or overwhelmed by circumstances. How does the psalmist's journey from despair to hope resonate with your own experiences of trusting in God's faithfulness in difficult times?

Matthew 6:19-34

Reflection: Jesus teaches about storing up treasures in heaven, seeking God's kingdom first, and trusting in God's provision. Reflect on your priorities and concerns in life. How can you shift your focus from earthly worries to seeking God's kingdom and righteousness above all else?

Day 14: Gn 25:19-26:35 Ps 14 Mt 7

Genesis 25:19-26:35

Reflection: These chapters cover the birth of Jacob and Esau, Jacob's acquisition of Esau's birthright and blessing, and Isaac's interaction with Abimelech. Reflect on the themes of family dynamics, sibling rivalry, and God's sovereignty in these passages. How do the complex relationships and decisions of Isaac, Rebekah, Jacob, and Esau reveal God's providential plan unfolding through imperfect human actions?

Psalm 14

Reflection: Psalm 14 describes the folly of those who deny God and the hope of salvation for the righteous. Reflect on the psalmist's observations about human nature and the need for God's intervention. How does this psalm prompt you to examine your own heart and align yourself with God's truth and righteousness?

Matthew 7

Reflection: Jesus teaches about judging others, asking, seeking, and knocking, and the narrow and wide gates in these verses. Reflect on the call to discernment, persistence in prayer, and the importance of entering through the narrow gate of following Jesus. How can you cultivate humility, discernment, and steadfastness in your journey of faith?

WEEK 3: Loyalty, Love, and Redemption for a Woman

Welcome, Faithful and Fierce women! This week, we delve into the beautiful and heartwarming story of Ruth, a Moabite woman who embodies the power of loyalty, love, and unwavering faith. The Book of Ruth, a short gem nestled amongst the historical books of the Old Testament, offers timeless lessons about commitment, resilience, and God's redemptive plan working through unlikely heroes.

A Story of Loss and Loyalty:

The narrative opens with a heartbreaking scene. Naomi, an Israelite woman, faces devastating loss. Her husband and two sons die in a foreign land, Moab. Devastated and alone, Naomi decides to return to her homeland, Bethlehem. Her daughters-in-law, Orpah and Ruth, offer to accompany her.

At this pivotal moment, Ruth's unwavering loyalty shines brightly. While Orpah tearfully bids farewell and returns to her Moabite family, Ruth clings to Naomi with unwavering devotion. She declares, "Where you go I will go, and where you lodge I will lodge. Your people shall be my people, and your God my God" (Ruth 1:16). This powerful verse transcends cultural norms. Ruth chooses a life of faith and commitment over comfort and familiarity.

A Glimmer of Hope: Gleaning in the Fields of Boaz

Ruth accompanies Naomi to Bethlehem, a land unfamiliar and potentially hostile. To survive, they glean leftover grain in the fields during harvest season (Ruth 2:3). Gleaning was a practice that allowed the poor to gather leftover crops after the main harvest. It was an act of both humility and resourcefulness.

Here, Ruth encounters Boaz, a wealthy landowner and relative of Naomi's deceased husband. Boaz is impressed by Ruth's diligence and kindness. He instructs his workers to leave extra grain for her and even offers her protection (Ruth 2:8-16).

Ruth's Initiative and Cunning Plan:

Naomi, recognizing Boaz as a potential kinsman redeemer, hatches a daring plan. According to Mosaic Law, a close male relative had the responsibility to marry a childless widow and ensure the continuation of the family line (Leviticus 25:25-28). Naomi coaches Ruth on how to approach Boaz at the threshing floor, a place where winnowed grain was separated from the chaff.

Following Naomi's instructions, Ruth discreetly positions herself at Boaz's feet after the celebratory meal (Ruth 3:7). Startled but intrigued, Boaz listens attentively as Ruth reveals her situation and respectfully requests that he fulfill his role as kinsman redeemer. Boaz, struck by Ruth's loyalty, humility, and courage, assures her of his intentions (Ruth 3:11).

A Redemptive Ending and a Glimpse of Christ's Lineage

However, there's a closer relative who has a prior claim as redeemer. Boaz cleverly devises a plan. He approaches the closer relative in the presence of witnesses and proposes the redemption. The relative declines due to the burden of acquiring Ruth's Moabite land (Ruth 4:5-6). This paves the way for Boaz to fulfill his role.

Boaz marries Ruth, and they have a son named Obed, who becomes the grandfather of King David, a pivotal figure in the lineage of Jesus Christ. The Book of Ruth ends on a joyous note, celebrating the birth of Obed and the redemption Naomi and Ruth experienced through God's providence (Ruth 4:13-22).

Self-Reflection: The Power of Loyalty and Faithfulness

The story of Ruth is a powerful testament to the importance of loyalty and faithfulness. Ruth's unwavering commitment to Naomi serves as an inspiration to women. Consider the following questions:

- **How do you demonstrate loyalty in your relationships with husband, family and friends?**

- **Have you ever faced a situation where your faith or commitment was challenged? How did you navigate that challenge?**

- **Think about a time when you experienced God's faithfulness in your life, even during difficult times.**

Discussion Starter (For Group Bible Study):

- How does the Book of Ruth challenge traditional societal expectations of women during this time period?

- Discuss the significance of Ruth, a Moabite woman, being included in the lineage of Jesus Christ.

- How can we, as women of faith, cultivate the kind of unwavering loyalty and trust in God that Ruth exemplifies?

Remember, dear sisters, loyalty and faithfulness are not passive qualities. They require courage, commitment, and a willingness to stand by our convictions even when it's difficult. Let the story of Ruth inspire you this week.

Day 15: Gn 27-28 Ps 15 Mt 8:1-17

Genesis 27-28

Reflection: These chapters recount Jacob's deception to receive Isaac's blessing and his dream at Bethel. Reflect on the themes of deceit, blessings, and divine encounters. How does Jacob's journey, including his failures and God's revelation at Bethel, encourage you to seek God's presence and guidance despite your shortcomings?

Psalm 15

Reflection: Psalm 15 describes the character of those who may dwell with God. Reflect on the qualities listed in this psalm. How can you cultivate integrity, righteousness, and honesty in your daily life to live in close fellowship with God?

Matthew 8:1-17

Reflection: Jesus heals a leper, a centurion's servant, and Peter's mother-in-law, demonstrating His authority and compassion. Reflect on Jesus' willingness to heal and restore. How does His compassion for those who are suffering challenge you to extend grace and care to those in need around you?

Day 16: Genesis 46-48; Matthew 12:24-50

Genesis 29-30

Reflection: These chapters cover Jacob's marriages to Leah and Rachel, and the birth of his children. Reflect on the themes of love, rivalry, and God's provision in these family dynamics. How do the complex relationships and God's faithfulness in Jacob's life encourage you to trust in God's plan for your own family and relationships?

Psalm 16

Reflection: Psalm 16 is a psalm of trust and confidence in God. Reflect on the psalmist's declaration of God as his refuge and portion. How can you find contentment and security in God's presence and promises, especially in times of uncertainty?

Matthew 8:18-34

Reflection: Jesus calms a storm and heals two demon-possessed men, demonstrating His authority over nature and evil spirits. Reflect on Jesus' power and authority in your life. How can you deepen your faith in His ability to calm the storms you face and deliver you from spiritual oppression?

Day 17: Gn 31-32 Ps 17 Mt 9:1-17

Genesis 31-32

Reflection: These chapters describe Jacob's departure from Laban and his preparation to meet Esau. Reflect on Jacob's encounters with God and his transformation through these experiences. How do moments of wrestling with God and seeking reconciliation with others shape your own journey of faith?

Psalm 17

Reflection: Psalm 17 is a prayer for protection and vindication. Reflect on the psalmist's confidence in God's justice and righteousness. How does this psalm inspire you to seek God's protection and maintain integrity in the face of opposition or adversity?

Matthew 9:1-17

Reflection: Jesus heals a paralytic, calls Matthew, and discusses fasting with John's disciples. Reflect on the transformative power of Jesus' healing and calling. How can you respond to Jesus' invitation to follow Him and experience His forgiveness and renewal in your life?

Day 18: Gn 33-34 Ps 18 Mt 9:18-38

Genesis 33-34

Reflection: These chapters cover Jacob's reconciliation with Esau and the tragic incident involving Dinah. Reflect on the themes of forgiveness, reconciliation, and justice. How does Jacob's reunion with Esau encourage you to pursue reconciliation in strained relationships, and how does the incident with Dinah highlight the need for justice and protection in your community?

Psalm 18

Reflection: Psalm 18 is a song of thanksgiving for God's deliverance and victory. Reflect on a time when God delivered you from a difficult situation. How does this psalm of praise inspire you to express gratitude for God's faithfulness and strength in your life?

Matthew 9:18-38

Reflection: Jesus performs several miracles, including raising a dead girl and healing the blind and mute. Reflect on Jesus' compassion and power to bring life and healing. How can you bring your needs and the needs of others to Jesus in faith, trusting in His ability to restore and transform?

Day 19: Gn 35-36 Ps 19 Mt 10:1-15

Genesis 35-36

Reflection: These chapters recount Jacob's return to Bethel, the deaths of Rachel and Isaac, and the genealogy of Esau. Reflect on the themes of renewal, loss, and legacy. How does Jacob's return to Bethel and the significant events in his family history remind you of God's faithfulness throughout life's transitions and challenges?

Psalm 19

Reflection: Psalm 19 celebrates God's revelation through creation and His Word. Reflect on the beauty and majesty of God's creation around you. How does meditating on God's creation and His perfect Word inspire you to live a life that honors Him?

Matthew 10:1-15

Reflection: Jesus sends out the twelve apostles with instructions for their mission. Reflect on the mission and authority Jesus gives to His followers. How can you be intentional about sharing the good news of the kingdom of God and serving others with the gifts and opportunities He has given you?

Day 20: Gn 37-38 Ps 20 Mt 10:16-33

Genesis 37-38

Reflection: These chapters begin the story of Joseph and cover Judah and Tamar. Reflect on the themes of betrayal, providence, and redemption. How does Joseph's experience of being sold into slavery and Judah's encounter with Tamar reveal God's ability to work through difficult and unexpected circumstances in your life?

Psalm 20

Reflection: Psalm 20 is a prayer for victory and blessing. Reflect on the psalmist's trust in God's power to save and deliver. How can you incorporate prayers for God's guidance, protection, and success in your endeavors, relying on His strength rather than your own?

Matthew 10:16-33

Reflection: Jesus warns His disciples about persecution and encourages them to stand firm in their faith. Reflect on Jesus' call to courage and faithfulness in the face of opposition. How can you remain steadfast and unafraid in living out your faith, knowing that God values and protects you?

Day 21: Gn 39-40 Ps 21 Mt 10:34-11:1

Genesis 39-40

Reflection: These chapters describe Joseph's time in Potiphar's house and in prison. Reflect on Joseph's faithfulness and integrity despite unjust treatment. How does Joseph's steadfastness and trust in God's presence during trials encourage you to remain faithful in your own challenging circumstances?

Psalm 21

Reflection: Psalm 21 is a song of praise for the king's victory and blessings. Reflect on the ways God has blessed and granted you success. How can you offer thanks and acknowledge God's role in your achievements and joys?

Matthew 10:34-11:1

Reflection: Jesus speaks about the cost of discipleship and the division it may bring, followed by instructions to His disciples. Reflect on the challenges and sacrifices involved in following Jesus. How can you prioritize your commitment to Christ above all else, even when it requires difficult choices or causes conflict?

WEEK 4: Courage and Faith in Action

Welcome back, Faithful and Fierce women! This week, we delve into the captivating story of Esther, a young Jewish woman who embodies courage, faith, and decisive action in the face of immense danger. The Book of Esther, a thrilling narrative filled with palace intrigue and daring exploits, reminds us that God can use even the most unlikely heroes to accomplish His purposes.

A Queen Crowned by Fate:

The story opens in the opulent Persian court of King Ahasuerus. Queen Vashti, renowned for her beauty, refuses the king's command to appear at a royal banquet (Esther 1:1-22). This act of defiance leads to her dismissal, paving the way for a nationwide search for a new queen. Esther, a beautiful young orphan raised by her cousin Mordecai, finds herself among the chosen candidates (Esther 2:1-17).

Mordecai's Plot and Haman's Hateful Edict

Esther, upon Mordecai's instruction, keeps her Jewish heritage hidden from the king (Esther 2:10). Meanwhile, Mordecai uncovers a plot by Haman, the king's arrogant advisor, to annihilate all the Jews in the Persian Empire (Esther 3:1-15). Mordecai pleads with Esther to intervene and risk her own life by appealing directly to the king, even though approaching the king uninvited is punishable by death (Esther 4:7-11).

A Decision Steeped in Faith and Courage:

Esther grapples with a terrifying choice. Remaining silent means the destruction of her people, yet approaching the king without a summons is a gamble with her own life. She recognizes the gravity of the situation and declares, "For if I perish, I perish" (Esther 4:16). This powerful statement underscores her unwavering faith and her willingness to act courageously even in the face of potential death.

Esther's Bold Move and Triumphant Reversal

Esther devises a daring plan. She invites the king to two banquets, strategically creating a space for her to plead her case. During the second banquet, she reveals her Jewish identity and exposes Haman's evil plot (Esther 7:3-4). Enraged by Haman's treachery, the king orders Haman's execution and grants Esther and Mordecai the authority to issue a decree reversing Haman's edict (Esther 7:9-8:11).

The Triumph of Faith and the Legacy of Esther

Esther's courage and quick thinking save the Jewish people from annihilation. The Book of Esther concludes by celebrating the joyous festival of Purim, established to commemorate the Jews' deliverance (Esther 9:1-32).

Action Step: Unleashing Your Inner Esther

Esther's story is a powerful reminder that God can use ordinary people to achieve extraordinary things. Consider the following:

- **Identify a Skill You Want to Develop:** Think about a skill or talent you'd like to cultivate, perhaps public speaking, leadership, or a creative pursuit.

- **Challenge Yourself:** Set a specific, achievable goal related to this skill. For example, if you want to become a more confident speaker, you could volunteer to give a short presentation at a local group meeting.

- **Embrace Faith-Based Growth:** Pray for the courage and confidence to step outside your comfort zone. Seek guidance from scripture verses that emphasize God's love and support. Consider seeking mentorship from a woman in your faith community who has developed this skill.

- **Remember:** Growth often happens outside our comfort zone. Trust that God will equip you with the skills and confidence you need to succeed as you embark on this journey of development.

Discussion Starter (For Group Bible Study):

- Discuss the challenges Esther faces in a foreign court and a patriarchal society.

- How does Esther's story challenge the notion of female passivity?

- Share stories of women in your own lives who have displayed courage and used their skills to make a positive impact.

- How can we, as women of faith, support and empower each other to step outside our comfort zones and develop our unique gifts and talents?

Dear sisters, courage isn't the absence of fear; it's the willingness to act in spite of it. Esther's story reminds us that with faith as our compass and God's strength as our foundation, we can overcome any obstacle and achieve remarkable things. Let her bravery inspire you to unleash your inner Esther and embrace the extraordinary potential within you.

With our weekly lesson completed, let's continue our Catholic Bible study and reflection, one passage at a time.

BIBLE READING: Week 4

Day 22: Gn 41-43 Ps 22 Mt 11:2-19

Genesis 41-43

Reflection: These chapters recount Joseph's rise to power in Egypt and his initial encounters with his brothers. Reflect on God's sovereignty and the unfolding of His plans through Joseph's trials and triumphs. How does Joseph's story encourage you to trust in God's timing and purposes, even when they are not immediately clear?

Psalm 22

Reflection: Psalm 22 is a prophetic lament that foreshadows the suffering of Christ. Reflect on the themes of abandonment and ultimate deliverance in this psalm. How does identifying with the psalmist's cries deepen your understanding of Jesus' suffering on the cross and God's faithfulness to redeem?

Matthew 11:2-19

Reflection: Jesus responds to John's disciples and speaks about John the Baptist. Reflect on the themes of doubt and affirmation in these verses. How does Jesus' reassurance to John and His praise for John inspire you to find assurance in your own faith journey, especially in times of doubt or questioning?

Day 23: Gn 44-45 Ps 23 Mt 11:20-30

Genesis 44-45

Reflection: These chapters detail Joseph's revelation of his identity to his brothers and their reconciliation. Reflect on the themes of forgiveness and restoration. How does Joseph's willingness to forgive and his perspective on God's hand in his circumstances challenge you to extend grace and seek reconciliation in your own relationships?

Psalm 23

Reflection: Psalm 23 is a beloved psalm of trust and comfort in God's guidance. Reflect on the imagery of God as your Shepherd. How does this psalm provide reassurance and peace in your current circumstances, knowing that God leads, restores, and protects you?

Matthew 11:20-30

Reflection: Jesus denounces unrepentant cities and invites the weary to find rest in Him. Reflect on Jesus' call to come to Him for rest and take His yoke upon you. How can you experience the rest and peace that Jesus offers in the midst of life's burdens and challenges?

Day 24: Gn 46-48 Ps 24 Mt 12:1-14

Genesis 46-48

Reflection: These chapters describe Jacob's journey to Egypt and his blessings on Joseph's sons. Reflect on God's faithfulness in bringing Jacob and his family to Egypt. How do Jacob's blessings and his reflection on God's promises encourage you to recognize and proclaim God's faithfulness in your own life?

Psalm 24

Reflection: Psalm 24 celebrates God's sovereignty and the entrance of the King of Glory. Reflect on the majesty and holiness of God as described in this psalm. How can you prepare your heart to welcome God's presence and live in a way that honors His holiness and lordship?

Matthew 12:1-14

Reflection: Jesus addresses the Pharisees' criticism regarding the Sabbath. Reflect on the themes of mercy and legalism in these verses. How does Jesus' teaching about the Sabbath challenge you to prioritize compassion and understanding over rigid adherence to rules in your walk with God?

Day 25: Gn 49-50 Ps 25 Mt 12:15-37

Genesis 49-50

Reflection: These chapters cover Jacob's blessings on his sons and his death, as well as Joseph's continued faithfulness. Reflect on the prophetic blessings Jacob gives to his sons and the legacy he leaves. How does Joseph's response to his brothers after Jacob's death demonstrate a commitment to God's purposes and forgiveness?

Psalm 25

Reflection: Psalm 25 is a prayer for guidance, forgiveness, and protection. Reflect on the psalmist's trust in God's direction and mercy. How can you incorporate prayers for guidance and a heart of humility and trust in your own spiritual practice?

Matthew 12:15-37

Reflection: Jesus heals many and speaks about the power of the Holy Spirit and the importance of our words. Reflect on Jesus' teachings about the impact of our words and the unforgivable sin. How can you ensure that your speech reflects your faith and aligns with God's will?

Day 26: Phil 1:1-2:18 Ps 26 Mt 12:38-50

Philippians 1:1-2:18

Reflection: Paul writes about joy, humility, and shining as lights in the world. Reflect on Paul's exhortations to live in a manner worthy of the gospel, including humility and obedience. How can you embody the mindset of Christ and live out your faith joyfully and humbly in your daily interactions?

Psalm 26

Reflection: Psalm 26 is a prayer for vindication and a declaration of integrity. Reflect on the psalmist's desire to live blamelessly and his trust in God's justice. How can you strive to maintain integrity and seek God's guidance and vindication in your life?

Matthew 12:38-50

Reflection: Jesus addresses the request for a sign and teaches about spiritual renewal and kinship. Reflect on Jesus' words about seeking signs and the importance of true repentance and obedience. How can you focus on fostering a genuine relationship with God rather than seeking miraculous proofs of His presence?

Day 27: Phil 2:19-4:23 Ps 27 Mt 13:1-30

Philippians 2:19-4:23

Reflection: Paul expresses his gratitude, encouragement, and final exhortations to the Philippians. Reflect on the themes of joy, peace, and contentment that permeate these chapters. How can you practice gratitude, seek peace, and find contentment in God's provision and presence, regardless of your circumstances?

Psalm 27

Reflection: Psalm 27 is a declaration of confidence in God's protection and a desire to dwell in His presence. Reflect on the psalmist's unwavering trust in God's goodness and protection.

How can you cultivate a deep sense of trust and a desire to seek God's presence in all areas of your life?

Matthew 13:1-30

Reflection: Jesus shares parables about the kingdom of heaven, including the sower and the weeds. Reflect on the different responses to God's Word as described in the parable of the sower. How can you ensure that your heart is receptive to God's Word and bears fruit in your life?

Day 28: Exodus 1-3 Ps 28 Mt 13:31-53

Exodus 1-3

Reflection: These chapters describe the Israelites' oppression in Egypt and God's call to Moses. Reflect on God's concern for the suffering of His people and His call to Moses. How does God's awareness of the Israelites' plight and His commissioning of Moses inspire you to respond to God's call to address injustice and serve others?

Psalm 28

Reflection: Psalm 28 is a prayer for help and a thanksgiving for God's response. Reflect on the psalmist's plea for mercy and trust in God's deliverance. How can you express your dependence on God in times of need and offer thanks for His faithful answers to your prayers?

Matthew 13:31-53

Reflection: Jesus shares more parables about the kingdom of heaven, including the mustard seed and the yeast. Reflect on the transformative and pervasive nature of God's kingdom as described in these parables. How can you participate in the growth of God's kingdom in your community and daily life?

WEEK 5: Woman: A Model of Strength and Virtue

Welcome back, Faithful and Fierce women! This week, we delve into a captivating passage from the book of Proverbs: the description of the "Proverbs 31 Woman." Often misconstrued as a rigid checklist of wifely duties, this passage offers a far richer and more nuanced portrayal of a woman who embodies strength, faith, resourcefulness, and unwavering trust in God.

Beyond Domesticity: A Woman of Many Facets

Proverbs 31:10-31 paints a portrait of a woman who thrives in various spheres of life. She's not confined to the domestic realm; she's an entrepreneur, a skilled laborer, a compassionate caregiver, a wise advisor, and a woman of unwavering faith.

Let's explore some of her key characteristics:

- **Industrious and Capable (vv. 13-19):** This woman is a diligent worker, managing her household with efficiency. She's not afraid of hard work, whether it's acquiring raw materials, weaving garments, or overseeing her servants.

- **Business Acumen and Resourcefulness (vv. 16-18):** She possesses a keen business sense, investing in land and managing her affairs with wisdom. She's not afraid to take calculated risks and leverage her skills to ensure her family's well-being.

- **Strength and Dignity (v. 25):** This woman's strength isn't just physical; it's a core aspect of her character. She approaches life's challenges with resilience and dignity, inspiring confidence in those around her.

- **Compassion and Generosity (v. 20):** She extends a helping hand to those in need, readily offering assistance to the poor and vulnerable. Her generosity flows from a heart of compassion and a desire to make a positive impact on the world around her.

- **Wisdom and Trust in God (vv. 30-31):** Above all, this woman fears the Lord. Her wisdom is rooted in her faith, and she trusts in God's guidance for every aspect of her life.

Journaling: Unveiling Your Inner Strength

The Proverbs 31 Woman serves as an inspiration, not an impossible ideal. Take some time to reflect on the following questions:

- Which aspects of the Proverbs 31 Woman resonate most with you?

- How do you demonstrate strength, resourcefulness, and compassion in your own life?

- Is there an area where you'd like to develop your skills or step outside your comfort zone, drawing inspiration from the Proverbs 31 Woman?

_____

_____

_____

_____

_____

_____

_____

_____

_____

_____

_____

_____

_____

_____

_____

_____

Discussion Starter (For Group Bible Study):

- How can we avoid misinterpreting the Proverbs 31 Woman as a legalistic ideal rather than an inspirational model?

- Discuss the importance of women having a strong work ethic and financial independence, even in the context of family life.

- Share ways you cultivate your faith and integrate your values into your daily life.

- How can we, as women of faith, support each other in developing our strengths and pursuing our God-given dreams?

Remember, dear sisters, the Proverbs 31 Woman is like a beautiful fabric woven with diverse threads. She's not a one-dimensional stereotype; she's a multifaceted woman of faith who excels in various areas of life. Let her story inspire you to embrace your own unique strengths, cultivate your skills, and live a life that reflects God's love and wisdom in all that you do.

With our weekly lesson completed, let's continue with our Catholic Bible study plan and reflection, one passage at a time.

BIBLE READING: Week 5

Day 29: Exodus 4:1-6:27, Psalm 29, Matthew 13:54-14:21

Exodus 4:1-6:27

Reflection: These chapters describe Moses' initial reluctance, his encounters with Pharaoh, and the increasing oppression of the Israelites. Reflect on Moses' doubts and God's assurances. How do you handle moments of doubt and opposition in your calling? How can you find strength in God's promises and faithfulness?

Psalm 29

Reflection: Psalm 29 is a psalm of praise for God's majestic voice and power. Reflect on the imagery of God's voice in this psalm. How does recognizing the power and majesty of God's voice deepen your reverence for Him and your sense of His presence in your life?

Matthew 13:54-14:21

Reflection: These verses cover Jesus being rejected in His hometown, John the Baptist's death, and the feeding of the five thousand. Reflect on the themes of rejection, sacrifice, and provision. How do Jesus' experiences of rejection and His compassionate provision for the crowd encourage you to trust in His care and continue your mission despite opposition?

Day 30: Exodus 7-8, Psalm 30, Matthew 14:22-36

Exodus 7-8

Reflection: These chapters recount the first plagues that God sent upon Egypt. Reflect on the power and purpose of these plagues. How does God's demonstration of power through these events shape your understanding of His sovereignty and justice?

Psalm 30

Reflection: Psalm 30 is a thanksgiving psalm for deliverance from death. Reflect on a time when you experienced God's deliverance or healing. How does this psalm inspire you to give thanks and testify to God's faithfulness?

Matthew 14:22-36

Reflection: Jesus walks on water and calms the storm. Reflect on Peter's initial faith and subsequent doubt. How can you strengthen your faith to step out of your comfort zone and trust Jesus more fully, especially in times of fear and uncertainty?

Day 31: Exodus 9-11, Psalm 31, Matthew 15:1-20

Exodus 9-11

Reflection: These chapters detail the escalating plagues and Pharaoh's hardened heart. Reflect on the themes of judgment and mercy. How does the account of the plagues challenge you to consider the seriousness of resisting God's will and the need for a responsive heart?

Psalm 31

Reflection: Psalm 31 is a plea for refuge and deliverance. Reflect on the psalmist's trust in God's protection. How can you find refuge in God amidst your trials and express your trust in His deliverance?

Matthew 15:1-20

Reflection: Jesus addresses issues of tradition and inner purity. Reflect on Jesus' teaching about the heart's condition. How can you ensure that your worship and actions are genuinely rooted in a pure heart and not just outward rituals?

Day 32: Exodus 12-14, Psalm 32, Matthew 15:21-39

Exodus 12-14

Reflection: These chapters recount the Passover, the exodus from Egypt, and the crossing of the Red Sea. Reflect on the themes of deliverance and faith. How does the story of the Israelites' liberation and their journey through the Red Sea inspire you to trust in God's power to deliver and guide you through life's challenges?

Psalm 32

Reflection: Psalm 32 celebrates the joy of forgiveness. Reflect on the relief and joy that come from confessing your sins and receiving God's forgiveness. How can you embrace and live out the freedom that comes from being forgiven?

Matthew 15:21-39

Reflection: Jesus heals a Canaanite woman's daughter and feeds the four thousand. Reflect on the themes of faith and compassion. How can you show persistent faith like the Canaanite woman and extend compassion to those in need around you?

Day 33: Exodus 15-16, Psalm 33, Matthew 16:1-12

Exodus 15-16

Reflection: These chapters include the song of Moses and the Israelites and the provision of manna and quail. Reflect on the themes of praise and provision. How can you cultivate a habit of praising God for His past deliverances and trust Him for your daily needs?

Psalm 33

Reflection: Psalm 33 is a call to worship and trust in God's steadfast love. Reflect on God's sovereignty and faithfulness. How does recognizing God's control over all creation and His unfailing love encourage you to place your hope and trust in Him?

Matthew 16:1-12

Reflection: Jesus warns against the yeast of the Pharisees and Sadducees. Reflect on the dangers of false teachings and hypocrisy. How can you stay vigilant and discerning in your faith, ensuring that your beliefs and practices align with the truth of God's Word?

Day 34: Exodus 17-18, Psalm 34, Matthew 16:13-28

Exodus 17-18

Reflection: These chapters describe the Israelites' battles and Moses' interaction with Jethro. Reflect on the importance of community and delegation in leadership. How can you rely on others' support and share responsibilities to effectively fulfill God's mission in your life?

Psalm 34

Reflection: Psalm 34 is a psalm of praise and testimony of God's deliverance. Reflect on the ways God has delivered and provided for you. How can you continually praise God and share your testimonies to encourage others?

Matthew 16:13-28

Reflection: Peter declares Jesus as the Messiah, and Jesus speaks about His death and the cost of discipleship. Reflect on Peter's confession and the call to take up your cross. How does recognizing Jesus as Lord and Savior shape your daily decisions and willingness to sacrifice for His sake?

Day 35: Exodus 19-20, Psalm 35, Matthew 17:1-13

Exodus 19-20

Reflection: These chapters include the Israelites' preparation to receive the Law and the Ten Commandments. Reflect on the themes of holiness and covenant. How do God's commandments and His call to holiness guide your behavior and relationship with Him?

Psalm 35

Reflection: Psalm 35 is a plea for God's justice against enemies. Reflect on the psalmist's cry for vindication and protection. How can you trust in God's justice and protection when you face opposition or feel wronged?

Matthew 17:1-13

Reflection: The Transfiguration of Jesus is described in these verses. Reflect on the revelation of Jesus' divine glory. How does the Transfiguration deepen your understanding of who Jesus is and strengthen your faith in His divine authority and purpose?

WEEK 6: The Virgin Mary: Model of Faithfulness and Motherhood (The Gospels)

Welcome back, Faithful and Fierce women! This week, we turn our hearts to the Blessed Virgin Mary, the mother of Jesus. Her presence throughout the Gospels is a beacon of unwavering faith, humility, and unwavering love. As we explore various Gospel accounts, Mary emerges not just as the mother of the God-man, but as a powerful role model for women of faith.

The Annunciation: A Call to Faithfulness (Luke 1:26-38)

The pivotal moment of the Annunciation, recounted in the Gospel of Luke, sets the stage for Mary's exceptional role in salvation history. An angel appears to Mary, announcing that she will bear the Son of God. Despite her initial fear and confusion, Mary's response is one of complete surrender and faith: "Behold, I am the servant of the Lord; let it be to me according to your word" (Luke 1:38).

> **Discussion Prompt 1:**
>
> Consider the significance of Mary's "Fiat" ("Yes" in Latin). How does her complete trust in God serve as an example of unwavering faith?

The Visitation: A Song of Love and Service (Luke 1:39-56)

Mary's response to the Annunciation is not one of passive acceptance. Filled with joy and the Holy Spirit, she journeys to visit her cousin Elizabeth, who is also pregnant (Luke 1:39-45). Mary's Magnificat, a beautiful song of praise and thanksgiving, expresses her profound faith and her understanding of God's work in her life (Luke 1:46-55). This act of service to Elizabeth further highlights Mary's willingness to use her gifts to bless others.

> **Discussion Prompt 2:**
>
> Discuss the importance of supporting other women on their faith journeys. How can we, like Mary, extend a helping hand and offer encouragement to those in need?

The Presentation in the Temple and the Flight to Egypt (Luke 2:22-40 & Matthew 2:13-18)

Mary's faithfulness is further tested as she faithfully follows Jewish customs, presenting Jesus at the Temple (Luke 2:22-40). Simeon's prophecy foreshadows the challenges Jesus will face, and Mary's heart is pierced with a "sword" of sorrow (Luke 2:35). When danger arises due to Herod's murderous decree, Mary flees to Egypt with Joseph and the infant Jesus, demonstrating her courage and willingness to protect her son (Matthew 2:13-18).

> **Discussion Prompt 3:**
>
> Mary's journey mirrors themes of exile and refuge found throughout scripture. How can we relate to Mary's experience of facing challenges and uncertainties as women of faith?

The Finding in the Temple: A Mother's Deep Love (Luke 2:41-52)

At the age of twelve, Jesus stays behind in the Temple after a family trip to Jerusalem. Frantic with worry, Mary and Joseph search for him (Luke 2:41-45). When they finally find Jesus engaged in theological discussions with the teachers, Mary expresses her concern and gentle rebuke (Luke 2:48). This scene underscores Mary's deep love for her son and her attentiveness to his well-being.

> **Discussion Prompt 4:**
>
> The story of the Finding in the Temple highlights the complex emotions of motherhood. Share your thoughts on Mary's experience and how it relates to the joys and challenges of motherhood in general.

The Wedding at Cana: A Mother's Intercession (John 2:1-11)

At the wedding at Cana, Mary witnesses the limitations of the wine supply and intuitively recognizes a need (John 2:1-3). She approaches Jesus, suggesting, "They have no more wine" (John 2:3). This seemingly simple act highlights Mary's attentiveness to others' needs and her faith in Jesus' power to intervene. While Jesus initially seems hesitant, He ultimately grants her request, performing the first miracle recorded in John's Gospel.

> **Discussion Prompt 5:**
>
> Discuss the power of a mother's intercession. Share stories (if comfortable) of times when you prayed for your loved ones or intervened on their behalf.

Action Step: Reflecting on Mary's Virtues

The Virgin Mary offers a wealth of inspiration for women of faith. This week, take some time for prayer or reflection. Meditate on Mary's virtues – her unwavering faith, her selfless love, her courage, and her unwavering trust in God's plan.

You can consider how Mary's virtues can be applied to your own life. Here are some prompts to guide your reflection:

- **Identify an area in your life where you need more faith.** Perhaps it's a personal challenge you're facing, a decision you need to make, or a relationship that needs healing. Ask Mary to intercede for you and to strengthen your faith in God's goodness and power.

- **Reflect on how you can extend love and service to others.** Think about someone in your life who might need your support, encouragement, or simply a listening ear. Pray for opportunities to be a blessing to those around you, just as Mary extended a helping hand to Elizabeth.

- **Consider a situation where you might need courage.** Maybe it's speaking up for what you believe in, pursuing a dream that seems daunting, or facing a personal fear. Draw strength from Mary's example and trust that God will be with you every step of the way.

Remember, dear sisters, the Virgin Mary is not just a revered figure; she's a relatable woman of faith who faced challenges, experienced joy, and ultimately played a pivotal role in God's plan. Let her story inspire you to embrace your own faith journey, nurture your strengths, and live a life that reflects God's love in all that you do.

BIBLE READING: Week 6

Day 36: Exodus 21-22, Psalm 36, Matthew 17:14-27

Exodus 21-22

Reflection: These chapters outline various laws for the Israelites, covering justice, property, and social responsibilities. Reflect on the importance of justice and fairness in your community. How do these laws help you understand God's heart for justice and how you can apply principles of fairness and compassion in your interactions with others?

Psalm 36

Reflection: Psalm 36 contrasts the wickedness of humanity with the steadfast love of God. Reflect on the descriptions of God's love and faithfulness. How does meditating on God's unfailing love and righteousness inspire you to trust Him more and seek to reflect His love in your life?

Matthew 17:14-27

Reflection: These verses include Jesus healing a demon-possessed boy and speaking about His death and resurrection. Reflect on the power of faith and the importance of understanding Jesus' mission. How can you strengthen your faith to overcome obstacles and better grasp the significance of Jesus' sacrifice?

Day 37: Exodus 23-24, Psalm 37, Matthew 18:1-20

Exodus 23-24

Reflection: These chapters include laws about justice and mercy, the Sabbath, and festivals, and the confirmation of the covenant. Reflect on the themes of justice, rest, and covenant. How can you implement principles of justice and mercy in your daily life, and how do you observe rest and renewal?

Psalm 37

Reflection: Psalm 37 encourages trust in the Lord and patience for His justice. Reflect on the call to trust and delight in the Lord amidst life's challenges. How can you cultivate trust in God's timing and justice, and find peace in His promises?

Matthew 18:1-20

Reflection: Jesus teaches about humility, dealing with sin, and the value of each believer. Reflect on the importance of humility and reconciliation. How can you practice humility and take steps to reconcile with others, valuing each person as Jesus does?

Day 38: Exodus 25-27, Psalm 38, Matthew 18:21-35

Exodus 25-27

Reflection: These chapters describe the instructions for the Tabernacle and its furnishings. Reflect on the detailed instructions and the significance of the Tabernacle as a dwelling place for God. How do you create space in your life for God's presence, and what steps can you take to ensure your life is a fitting dwelling for Him?

Psalm 38

Reflection: Psalm 38 is a prayer for healing and forgiveness. Reflect on the psalmist's plea for mercy and God's response. How can you seek God's forgiveness and healing in your life, and how does acknowledging your need for His mercy deepen your relationship with Him?

Matthew 18:21-35

Reflection: Jesus teaches about forgiveness through the parable of the unmerciful servant. Reflect on the importance of forgiveness. How can you embrace a lifestyle of forgiveness, extending the same mercy to others that God has shown to you?

Day 39: Exodus 28-29, Psalm 39, Matthew 19:1-15

Exodus 28-29

Reflection: These chapters detail the garments for the priests and the consecration of Aaron and his sons. Reflect on the themes of holiness and consecration. How can you dedicate your life and actions to God, striving for holiness in all that you do?

Psalm 39

Reflection: Psalm 39 is a meditation on the brevity of life. Reflect on the transient nature of life and the psalmist's plea for wisdom. How does recognizing the shortness of life affect your priorities and your dependence on God?

Matthew 19:1-15

Reflection: Jesus teaches about marriage and blesses the little children. Reflect on the value Jesus places on marriage and children. How can you honor your relationships and approach God with childlike faith and trust?

Day 40: Exodus 30-31, Psalm 40, Matthew 19:16-30

Exodus 30-31

Reflection: These chapters include further instructions for worship and the appointment of Bezalel and Oholiab. Reflect on the importance of obedience in worship and using your talents for God's glory. How can you use your skills and gifts to serve God and His community?

Psalm 40

Reflection: Psalm 40 is a song of deliverance and thanksgiving. Reflect on the psalmist's gratitude for God's help. How can you remember and give thanks for God's past deliverances in your life, and how does gratitude shape your outlook on current challenges?

Matthew 19:16-30

Reflection: Jesus speaks with the rich young man and teaches about the cost of following Him. Reflect on the challenges of letting go of material possessions to follow Jesus. How can you prioritize your relationship with God over material wealth and other distractions?

Day 41: Exodus 32-33, Psalm 41, Matthew 20:1-16

Exodus 32-33

Reflection: These chapters cover the golden calf incident and Moses' intercession for the people. Reflect on the themes of idolatry and intercession. How can you guard against modern-day idolatry in your life, and how can you intercede for others as Moses did?

Psalm 41

Reflection: Psalm 41 is a prayer for mercy and a declaration of God's blessing on the righteous. Reflect on the assurance of God's care for the faithful. How does knowing God's care and blessing inspire you to live righteously and show mercy to others?

Matthew 20:1-16

Reflection: Jesus tells the parable of the workers in the vineyard. Reflect on the themes of grace and fairness. How does this parable challenge your views on fairness and the generosity of God's grace?

Day 42: Exodus 34-36, Psalm 42, Matthew 20:17-34

Exodus 34-36

Reflection: These chapters describe the renewal of the covenant and the construction of the Tabernacle. Reflect on the themes of renewal and dedication. How can you renew your commitment to God and dedicate your efforts to building His kingdom?

Psalm 42

Reflection: Psalm 42 expresses a deep longing for God. Reflect on the psalmist's thirst for God's presence. How can you cultivate a deeper longing and dependence on God in your own life?

Matthew 20:17-34

Reflection: Jesus predicts His death a third time, and a mother's request is made for her sons. Reflect on the themes of service and sacrifice. How can you embrace a heart of service and follow Jesus' example of sacrificial love?

WEEK 7: Prayers for Every Woman

Welcome back, Faithful and Fierce women! This week, we delve into the beautiful and soul-stirring world of the Psalms. Often referred to as the "prayer book" of the Bible, the Psalms offer a rich Journey of emotions, struggles, and triumphs expressed through poetic language. As women of faith, we can find solace, strength, and inspiration within these ancient prayers.

A Journey of Emotions:

The Psalms capture the full spectrum of human experience – joy, sorrow, fear, doubt, and unwavering faith. They allow us to express our deepest emotions to God, knowing He understands our hearts.

- **Psalms of Lament (e.g., Psalm 3, 13):** In these Psalms, we find raw expressions of grief, despair, and cries for help. They offer solace for those facing difficult times, reminding us that it's okay to pour out our hearts to God.

- **Psalms of Thanksgiving (e.g., Psalm 100, 136):** These Psalms overflow with gratitude for God's blessings, His faithfulness, and His presence in our lives. They remind us to cultivate an attitude of gratitude, even amidst challenges.

- **Psalms of Praise (e.g., Psalm 18, 145):** These Psalms celebrate God's power, majesty, and love. They uplift our spirits and inspire us to worship God with joy and awe.

- **Psalms of Trust (e.g., Psalm 23, 91):** These Psalms offer comfort and assurance, reminding us of God's unfailing love and protection. They provide a sense of peace and security in times of uncertainty.

Finding Your Psalm:

With over 150 Psalms, there's a prayer waiting to resonate with your current situation. Perhaps you're facing a season of overwhelming challenges, or maybe your heart overflows with thanksgiving. Here are a few suggestions to get you started:

- **Feeling overwhelmed?** Read Psalm 55, a lament that expresses burdens and anxieties, but ultimately trusts in God's deliverance.

- **Need a reminder of God's faithfulness?** Turn to Psalm 36, which celebrates God's unfailing love, righteousness, and steadfastness.

- **Seeking inner strength?** Find encouragement in Psalm 18, a song of David praising God for his deliverance and expressing unwavering trust.

Challenge: A Week of Prayerful Reflection

This week, I challenge you to choose a Psalm that resonates with your current emotions or needs. Here's how you can make this a meaningful experience:

1. **Read the chosen Psalm several times.** Pay attention to the words and allow the emotions to wash over you.

2. **Reflect on how the Psalm relates to your life.** Are there verses that particularly speak to your current situation?

3. **Pray the Psalm back to God.** Use the words of the Psalm to express your emotions, petitions, or thanksgiving to God.

4. **Journal your reflections.** Write down your thoughts and feelings as you meditate on the Psalm.

Remember, dear sisters, the Psalms are a gift from God, offering a space for honest communication and heartfelt connection with Him. Don't be afraid to express your true feelings, knowing that God is a loving and compassionate listener.

Discussion Starter (For Group Bible Study):

- Share which Psalm resonated most with you this week, and why.

- Discuss how the Psalms can help us navigate difficult emotions and challenges.

- How can we incorporate praying the Psalms into our daily lives?

- In addition to the Psalms, what other scripture passages offer comfort and inspiration for women of faith?

Remember, the Psalms are a wellspring of strength, solace, and inspiration. Let their words guide you as you navigate the joys and challenges of life, drawing closer to God with each heartfelt prayer.

BIBLE READING: Week 7

Day 43: Exodus 37-38, Psalm 43, Matthew 21:1-17

Exodus 37-38

Reflection: These chapters describe the construction of the Ark of the Covenant, the table, the lampstand, the altar of incense, and other Tabernacle furnishings. Reflect on the meticulous care taken to prepare a dwelling place for God. How can you prepare your heart and life to be a worthy dwelling for God's presence?

Psalm 43

Reflection: Psalm 43 is a plea for vindication and a call to hope in God. Reflect on the psalmist's trust in God's light and truth. How can you seek God's guidance and place your hope in Him during times of uncertainty or distress?

Matthew 21:1-17

Reflection: These verses describe Jesus' triumphal entry into Jerusalem and the cleansing of the temple. Reflect on the significance of Jesus being welcomed as King and His zeal for God's house. How do you welcome Jesus into your life and what steps can you take to maintain the purity and sanctity of your worship?

Day 44: Exodus 39-40, Psalm 44, Matthew 21:18-32

Exodus 39-40

Reflection: These chapters cover the making of priestly garments and the setting up of the Tabernacle. Reflect on the themes of preparation and dedication. How can you dedicate your daily actions and roles to God's service, ensuring they are aligned with His purpose?

Psalm 44

Reflection: Psalm 44 is a communal lament for past defeats and a plea for God's help. Reflect on the community's cry for deliverance despite their faithfulness. How can you maintain faith and seek God's help when facing communal or personal challenges?

Matthew 21:18-32

Reflection: Jesus curses the fig tree and teaches about faith and obedience through parables. Reflect on the importance of bearing fruit and acting on God's will. How can you ensure that your faith is active and productive, producing the fruits of obedience and righteousness?

Day 45: Romans 1-2, Psalm 45, Matthew 21:33-46

Romans 1-2

Reflection: These chapters introduce Paul's letter to the Romans, focusing on humanity's unrighteousness and God's righteous judgment. Reflect on the themes of sin, judgment, and grace. How can you live in awareness of God's righteousness and grace, striving to reflect His righteousness in your life?

Psalm 45

Reflection: Psalm 45 is a wedding song celebrating the king's marriage. Reflect on the imagery of the king and his bride. How can this psalm inspire you to view your relationship with Christ as a beautiful and committed union, honoring Him with your devotion and faithfulness?

Matthew 21:33-46

Reflection: Jesus tells the parable of the tenants. Reflect on the themes of stewardship and accountability. How can you faithfully steward the responsibilities and blessings God has entrusted to you, ensuring you bear fruit for His kingdom?

Day 46: Romans 3-4, Psalm 46, Matthew 22:1-14

Romans 3-4

Reflection: These chapters discuss justification by faith and the example of Abraham's faith. Reflect on the significance of being justified by faith apart from works. How can you embrace and live out the truth that your righteousness comes through faith in Christ, and not by your own efforts?

Psalm 46

Reflection: Psalm 46 is a declaration of God as a refuge and strength. Reflect on the assurance of God's presence and protection. How can you find peace and confidence in knowing that God is your refuge and strength, especially in times of trouble?

Matthew 22:1-14

Reflection: Jesus tells the parable of the wedding banquet. Reflect on the themes of invitation and readiness. How can you ensure that you are responding to God's invitation with readiness and living in a way that honors Him?

Day 47: Romans 5-6, Psalm 47, Matthew 22:15-33

Romans 5-6

Reflection: These chapters explore the implications of being justified by faith, including peace with God and freedom from sin. Reflect on the transformative power of grace and the call to live a new life in Christ. How can you live out the reality of being dead to sin and alive to God in your daily choices?

Psalm 47

Reflection: Psalm 47 is a call to praise God as the King of all the earth. Reflect on the universal kingship of God. How does acknowledging God's sovereignty over all the earth inspire your worship and affect your perspective on global events?

Matthew 22:15-33

Reflection: Jesus responds to questions about paying taxes to Caesar and the resurrection. Reflect on His wisdom in addressing these challenges. How can you apply Jesus' wisdom in navigating difficult conversations and staying true to God's principles?

Day 48: Romans 7-8, Psalm 48, Matthew 22:34-46

Romans 7-8

Reflection: These chapters discuss the struggle with sin and the victory through the Spirit. Reflect on the inner conflict described in Romans 7 and the assurance of no condemnation in Romans 8. How can you rely on the Holy Spirit to overcome sin and live in the freedom and life that Christ offers?

Psalm 48

Reflection: Psalm 48 celebrates the beauty and security of Zion, the city of God. Reflect on the imagery of God's city and His protection. How can you find security and joy in the knowledge that God is your fortress and that you belong to His unshakable kingdom?

Matthew 22:34-46

Reflection: Jesus teaches about the greatest commandment and questions the Pharisees about the Messiah. Reflect on the command to love God and love your neighbor. How can you prioritize these commandments in your daily life, ensuring that love is at the center of all your actions?

Day 49: Romans 9-10, Psalm 49, Matthew 23

Romans 9-10

Reflection: These chapters address God's sovereignty in salvation and the righteousness that comes by faith. Reflect on the themes of God's mercy and human responsibility. How can you trust in God's sovereign plan for salvation while actively sharing the message of faith and righteousness through Christ?

Psalm 49

Reflection: Psalm 49 reflects on the futility of wealth and the certainty of death. Reflect on the transient nature of earthly riches and the eternal value of a relationship with God. How can you focus on storing up treasures in heaven rather than being consumed by the pursuit of worldly wealth?

Matthew 23

Reflection: Jesus pronounces woes on the scribes and Pharisees for their hypocrisy. Reflect on the dangers of hypocrisy and the call to genuine faith. How can you examine your own life for any traces of hypocrisy and strive to live authentically in accordance with Jesus' teachings?

WEEK 8: Women and the Sacraments: Receiving God's Grace

Welcome back, Faithful and Fierce women! This week, we delve into the beautiful and life-giving tradition of the Sacraments in the Catholic Church. The seven Sacraments – Baptism, Confirmation, Eucharist, Reconciliation, Anointing of the Sick, Holy Orders, and Matrimony – are outward signs of inward grace, instituted by Christ to nourish and strengthen us on our faith journey. But how do women participate in these Sacraments, and can they play a more fulfilling role within the Sacramental life of the Church?

Women: Recipients and Instruments of Grace

From the very beginning, women have been active participants in the Sacramental life of the Church.

- **Women as Recipients of Grace:** Women receive the Sacraments just as men do, experiencing God's transforming grace through Baptism, Confirmation, Eucharist, Reconciliation, and Anointing of the Sick.

- **Women as Instruments of Grace:** Mothers play a vital role in the initiation of their children into the faith, nurturing their faith formation and preparing them for the Sacraments of Baptism and First Communion. Women also serve as catechists, teachers, and spiritual directors, guiding others on their faith journeys.

A Call for Deeper Participation

While women play a crucial role in the Sacramental life, there are ongoing discussions about expanding their involvement. Here are some areas to consider:

- **Women in Ministries:** The Church offers a variety of ministries open to women, such as Lectors, Extraordinary Ministers of Holy Communion, and leaders of prayer groups. Encouraging women to participate actively in these ministries enriches the liturgical experience for the entire community.

- **Women and the Diaconate:** The possibility of women serving as Deacons is a topic of ongoing theological discussion. While the Church's position on female ordination to the priesthood remains unchanged, a renewed exploration of the female diaconate could offer women additional opportunities for service within the Church.

- **Women and Decision-Making:** While women can't be ordained priests or bishops, their voices are crucial in shaping the Church's future. Encouraging women to participate in advisory roles and decision-making processes can lead to a more inclusive and representative Church.

Discussion Starter:

Let's delve deeper into the role of women in the Sacraments:

- Share your experiences as recipients and instruments of grace within the Sacramental life.

- How can women be further empowered to use their gifts and talents in various ministries within the Church?

- What are your thoughts on the possibility of a female diaconate?

- How can women have a greater voice in shaping the Church's future, particularly regarding matters related to women's roles and experiences?

Remember, dear sisters, the Sacraments are gifts from God, offering us opportunities to encounter His grace and strengthen our faith. By actively participating in the Sacramental life and advocating for a more inclusive Church community, we can create a space where women can flourish and utilize their God-given gifts to serve the Church and the world.

Beyond the Discussion:

- Research the history of women's roles in the Church throughout the centuries.

- Explore the writings of female Catholic theologians and thinkers.

- Consider attending workshops or conferences that address the evolving role of women in the Church.

As we continue this faith journey, let us remember the words of St. Teresa of Avila: "Christ has no body now but yours. No eyes but yours to see with. No feet but yours to go by with. Yours are the hands with which He blesses all the world." May we, as women of faith, continue to be active participants in the Sacramental life of the Church, using our voices and gifts to build a more inclusive and vibrant community of faith.

BIBLE READING: Week 8

Day 50: Romans 11-12, Psalm 50, Matthew 24:1-28

Romans 11-12

Reflection: These chapters cover God's mercy to Israel and the call to live a transformed life. Reflect on the themes of mercy, renewal, and spiritual gifts. How can you present yourself as a living sacrifice and use your gifts to serve others, acknowledging God's mercy in your life?

Psalm 50

Reflection: Psalm 50 speaks of God's judgment and the true worship He desires. Reflect on the contrast between empty rituals and sincere worship. How can you ensure that your worship is genuine and that you are living in a way that pleases God?

Matthew 24:1-28

Reflection: Jesus discusses the signs of the end times and urges vigilance. Reflect on the call to be watchful and prepared for Jesus' return. How can you live with a sense of urgency and readiness, focusing on what truly matters in light of eternity?

Day 51: Romans 13-14, Psalm 51, Matthew 24:29-51

Romans 13-14

Reflection: These chapters address the Christian's responsibilities to the government and to weaker believers. Reflect on the themes of love, respect, and mutual acceptance. How can you show love and respect in your community and be considerate of others' consciences?

Psalm 51

Reflection: Psalm 51 is a heartfelt confession and plea for forgiveness. Reflect on David's contrition and God's mercy. How can you seek God's forgiveness with a sincere heart and experience the joy of His salvation?

Matthew 24:29-51

Reflection: Jesus continues teaching about His return, emphasizing the need for readiness. Reflect on the importance of being faithful and prepared for Christ's coming. How can you stay spiritually alert and faithful in your daily walk with God?

Day 52: Romans 15-16, Psalm 52, Matthew 25:1-30

Romans 15-16

Reflection: These chapters focus on Paul's ministry and personal greetings. Reflect on the themes of unity, service, and commendation. How can you work towards unity in your community and appreciate the contributions of others in your ministry?

Psalm 52

Reflection: Psalm 52 contrasts the wicked and the righteous, focusing on God's justice. Reflect on the assurance of God's justice and the importance of trusting in His steadfast love. How can you remain steadfast in your trust in God despite the actions of the wicked?

Matthew 25:1-30

Reflection: Jesus tells the parables of the ten virgins and the talents. Reflect on the themes of preparedness and faithful stewardship. How can you ensure that you are spiritually prepared and faithfully using the resources and gifts God has entrusted to you?

Day 53: Leviticus 1-3, Psalm 53, Matthew 25:31-46

Leviticus 1-3

Reflection: These chapters describe the offerings made to God, including burnt offerings, grain offerings, and peace offerings. Reflect on the significance of these offerings and the principles of sacrifice and thanksgiving they represent. How can you offer your best to God and express your gratitude through your actions?

Psalm 53

Reflection: Psalm 53 speaks about the foolishness of denying God. Reflect on the psalmist's description of human wickedness and the hope for God's salvation. How can you remain conscious of God's presence and live wisely according to His truth?

Matthew 25:31-46

Reflection: Jesus teaches about the final judgment and the separation of the sheep and goats. Reflect on the criteria Jesus uses for judgment, focusing on acts of compassion and service. How can you actively serve others and demonstrate Christ's love in tangible ways?

Day 54: Leviticus 4-5, Psalm 54, Matthew 26:1-25

Leviticus 4-5

Reflection: These chapters discuss sin offerings and guilt offerings. Reflect on the importance of acknowledging sin and seeking atonement. How can you cultivate a heart of repentance and seek God's forgiveness for your shortcomings?

Psalm 54

Reflection: Psalm 54 is a prayer for deliverance and a declaration of trust in God. Reflect on the psalmist's confidence in God's help and protection. How can you trust in God's deliverance in times of trouble and express your reliance on Him?

Matthew 26:1-25

Reflection: These verses describe the plot to arrest Jesus and the Last Supper. Reflect on Jesus' awareness of His impending suffering and His willingness to endure it. How can you find strength and purpose in the face of trials, knowing that Jesus willingly faced His for your salvation?

Day 55: Leviticus 6-7, Psalm 55, Matthew 26:26-56

Leviticus 6-7

Reflection: These chapters provide further instructions on offerings, including the guilt offering and peace offering. Reflect on the meticulous care required in offering sacrifices and the principles of restitution and fellowship they involve. How can you practice making amends and fostering fellowship in your relationships?

Psalm 55

Reflection: Psalm 55 is a lament about betrayal by a close friend. Reflect on the pain of betrayal and the psalmist's turning to God for comfort. How can you seek God's comfort and strength when dealing with betrayal or relational pain?

Matthew 26:26-56

Reflection: These verses cover the institution of the Lord's Supper and Jesus' arrest. Reflect on the significance of the Lord's Supper and Jesus' submission to God's will. How can you commemorate Jesus' sacrifice and submit to God's will in your own life?

Day 56: Leviticus 8-10, Psalm 56, Matthew 26:57-75

Leviticus 8-10

Reflection: These chapters describe the consecration of Aaron and his sons as priests and the tragic incident of Nadab and Abihu. Reflect on the themes of consecration, obedience, and the holiness of God. How can you dedicate yourself to God's service and live in obedience to His commands?

Psalm 56

Reflection: Psalm 56 is a prayer of trust in God amidst adversity. Reflect on the psalmist's expression of trust in God's protection. How can you trust God's promises and find courage in His Word when facing fear or opposition?

Matthew 26:57-75

Reflection: These verses describe Jesus' trial before the Sanhedrin and Peter's denial. Reflect on Jesus' steadfastness and Peter's failure. How can you find strength to stand firm in your faith and seek restoration when you fall short?

WEEK 9: The Mass: The Source and Summit of Our Faith

Welcome back, Faithful and Fierce women! This week, we journey to the heart of our Catholic faith: the Holy Mass. Often referred to as the Eucharist or the Lord's Supper, the Mass is more than just a weekly gathering; it's a sacred encounter with the living God, a re-presentation of Christ's sacrifice on the cross, and a source of immense grace and nourishment for our souls.

A Journey through the Mass:

The Mass unfolds in a beautiful sequence, each element rich with meaning and significance. Let's explore the key parts:

- **The Introductory Rites:** We gather in prayer, acknowledging our sins and seeking God's forgiveness. Here, you can actively participate by responding to the greetings, joining the Litany of the Saints, and saying the Gloria.

- **The Liturgy of the Word:** We listen attentively to Scripture readings from the Old and New Testaments, followed by a homily (reflection) by the priest. This is a time for focused listening, allowing God's word to speak to your heart.

- **The Liturgy of the Eucharist:** The heart of the Mass, here we witness the transformation of bread and wine into the Body and Blood of Christ (Transubstantiation). Join in praying the Eucharistic Prayer, the pinnacle of the Mass.

- **The Communion Rite:** We receive the Eucharist, the very source and summit of our faith. Approach this sacrament with reverence and devotion, preparing your heart through silent prayer.

- **The Concluding Rites:** We express thanks for the gift of the Eucharist and receive a blessing to go forth and live out our faith in the world. Actively participate by responding to the final blessings.

More than Just Going through the Motions:

The Mass is not a passive experience; it requires our active participation. Here's how you can deepen your engagement:

- **Arrive early for quiet reflection and preparation.**

- **Sing hymns and recite prayers with intention and devotion.**

- **Focus on the readings and the homily, allowing Scripture to speak to your heart.**

- **Participate in the gestures and responses, such as standing, sitting, kneeling, and bowing.**

- **Most importantly, come with an open heart, ready to receive God's grace and encounter His presence in the Eucharist.**

Action Step: Deepen Your Connection

This week, choose a specific aspect of the Mass to focus on and deepen your engagement. Here are some ideas:

- **Active Participation:** Pay close attention to the responses and prayers throughout the Mass. Participate with enthusiasm and focus on connecting with the meaning behind the words.

- **Focus on a Specific Prayer:** Choose a prayer that resonates with you, such as the Our Father or the Prayer of the Faithful. Pray this prayer slowly and meditatively, allowing its words to wash over you.

- **Contemplative Receiving of the Eucharist:** As you approach to receive Communion, take a moment for quiet reflection. Express gratitude for this incredible gift and focus on the spiritual encounter with Christ.

Remember, dear sisters, the Mass is a beautiful gift from God, a sacred space to encounter His love and deepen your faith. By actively participating and focusing your heart, you can transform your weekly Mass experience into a life-changing encounter with the divine.

Discussion Starter (For Group Bible Study):

- Share your experiences of the Mass: What elements resonate most with you?

- How can we create a more inviting and engaging atmosphere during the Mass, especially for newcomers?

- Discuss ways to encourage active participation among all members of the congregation.

- Share resources or strategies for deepening your personal prayer life before, during, and after the Mass.

As we conclude this exploration of the Mass, let us remember the words of Pope Saint John Paul II: "The Eucharist is not just a commemoration of the past; it is the real presence of Christ in the present." May each Mass be a transformative encounter with the living God, nourishing your soul and empowering you to live out your faith in the world.

BIBLE READING: Week 9

Day 57: Leviticus 11-13, Psalm 57, Matthew 27:1-26

Leviticus 11-13

Reflection: These chapters provide laws about clean and unclean animals, purification after childbirth, and diagnosing skin diseases. Reflect on the importance of holiness and purity in God's instructions. How can you apply the principles of spiritual cleanliness and holiness in your life today?

Psalm 57

Reflection: Psalm 57 is a prayer for mercy and refuge in God amidst danger. Reflect on David's trust in God's protection and faithfulness. How can you seek God's refuge and express your confidence in His steadfast love during times of distress?

Matthew 27:1-26

Reflection: These verses describe Jesus being handed over to Pilate, Judas' remorse, and Jesus' trial. Reflect on Jesus' willingness to endure suffering and injustice. How can you draw strength from Jesus' example when facing your own trials and unjust situations?

Day 58: Leviticus 14-16, Psalm 58, Matthew 27:27-66

Leviticus 14-16

Reflection: These chapters detail the purification rituals for skin diseases and bodily discharges, and the Day of Atonement. Reflect on the meticulousness of these rituals and the significance of atonement. How can you appreciate the depth of Christ's atonement for your sins and strive to live a purified life?

Psalm 58

Reflection: Psalm 58 is a lament against unjust rulers. Reflect on the psalmist's cry for justice and God's righteous judgment. How can you trust in God's ultimate justice and seek to promote fairness and righteousness in your own sphere of influence?

Matthew 27:27-66

Reflection: These verses describe Jesus' crucifixion and burial. Reflect on the immense sacrifice of Jesus and the fulfillment of prophecy. How does Jesus' sacrifice impact your faith and daily living, and how can you honor His sacrifice in your actions and decisions?

Day 59: 2 John, 3 John, Psalm 59, Matthew 28

2 John and 3 John

Reflection: These epistles focus on walking in truth and love, and offering hospitality to fellow believers. Reflect on the importance of truth, love, and hospitality in your Christian walk. How can you practice living out these values in your interactions with others?

Psalm 59

Reflection: Psalm 59 is a prayer for deliverance from enemies. Reflect on the psalmist's reliance on God's strength and protection. How can you seek God's deliverance in your struggles and trust in His power to save?

Matthew 28

Reflection: This chapter describes the resurrection of Jesus and the Great Commission. Reflect on the significance of the resurrection and the call to make disciples of all nations. How can you live in the power of the resurrection and actively participate in the mission of sharing the gospel?

Day 60: Leviticus 17-18, Psalm 60, Mark 1:1-13

Leviticus 17-18

Reflection: These chapters provide laws about the sanctity of blood and moral behavior. Reflect on the importance of respecting life and maintaining moral purity. How can you uphold these principles in your personal life and relationships?

Psalm 60

Reflection: Psalm 60 is a plea for God's help in a time of national defeat. Reflect on the psalmist's cry for restoration and God's promise of victory. How can you seek God's help and remain hopeful during times of personal or communal setback?

Mark 1:1-13

Reflection: These verses describe the beginning of Jesus' ministry, including His baptism and temptation. Reflect on the preparation and affirmation of Jesus' ministry. How can you prepare yourself for the ministry or tasks God has for you, and how can you rely on His guidance and strength?

Day 61: Leviticus 19-20, Psalm 61, Mark 1:14-31

Leviticus 19-20

Reflection: These chapters outline various laws for holy living. Reflect on the call to be holy because God is holy. How can you strive to live a holy life, reflecting God's character in your actions and decisions?

Psalm 61

Reflection: Psalm 61 is a prayer for protection and refuge in God. Reflect on the psalmist's longing for God's presence and protection. How can you seek God as your refuge and find comfort in His eternal protection?

Mark 1:14-31

Reflection: These verses describe Jesus' early ministry, including His preaching and healing. Reflect on Jesus' message of repentance and the power of His healing. How can you respond to Jesus' call to repentance and seek His healing in areas of your life that need restoration?

Day 62: Leviticus 21-23, Psalm 62, Mark 1:32-45

Leviticus 21-23

Reflection: These chapters cover the holiness of priests and the appointed festivals. Reflect on the significance of the festivals and the call to holiness for those who serve God. How can you incorporate times of worship and reflection in your life to honor God's holiness?

Psalm 62

Reflection: Psalm 62 emphasizes trust in God alone as a rock and refuge. Reflect on the psalmist's unwavering trust in God's salvation and protection. How can you cultivate a deep trust in God as your sole source of hope and security?

Mark 1:32-45

Reflection: These verses describe Jesus' healing ministry and His compassion for the sick. Reflect on Jesus' willingness to heal and restore. How can you seek Jesus' healing in your own life and extend His compassion to others in need?

Day 63: Leviticus 24-25, Psalm 63, Mark 2:1-17

Leviticus 24-25

Reflection: These chapters discuss the care of the Tabernacle lamps, the showbread, and the Year of Jubilee. Reflect on the principles of light, provision, and freedom. How can you bring light to others, provide for those in need, and promote freedom and restoration in your community?

Psalm 63

Reflection: Psalm 63 is a psalm of longing for God's presence. Reflect on the psalmist's deep desire for God and satisfaction in His love. How can you cultivate a deeper thirst for God's presence and find fulfillment in His love?

Mark 2:1-17

Reflection: These verses describe the healing of a paralytic and the calling of Levi. Reflect on Jesus' authority to forgive sins and His call to follow Him. How can you embrace Jesus' forgiveness and respond to His invitation to follow Him wholeheartedly?

WEEK 10: Women and the Holy Spirit: Gifts for Everyday Life

Welcome back, Faithful and Fierce women! As we continue our journey, let's turn our hearts towards the Holy Spirit, the third person of the Trinity. Often depicted as a dove or a rushing wind, the Holy Spirit is the force that empowers believers, bestowing gifts and guidance on our faith walk. This week, we explore the unique role the Holy Spirit plays in a woman's life.

The Advocate Within:

The Holy Spirit is not a distant force; He resides within us, acting as our Advocate (John 14:16). He guides us, strengthens us, and equips us with the gifts we need to navigate life's challenges and live out our faith authentically.

The Seven Gifts of the Holy Spirit:

The Catechism of the Catholic Church identifies seven Gifts of the Holy Spirit: Wisdom, Understanding, Counsel, Fortitude, Knowledge, Piety, and Fear of the Lord (CCC 783-787). These are not mere talents, but supernatural gifts that empower us to live a Christ-centered life. Here's a glimpse at how these gifts might manifest in a woman's life:

- **Wisdom:** The ability to discern God's will and make sound decisions, particularly in challenging situations.

- **Understanding:** The capacity to grasp the deeper meaning of Scripture, teachings, and life experiences.

- **Counsel:** The ability to offer wise advice and guidance to others, drawing from faith and discernment.

- **Fortitude:** The strength to persevere through trials, overcome obstacles, and remain faithful regardless of challenges.

- **Knowledge:** A deep understanding of God and His plan for humanity, allowing women to share their faith confidently.

- **Piety:** A deep devotion to God, expressed through prayer, worship, and a desire to live a holy life.

- **Fear of the Lord:** Not a sense of dread, but a profound reverence and respect for God, motivating us to live according to His will.

Unveiling Your Unique Gifts:

The Holy Spirit doesn't distribute these gifts in a cookie-cutter fashion; He tailors them to each individual's strengths and callings. Here's how to discover your unique Journey of gifts:

- **Reflect on your strengths and passions.** What are you naturally good at? What activities bring you joy and fulfillment?

- **Pay attention to how you've served others.** Have you offered comfort, guidance, or encouragement? These actions might be expressions of the Holy Spirit's gifts working through you.

- **Pray for discernment.** Ask the Holy Spirit to reveal your unique gifts and how you can use them to serve Him and His Church.

Self-Reflection:

Take some time for quiet reflection:

- **Identify a situation where you felt particularly empowered or guided by the Holy Spirit.** What qualities did you experience (wisdom, courage, compassion)?

- **Consider your natural strengths and passions.** How could these strengths be expressions of the Holy Spirit's gifts in your life?

- **Brainstorm ways to use your gifts to serve others in your daily life.** This could involve volunteering, mentoring, sharing your knowledge with others, or simply offering a listening ear.

Remember, dear sisters, the Holy Spirit is not an afterthought; He is the active force within us, guiding our steps and equipping us with the gifts we need to live out our faith with passion and purpose. Be open to His promptings, pray for discernment, and allow your unique gifts to shine forth, enriching the lives of those around you.

Discussion Starter (For Group Bible Study):

- Share stories of times when you felt empowered by the Holy Spirit.

- Discuss how women can utilize their gifts to contribute to the life of the Church and the wider community.

- Explore resources on the Holy Spirit and the Gifts of the Holy Spirit.

- How can we encourage and support each other in using our gifts to glorify God and serve others?

As we conclude this exploration of the Holy Spirit, let us remember the words of Pope John XXIII: "The renewal of the Church necessarily entails an ever increasing understanding of the Holy Spirit." May we continue to deepen our understanding of the Holy Spirit's role in our lives, allowing His gifts to transform us into women of strength, compassion, and unwavering faith.

BIBLE READING: Week 10

Day 64: Leviticus 26-27, Psalm 64, Mark 2:18-28

Leviticus 26-27

Reflection: These chapters outline blessings for obedience and curses for disobedience, and regulations about vows. Reflect on the importance of obedience to God and the consequences of disobedience. How can you commit to living in obedience to God's commands and honor any vows or commitments you have made to Him?

Psalm 64

Reflection: Psalm 64 is a plea for protection against enemies and a declaration of trust in God. Reflect on the psalmist's confidence in God's justice. How can you trust in God's protection and justice when faced with opposition or malicious attacks?

Mark 2:18-28

Reflection: These verses discuss fasting and Jesus' lordship over the Sabbath. Reflect on the significance of Jesus' teaching about the new covenant and the true purpose of the Sabbath. How can you embrace the freedom that comes from following Jesus and find rest in Him?

Day 65: 1 Corinthians 1-3, Psalm 65, Mark 3:1-19

1 Corinthians 1-3

Reflection: These chapters address divisions in the church and the wisdom of God versus human wisdom. Reflect on the call for unity and the message of Christ crucified. How can you contribute to unity in the body of Christ and seek God's wisdom over human wisdom in your life?

Psalm 65

Reflection: Psalm 65 is a song of praise for God's provision and care for the earth. Reflect on God's abundant blessings and faithfulness. How can you express gratitude for God's provision and recognize His hand in the blessings you receive?

Mark 3:1-19

Reflection: These verses describe Jesus healing on the Sabbath, the growing opposition, and the calling of the twelve apostles. Reflect on Jesus' compassion, authority, and His selection of His disciples. How can you follow Jesus' example of compassion and respond to His call to be His disciple?

Day 66: 1 Corinthians 4-6, Psalm 66, Mark 3:20-35

1 Corinthians 4-6

Reflection: These chapters address the role of apostles, sexual immorality, and lawsuits among believers. Reflect on the call to purity, humility, and resolving conflicts within the Christian community. How can you strive for personal holiness and handle disputes in a way that honors God?

Psalm 66

Reflection: Psalm 66 is a song of praise and thanksgiving for God's deliverance. Reflect on the ways God has delivered and blessed you. How can you testify to God's goodness and express your thankfulness for His deliverance in your life?

Mark 3:20-35

Reflection: These verses cover the opposition to Jesus, the accusation of being possessed, and the true family of Jesus. Reflect on the importance of spiritual kinship and Jesus' response to opposition. How can you identify as part of Jesus' true family and remain steadfast amidst opposition?

Day 67: 1 Corinthians 7-9, Psalm 67, Mark 4:1-25

1 Corinthians 7-9

Reflection: These chapters discuss marriage, singleness, and the rights of an apostle. Reflect on Paul's teachings about relationships and self-discipline for the sake of the gospel. How can you honor God in your relationships and exercise your freedoms responsibly for the sake of others?

Psalm 67

Reflection: Psalm 67 is a prayer for God's blessing and the spread of His salvation to all nations. Reflect on the desire for God's ways to be known on earth. How can you pray for and participate in the mission of making God's salvation known to all people?

Mark 4:1-25

Reflection: These verses include the Parable of the Sower and the purpose of parables. Reflect on the different responses to God's Word and the importance of hearing and understanding. How can you cultivate a receptive heart to God's Word and bear fruit in your life?

Day 68: 1 Corinthians 10-11, Psalm 68, Mark 4:26-41

1 Corinthians 10-11

Reflection: These chapters address warnings from Israel's history, the Lord's Supper, and proper worship. Reflect on the call to avoid idolatry and to honor God in worship. How can you ensure that your worship and communal practices are pleasing to God and free from idolatry?

Psalm 68

Reflection: Psalm 68 is a victorious hymn celebrating God's triumph and care for His people. Reflect on God's power and protection. How can you find encouragement in God's might and care, and how can you praise Him for His victories in your life?

Mark 4:26-41

Reflection: These verses include parables of the growing seed and the mustard seed, and Jesus calming the storm. Reflect on the kingdom of God and Jesus' authority over nature. How can you trust in the growth of God's kingdom and in Jesus' power to calm the storms in your life?

Day 69: 1 Corinthians 12-13, Psalm 69, Mark 5:1-20

1 Corinthians 12-13

Reflection: These chapters discuss spiritual gifts and the supremacy of love. Reflect on the diversity of gifts in the body of Christ and the importance of love. How can you use your spiritual gifts to serve others and ensure that love is the foundation of all you do?

Psalm 69

Reflection: Psalm 69 is a cry for help and a plea for God's deliverance. Reflect on the psalmist's earnest seeking of God in distress. How can you bring your struggles and burdens before God, trusting in His deliverance and timing?

Mark 5:1-20

Reflection: These verses describe Jesus healing a demon-possessed man. Reflect on Jesus' authority over evil and His power to bring restoration. How can you seek Jesus' deliverance in areas of your life that need His healing touch?

Day 70: 1 Corinthians 14-16, Psalm 70, Mark 5:21-43

1 Corinthians 14-16

Reflection: These chapters address prophecy, speaking in tongues, the resurrection of Christ, and the future resurrection. Reflect on the importance of orderly worship, the power of the resurrection, and the hope it brings. How can you live in the hope and power of the resurrection, and contribute to orderly and edifying worship?

Psalm 70

Reflection: Psalm 70 is a short prayer for deliverance. Reflect on the urgency of the psalmist's plea for God's help. How can you seek God's swift intervention in your times of need and trust in His timely deliverance?

Mark 5:21-43

Reflection: These verses describe the healing of a woman with a bleeding issue and the raising of Jairus' daughter. Reflect on Jesus' compassion and power over sickness and death. How can you approach Jesus with faith for healing and restoration in your life and in the lives of those around you?

WEEK 11: Women Saints and Role Models: Lessons from Inspiring Women

Welcome back, Faithful and Fierce women! This week, we delve into the lives of extraordinary women who have walked the path of faith before us. The Catholic Church boasts a rich Journey of female Saints – women of exceptional courage, unwavering faith, and a deep love for God. Their stories serve as beacons of inspiration, reminding us of the incredible things God can accomplish through ordinary women.

A Galaxy of Saints:

From the early martyrs who faced persecution with unwavering faith to the mystics who experienced profound encounters with God, the lives of women Saints offer a diverse range of inspiration. Here are just a few examples:

- **St. Joan of Arc:** A young peasant girl who led the French army to victory, guided by her unwavering faith and visions.

- **St. Teresa of Avila:** A Doctor of the Church, mystic, and reformer, known for her profound writings and unwavering faith.

- **St. Mother Teresa:** A Nobel Peace Prize laureate who dedicated her life to serving the poorest of the poor, embodying compassion and Christ-like love.

- **St. Katharine Drexel:** An American Saint who founded the Sisters of the Blessed Sacrament for Indians and Colored People, defying societal norms to serve marginalized communities.

- **St. Gianna Beretta Molla:** A young wife and mother who sacrificed her life to save her unborn child, exemplifying courage and selfless love.

Lessons from Holiness:

The lives of these women Saints offer us invaluable lessons that can be applied to our own lives:

- **Faith in the Face of Adversity:** Many Saints faced immense challenges, yet their faith remained unwavering. They inspire us to trust in God's presence even during difficult times.

- **Discerning Your Calling:** Each Saint discovered and pursued her unique calling in life. Their stories encourage us to seek God's will for our own lives.

- **The Power of Service:** Many Saints dedicated their lives to serving others. Their examples inspire us to use our gifts and talents to make a positive impact on the world.

- **Living a Life of Prayer:** These holy women cultivated a deep prayer life. Their stories remind us of the importance of prayer in nurturing our faith.

Challenge: Share the Light

This week, I challenge you to research a woman Saint who resonates with you. Here's how you can embark on this inspiring journey:

- **Browse the lives of Saints:** Many resources are available online or at your local library. Consider factors like your interests, challenges you face, or values you hold dear.

- **Delve deeper:** Once you've chosen a Saint, research their life story, significant accomplishments, and their impact on the Church and the world.

- **Share the inspiration:** Write a blog post, create a presentation, or simply share the story of your chosen Saint with friends and family. By sharing their light, you can inspire others on their faith journeys.

Remember, dear sisters, the lives of women Saints are not just historical stories; they are testaments to the power of God's grace working in ordinary women. As you learn from their stories, may their courage, faith, and love inspire you to become a radiant Saint in your own corner of the world.

> **Discussion Starter (For Group Bible Study):**
>
> - Share the stories of women Saints who inspire you.
>
> - Discuss the challenges women Saints faced in their historical context. How do these challenges relate to the experiences of women today?
>
> - How can we incorporate the lessons learned from women Saints into our daily lives?
>
> - Brainstorm ways to share the stories and inspiration of women Saints with others in your community.

As we close this week, let us remember the words of St. Catherine of Siena: "Be who God meant you to be and you will set the world on fire." May the stories of these extraordinary women ignite a fire within you, propelling you forward on your faith journey and inspiring you to live a life that reflects God's love and grace in all that you do.

Day 71: Numbers 1-3, Psalm 71, Mark 6:1-29

Numbers 1-3

Reflection: These chapters detail the census of the Israelites, the organization of the tribes, and the responsibilities of the Levites. Reflect on the importance of order, organization, and each person's role in God's plan. How can you embrace your role in God's kingdom work and serve faithfully according to His calling?

Psalm 71

Reflection: Psalm 71 is a prayer for deliverance and praise for God's faithfulness. Reflect on the psalmist's trust in God's protection and rescue. How can you express your confidence in God's faithfulness and seek His deliverance in your life?

Mark 6:1-29

Reflection: These verses describe Jesus' rejection in His hometown, the sending out of the twelve, and the death of John the Baptist. Reflect on the themes of rejection, obedience, and martyrdom. How can you respond faithfully to God's call, even in the face of rejection or persecution?

Day 72: Numbers 4-5, Psalm 72, Mark 6:30-56

Numbers 4-5

Reflection: These chapters provide instructions for the duties of the Kohathites and laws regarding restitution for wrongdoing. Reflect on the themes of service and justice. How can you serve faithfully in your responsibilities and seek reconciliation and restitution when necessary?

Psalm 72

Reflection: Psalm 72 is a prayer for the king's righteous reign and prosperity. Reflect on the desire for justice, righteousness, and blessings for the ruler and the people. How can you pray for and work towards justice and prosperity in your community?

Mark 6:30-56

Reflection: These verses include the feeding of the five thousand, Jesus walking on water, and healing the sick in Gennesaret. Reflect on Jesus' compassion, provision, and power. How can you trust in Jesus' ability to meet your needs and respond with faith and obedience?

Day 73: Numbers 6-7, Psalm 73, Mark 7:1-23

Numbers 6-7

Reflection: These chapters discuss the Nazirite vow and the offerings brought by the leaders for the dedication of the altar. Reflect on the themes of consecration and generosity. How can you consecrate yourself to God's service and demonstrate generosity towards His work and others?

Psalm 73

Reflection: Psalm 73 wrestles with the problem of evil and the prosperity of the wicked. Reflect on the psalmist's journey from doubt to renewed trust in God's justice. How can you maintain trust in God's goodness and justice, especially when faced with apparent injustices or hardships?

Mark 7:1-23

Reflection: These verses discuss Jesus' teachings on defilement and true defilement. Reflect on the importance of inner purity and the dangers of hypocrisy. How can you cultivate a heart that is pleasing to God and avoid outward religious practices that lack sincerity?

Day 74: Numbers 8:1-10:10, Psalm 74, Mark 7:24-37

Numbers 8:1-10:10

Reflection: These chapters cover the setting up of the lampstand, consecration of the Levites, and the celebration of Passover. Reflect on the themes of light, consecration, and remembrance. How can you be a light in the darkness, consecrate yourself to God's service, and remember His faithfulness in your life?

Psalm 74

Reflection: Psalm 74 is a lament over the destruction of the temple. Reflect on the psalmist's cry for God's intervention and restoration. How can you trust in God's sovereignty and faithfulness, even in times of devastation or loss?

Mark 7:24-37

Reflection: These verses describe Jesus' encounters with a Syrophoenician woman and a deaf and mute man. Reflect on Jesus' compassion and healing power. How can you approach Jesus with bold faith, seeking His mercy and restoration in your life and the lives of others?

Day 75: Numbers 10:11-12:16, Psalm 75, Mark 8:1-26

Numbers 10:11-12:16

Reflection: These chapters detail the Israelites' journey and complaints in the wilderness. Reflect on the themes of trust, complaint, and leadership. How can you trust in God's guidance and provision, even in the midst of challenging circumstances, and avoid the trap of grumbling and discontentment?

Psalm 75

Reflection: Psalm 75 is a song of praise for God's righteous judgment. Reflect on the psalmist's affirmation of God's sovereignty and justice. How can you trust in God's timing and judgment, even when it seems delayed or different from your expectations?

Mark 8:1-26

Reflection: These verses include the feeding of the four thousand and Jesus' warning about the yeast of the Pharisees. Reflect on Jesus' provision and the danger of spiritual blindness. How can you recognize and guard against the influence of hypocrisy and unbelief in your own life?

Day 76: Numbers 13-14, Psalm 76, Mark 8:27-38

Numbers 13-14

Reflection: These chapters describe the Israelite spies' report of the Promised Land and the people's lack of faith. Reflect on the consequences of fear and unbelief, and the importance of trusting in God's promises. How can you overcome fear and doubt and walk in faith, even when faced with seemingly insurmountable challenges?

Psalm 76

Reflection: Psalm 76 is a song celebrating God's victory over His enemies. Reflect on the themes of power, victory, and fear of God. How can you honor God's majesty and sovereignty and find assurance in His ultimate victory over all opposition?

Mark 8:27-38

Reflection: These verses include Peter's confession of Jesus as the Christ and Jesus' prediction of His death and resurrection. Reflect on Jesus' call to discipleship and the cost of following Him. How can you take up your cross and follow Jesus, surrendering your own desires and ambitions for the sake of His kingdom?

Day 77: Numbers 15-16, Psalm 77, Mark 9:1-32

Numbers 15-16

Reflection: These chapters discuss offerings for unintentional sins, Korah's rebellion, and Aaron's staff budding. Reflect on the themes of obedience, rebellion, and God's authority. How can you submit to God's authority and follow His commands, avoiding the pitfalls of rebellion and disobedience?

Psalm 77

Reflection: Psalm 77 is a prayer for God's comfort and remembrance of His past deeds. Reflect on the psalmist's trust in God's faithfulness and deliverance. How can you find solace in God's past acts of salvation and trust in His steadfast love and provision in times of trouble?

Mark 9:1-32

Reflection: These verses include Jesus' transfiguration, His teaching on Elijah, and the healing of a boy with an unclean spirit. Reflect on the revelation of Jesus' glory and His power over spiritual darkness. How can you fix your eyes on Jesus, the source of light and life, and rely on His power to overcome the darkness in your life and the world around you?

WEEK 12: Discernment: Making Faith-Based Decisions (Finding God's Will in Your Life)

Welcome back, Faithful and Fierce women! We've reached the final week of our journey together. This week, we delve into the often-challenging yet crucial process of discernment – discerning God's will for our lives, particularly when faced with significant decisions. Life throws curveballs, and navigating them with faith and clarity requires a willingness to listen to God's voice within us.

The Discernment Dance:

Discernment isn't a one-time event; it's an ongoing dance between seeking God's will and making choices aligned with our faith. Here are some key steps to guide you in this process:

- **Prayer:** Begin with heartfelt prayer, acknowledging your confusion and seeking God's guidance. Open your heart to listen for His promptings.

- **Self-Reflection:** Reflect deeply on the decision you face. Consider the potential consequences of each option and how they align with your values and faith.

- **Seek Wisdom:** Talk to trusted friends, mentors, or spiritual advisors who can offer guidance and a different perspective, informed by their faith.

- **Discerning God's Voice:** Pay attention to internal nudges, scripture readings that resonate with you, or signs that might point you in a certain direction. Remember, God speaks in many ways – through prayer, quiet moments of reflection, or even through the words of others.

- **Discerning Peace:** Ultimately, a faith-based decision should bring a sense of peace, not anxiety. Trust that God will guide you towards the path that aligns with His will for your life.

Journaling: Seeking Clarity

Take some quiet time for reflection and journaling:

1. **Identify a current decision you're facing.** This could be anything from a career change to a personal relationship dilemma.

2. **List the options you're considering.** Be honest and realistic about the potential outcomes of each choice.

3. **Reflect on your values and faith.** What principles are most important to you? How do these principles influence this decision?

4. **Pray for guidance.** Ask God to reveal His will for you in this situation and to grant you the wisdom to make a faith-filled choice.

5. **Pay attention to internal nudges or external signs.** Has anything resonated with you lately? Could it be a message from God?

6. **Imagine yourself down each path.** How does each choice make you feel? Does one path bring a greater sense of peace and purpose?

Remember, dear sisters, discernment is a journey, not a destination. There will be times when the path seems unclear, but trust that God is with you every step of the way. By following the steps outlined above, you can approach difficult decisions with a prayerful heart and the confidence that you're making choices aligned with your faith.

Beyond This Book:

As we continue this faith-enriching journey, remember that your growth continues! Here are some ways to keep the momentum going:

- **Continue your exploration of discernment.** Many resources are available online and in libraries, offering guidance on making faith-based decisions.

- **Develop a daily prayer practice.** Regular communication with God deepens your relationship with Him and allows Him to guide you throughout your life.

- **Join a faith-based community.** Surrounding yourself with supportive women who share your values can provide encouragement and inspiration.

- **Most importantly, trust in God's guidance.** Believe that He has a plan for your life, and surrender your decisions to His will, knowing that He will lead you towards your ultimate purpose.

Remember, you are a Faithful and Fierce woman, created by God with unique gifts and a purpose to fulfill. May the lessons learned on this journey empower you to navigate life's challenges with faith, courage, and the unwavering knowledge that you are loved and guided by the Almighty. Go forth and shine brightly, dear sisters, and let your light illuminate the world!

BIBLE READING: Week 12:

Day 78: Numbers 17-18, Psalm 78, Mark 9:33-50

Numbers 17-18

Reflection: These chapters discuss Aaron's budding staff and the duties of the priests and Levites. Reflect on the theme of God's choice and authority in selecting leaders and ministers. How can you honor and support those whom God has appointed for His service?

Psalm 78

Reflection: Psalm 78 recounts the history of Israel's rebellion and God's faithfulness. Reflect on the importance of remembering God's faithfulness and learning from Israel's mistakes. How can you pass down the stories of God's faithfulness to future generations and avoid repeating the errors of the past?

Mark 9:33-50

Reflection: These verses include Jesus' teaching on humility, causing others to stumble, and salt and peace. Reflect on the call to humility and the seriousness of sin. How can you cultivate a humble heart, strive for peace with others, and guard against anything that causes spiritual stumbling?

Day 79: Numbers 19:1-22:1, Psalm 79, Mark 10:1-31

Numbers 19:1-22:1

Reflection: These chapters cover the purification ritual of the red heifer, the death of Miriam and Aaron, and the story of Balaam. Reflect on the themes of purity, mortality, and God's sovereignty. How can you seek purity of heart and acknowledge God's control over life and death?

Psalm 79

Reflection: Psalm 79 is a lament over the destruction of Jerusalem. Reflect on the psalmist's cry for God's mercy and restoration. How can you intercede for those who are suffering and plead for God's intervention in times of crisis?

Mark 10:1-31

Reflection: These verses include Jesus' teachings on divorce, children, and wealth. Reflect on the values of God's kingdom compared to the world's standards. How can you align your priorities with the values of God's kingdom and trust in His provision for your needs?

Day 80: Numbers 22:2-24:25, Psalm 80, Mark 10:32-53

Numbers 22:2-24:25

Reflection: These chapters tell the story of Balaam and his encounter with Balak, the king of Moab. Reflect on Balaam's journey from disobedience to prophesying God's blessings over Israel. How can you remain faithful to God's commands and resist the temptation to pursue personal gain at the expense of obedience?

Psalm 80

Reflection: Psalm 80 is a plea for God's restoration and favor toward His people. Reflect on the psalmist's cry for God's intervention and salvation. How can you seek God's restoration and revival in your own life and in the life of your community?

Mark 10:32-53

Reflection: These verses include Jesus' third prediction of His death, James and John's request for positions of honor, and the healing of blind Bartimaeus. Reflect on Jesus' humility and compassion, and the significance of spiritual sight. How can you follow Jesus' example of selfless service and pray for spiritual insight to recognize His truth?

Day 81: Numbers 25-26, Psalm 81, Mark 11:1-14

Numbers 25-26

Reflection: These chapters cover the incident of Israel's idolatry with the Moabite women, the zeal of Phinehas, and the census of the new generation. Reflect on the consequences of sin and the importance of zeal for God's holiness. How can you remain faithful to God and stand against the temptations of idolatry and immorality?

Psalm 81

Reflection: Psalm 81 is a call to worship and obedience to God. Reflect on the blessings of obedience and the consequences of disobedience. How can you respond to God's invitation to worship Him wholeheartedly and follow His commands with joy?

Mark 11:1-14

Reflection: These verses include Jesus' triumphal entry into Jerusalem and His cleansing of the temple. Reflect on the symbolism of Jesus' actions and the response of the people. How can you welcome Jesus as your King and allow Him to cleanse your heart and life?

Day 82: Numbers 27-28, Psalm 82, Mark 11:15-33

Numbers 27-28

Reflection: These chapters cover the appointment of Joshua as Moses' successor and the laws concerning offerings. Reflect on the theme of succession and the importance of worship and sacrifice. How can you prepare for transitions in leadership and maintain a heart of worship and gratitude toward God?

Psalm 82

Reflection: Psalm 82 is a prayer for God's justice against unjust rulers. Reflect on the psalmist's cry for righteousness and judgment. How can you advocate for justice and mercy in your community and intercede for those in authority?

Mark 11:15-33

Reflection: These verses include Jesus' cleansing of the temple, His authority questioned, and His teaching on faith and forgiveness. Reflect on the significance of Jesus' authority and His call to faith and prayer. How can you submit to Jesus' authority in your life and demonstrate faith and forgiveness in your relationships?

Day 83: Numbers 29-30, Psalm 83, Mark 12:1-27

Numbers 29-30

Reflection: These chapters detail the offerings for the appointed festivals and the regulations concerning vows. Reflect on the importance of honoring God through worship and keeping vows made to Him. How can you commit to worshiping God faithfully and fulfilling any promises you have made to Him?

Psalm 83

Reflection: Psalm 83 is a prayer for God's deliverance from enemies. Reflect on the psalmist's plea for God's intervention and justice. How can you trust in God's sovereignty and seek His protection and deliverance from the challenges and adversaries you face?

Mark 12:1-27

Reflection: These verses include the parable of the tenants, the question about paying taxes to Caesar, and the discussion about the resurrection. Reflect on Jesus' teachings about stewardship, citizenship, and the afterlife. How can you faithfully steward the resources and opportunities God has given you, fulfill your obligations as a citizen, and live in the hope of the resurrection?

Day 84: Numbers 31-32, Psalm 84, Mark 12:28-44

Numbers 31-32

Reflection: These chapters describe the Israelites' victory over the Midianites and the request of the tribes of Reuben and Gad for land east of the Jordan. Reflect on the themes of obedience, warfare, and inheritance. How can you remain obedient to God's commands, engage in spiritual warfare, and claim the inheritance He has promised you?

Psalm 84

Reflection: Psalm 84 expresses a longing for God's presence and the blessings of dwelling in His house. Reflect on the psalmist's deep desire for intimacy with God. How can you cultivate a longing for God's presence in your life and find joy and strength in worshiping Him?

Mark 12:28-44

Reflection: These verses include the great commandment, Jesus' question about the Messiah, and the widow's offering. Reflect on the themes of love, identity, and sacrificial giving. How can you love God with all your heart, soul, mind, and strength, recognize Jesus as the Messiah, and sacrificially give of yourself to others in need?

WEEK 13: Wisdom for Women

Welcome back, Faithful and Fierce women! As we embark on a new week of exploration, we turn our hearts to the wisdom-filled Book of Sirach (Ecclesiasticus). Written around 180-170 BC, this book offers practical guidance for living a virtuous life, with specific themes that resonate particularly with women. This week, we delve into Sirach 25-36, uncovering gems of wisdom that can empower us in our daily lives.

A Journey of Wisdom:

The Book of Sirach is a treasure trove of practical advice on an array of topics, including:

- **Living a God-centered life (Sirach 25):** The opening verses emphasize the importance of fearing God and keeping His commandments, laying the foundation for a life of wisdom.

- **The Power of Speech (Sirach 28):** This chapter reminds us of the power of our words, urging us to speak with kindness and avoid gossip or slander.

- **Strength in Facing Challenges (Sirach 30-31):** These chapters offer encouragement for navigating difficult times, reminding us that God is our refuge and strength.

- **The Importance of Family (Sirach 31-32):** Sirach emphasizes the importance of honoring parents, offering guidance on raising children, and the value of a faithful wife.

- **The Value of Work (Sirach 37-39):** The book highlights the importance of honest work and craftsmanship, urging us to use our skills to serve others.

Strength and Perseverance: A Woman's Journey

The Book of Sirach offers a wealth of wisdom for women navigating the complexities of life. Here are some key themes that resonate with women's experiences:

- **Finding Strength in Faith:** Sirach emphasizes the importance of fearing God (meaning a deep respect and reverence) and living a life aligned with His will. This unwavering faith provides women with inner strength to face challenges and persevere through difficulties.

- **The Power of Wise Words:** Women are often underestimated in their communication skills. Sirach reminds us of the power of our words, encouraging us to use them for good – to build up others, offer encouragement, and speak truth with kindness.

- **Navigating Challenges with Resilience:** Life throws curveballs, and women are no strangers to hardship. Sirach reminds us that God is our refuge and strength, offering comfort and guidance during difficult times.

- **The Value of Family and Relationships:** Strong family bonds and healthy relationships are crucial for women's well-being. Sirach emphasizes honoring parents, nurturing children, and the importance of a faithful wife (or partner), highlighting the significance of these relationships in our lives.

- **Finding Dignity in Work:** Women are often the backbone of families and communities, contributing significantly through paid or unpaid work. The Book of Sirach affirms the value of honest work and craftsmanship, encouraging women to use their skills and talents to make a positive impact on the world.

Discussion Starter: A Modern Application

The Book of Sirach, though written centuries ago, offers timeless wisdom that remains relevant to women today. Let's delve deeper through discussion:

- Explore specific verses from Sirach 25-36 that resonate with you and your experiences as a woman.

- How can the themes of faith, strength, and perseverance empower women in facing the challenges of the 21st century?

- Discuss the concept of "fearing God" in Sirach. How can we cultivate a deep respect and reverence for God in our daily lives?

- How can women use their communication skills more effectively, as highlighted in the Book of Sirach?

- Share stories of women you admire who exemplify the virtues of strength, resilience, and faith.

Remember, dear sisters, the Book of Sirach is not a dusty relic; it's a wellspring of wisdom waiting to be tapped. As you explore its verses, allow its timeless truths to guide and empower you on your journey of faith.

BIBLE READING: Week 13

Day 85: Numbers 33-34, Psalm 85, Mark 13:1-23

Numbers 33-34

Reflection: These chapters recount Israel's journey from Egypt to the plains of Moab and the boundaries of the Promised Land. Reflect on the significance of remembering the past and looking forward to the future. How can you learn from your own journey and trust in God's guidance for the road ahead?

Psalm 85

Reflection: Psalm 85 is a prayer for God's restoration and favor. Reflect on the themes of forgiveness, salvation, and revival. How can you seek God's renewal in your life and community, and what steps can you take to foster reconciliation and peace?

Mark 13:1-23

Reflection: These verses include Jesus' predictions about the destruction of the temple and signs of the end times. Reflect on the themes of perseverance, discernment, and readiness. How can you remain vigilant in your faith and discern the signs of God's presence and activity in the world around you?

Day 86: Numbers 35-36, Psalm 86, Mark 13:24-37

Numbers 35-36

Reflection: These chapters discuss the cities of refuge and the inheritance of the daughters of Zelophehad. Reflect on the themes of justice, mercy, and inheritance. How can you advocate for justice and offer refuge to those in need, while also stewarding the blessings and responsibilities entrusted to you?

Psalm 86

Reflection: Psalm 86 is a prayer for God's mercy and protection. Reflect on the psalmist's trust in God's faithfulness and goodness. How can you cultivate a heart of humility and dependence on God, seeking His guidance and strength in every circumstance?

Mark 13:24-37

Reflection: These verses include Jesus' description of the coming of the Son of Man and the need for watchfulness. Reflect on the themes of anticipation, preparedness, and faithfulness. How can you live with a sense of expectancy for Christ's return and faithfully fulfill the tasks He has entrusted to you?

Day 87: 2 Corinthians 1-3, Psalm 87, Mark 14:1-21

2 Corinthians 1-3

Reflection: These chapters contain Paul's reflections on suffering, comfort, and the ministry of the new covenant. Reflect on the themes of consolation, integrity, and the transformative power of the Holy Spirit. How can you find comfort in God's presence during times of difficulty and embrace the call to live with sincerity and authenticity?

Psalm 87

Reflection: Psalm 87 celebrates Zion as the city of God's foundation and the birthplace of all who belong to Him. Reflect on the significance of belonging to God's kingdom and the privilege of being counted among His people. How can you rejoice in your identity as a citizen of God's heavenly kingdom and live accordingly?

Mark 14:1-21

Reflection: These verses include the plot against Jesus, the anointing at Bethany, and the betrayal of Judas. Reflect on the contrasts between love and betrayal, devotion and deceit. How can you cultivate a heart of love and loyalty toward Jesus, even in the face of opposition and temptation?

Day 88: 2 Corinthians 4-6, Psalm 88, Mark 14:22-52

2 Corinthians 4-6

Reflection: These chapters contain Paul's teachings on the ministry of reconciliation, the treasure of the gospel, and the call to holiness. Reflect on the themes of perseverance, spiritual warfare, and living as ambassadors for Christ. How can you stand firm in the face of trials, proclaim the message of reconciliation, and pursue holiness in your life?

Psalm 88

Reflection: Psalm 88 is a lament expressing deep distress and a sense of abandonment. Reflect on the psalmist's honesty before God and his plea for deliverance. How can you bring your own struggles and doubts before God, trusting in His faithfulness and mercy even in the midst of darkness?

Mark 14:22-52

Reflection: These verses include the Last Supper, Jesus' prayer in Gethsemane, and His betrayal and arrest. Reflect on the themes of communion, submission, and loyalty. How can you participate in the fellowship of Christ's body, surrender your will to God's, and remain faithful to Him in times of trial?

Day 89: 2 Corinthians 7-9, Psalm 89, Mark 14:53-72

2 Corinthians 7-9

Reflection: These chapters contain Paul's exhortations on repentance, generosity, and God's abundant grace. Reflect on the themes of repentance, generosity, and God's faithfulness. How can you cultivate a heart of repentance, embrace the joy of giving, and trust in God's promises of provision and blessing?

Psalm 89

Reflection: Psalm 89 is a meditation on God's covenant with David and His faithfulness to His promises. Reflect on the themes of covenant, sovereignty, and trust. How can you find assurance in God's unchanging character and trust in His faithfulness, even when circumstances seem uncertain?

Mark 14:53-72

Reflection: These verses include Jesus' trial before the Sanhedrin and Peter's denial. Reflect on the themes of injustice, betrayal, and forgiveness. How can you stand up for truth and justice, remain faithful to Jesus even in difficult circumstances, and extend forgiveness to those who have wronged you?

Day 90: 2 Corinthians 10-11, Psalm 90, Mark 15:1-15

2 Corinthians 10-11

Reflection: These chapters contain Paul's defense of his apostolic authority and his warnings against false apostles. Reflect on the themes of spiritual warfare, humility, and authenticity. How can you equip yourself for spiritual battle, embrace humility in your service to God, and discern truth from falsehood?

Psalm 90

Reflection: Psalm 90 is a meditation on the brevity of life and the eternal nature of God. Reflect on the themes of mortality, eternity, and wisdom. How can you live each day with a sense of urgency and purpose, seeking God's wisdom and making the most of the time He has given you?

Mark 15:1-15

Reflection: These verses include Jesus' trial before Pilate and the crowd's choice of Barabbas over Jesus. Reflect on the themes of injustice, substitution, and redemption. How can you respond to the injustice and suffering in the world with compassion and a willingness to stand up for what is right?

Day 91: 2 Corinthians 12-13, Psalm 91, Mark 15:16-47

2 Corinthians 12-13

Reflection: These chapters contain Paul's reflections on his visions and revelations, his thorn in the flesh, and his final exhortations to the Corinthians. Reflect on the themes of weakness, strength, and spiritual maturity. How can you find strength in your weakness, rely on God's grace, and pursue maturity in your faith?

Psalm 91

Reflection: Psalm 91 is a powerful affirmation of God's protection and faithfulness to those who trust in Him. Reflect on the psalmist's confidence in God's shelter and deliverance. How can you lean on God's promises of protection and find refuge in His presence, especially in times of trouble and uncertainty?

Mark 15:16-47

Reflection: These verses describe Jesus' crucifixion, death, and burial. Reflect on the profound sacrifice of Jesus and the significance of His death for humanity. How does the crucifixion deepen your understanding of God's love and redemption, and how does it inspire you to live in response to His grace?

Part 2: Living Your Faith Fiercely

(WEEKS 14-40)

Theme: Putting Faith into Action in Today's World

WEEK 14: The Call to Be Stewards: Caring for Creation

Welcome back, Faithful and Fierce women! This week, we embark on a journey of environmental stewardship, guided by the wisdom found in the very beginning of the Bible – the creation story in Genesis 1-2. As we delve into this sacred narrative, we discover not only the awe-inspiring power of God the Creator, but also our responsibility as stewards of His magnificent creation.

A Journey of Creation:

The opening chapters of Genesis paint a breathtaking picture of God's creative power. From the formless void to the teeming diversity of life, God meticulously crafts a world teeming with beauty and purpose. Here are some key themes to consider:

- **God, the Creator:** Genesis establishes God as the sole Creator, a powerful force who brings order out of chaos and imbues creation with inherent value.

- **The Interconnectedness of Creation:** The creation narrative emphasizes the interconnectedness of all living things. Humans are not separate from nature; we are intricately woven into the fabric of creation.

- **Human Dominion with Responsibility:** While entrusted with dominion over creation (Genesis 1:28), humans are not given the right to exploit or destroy. Our role is one of responsible stewardship, caring for and protecting the Earth and its resources.

The Challenge of Our Time:

Today, our planet faces unprecedented environmental challenges – climate change, pollution, and habitat destruction threaten the delicate balance of creation. As women of faith, we are called to be active participants in the solution, not bystanders to the problem.

From Words to Action: Your Role as a Steward

The Bible compels us to move beyond mere knowledge to action. Here's how you can embrace your role as a steward of creation:

- **Reduce Your Environmental Impact:** Simple changes in daily habits can make a significant difference. Consider actions like conserving energy, reducing waste, and opting for sustainable products.

- **Embrace Eco-Friendly Practices:** Explore ways to live a more sustainable lifestyle. This could involve composting food scraps, using reusable shopping bags, or planting a pollinator garden.

- **Raise Awareness:** Educate yourself and others about environmental issues. Talk to friends and family, get involved in advocacy efforts, and support organizations working to protect the planet.

- **Advocate for Change:** Use your voice to advocate for policies that promote environmental protection. Contact your elected officials and support legislation that safeguards our planet.

Action Step: Make a Difference

This week, take a concrete step towards becoming a better steward of creation. Here are some ideas to get you started:

- **Choose an eco-friendly practice:** This could be anything from switching to energy-efficient light bulbs to starting a backyard compost bin.

- **Participate in an environmental service project:** Volunteer for a local clean-up event, plant trees in your community, or support an organization working on environmental issues that resonate with you.

- **Educate yourself and others:** Research a specific environmental challenge and share your learnings with friends and family. Knowledge is power, and raising awareness is crucial for creating positive change.

Remember, dear sisters, we are not inheritors of the Earth; we are borrowers from future generations. By embracing our role as stewards, we can ensure a healthy planet for ourselves and for generations to come.

Discussion Starter:

- How does the creation story in Genesis shape your understanding of humanity's relationship with the Earth?

- Discuss the environmental challenges facing our planet today. What specific actions can we take as individuals to make a difference?

- Share your ideas for eco-friendly practices or environmental service projects that you find inspiring.

- How can we integrate our faith and our responsibility towards creation care in our daily lives?

As we conclude this exploration, let us remember the words of Pope Francis from his encyclical Laudato Si': "This world... is fundamentally marked by gratuitous love on the part of the Creator; love which precedes any human merit, love which persists despite our constant failures." May our love for God be reflected in our love for His creation, inspiring us to become faithful stewards of the magnificent world entrusted to our care.

BIBLE READING: Week 14

Day 92: Deuteronomy 1-3, Psalm 92, Mark 16

Deuteronomy 1-3

Reflection: These chapters recount Moses' retelling of Israel's journey from Horeb to the plains of Moab. Reflect on the importance of remembering God's faithfulness and provision throughout your life's journey. How can you learn from Israel's experiences in the wilderness and trust in God's guidance in your own journey?

Psalm 92

Reflection: Psalm 92 is a song of praise for the works of the Lord, especially His righteousness and faithfulness. Reflect on the significance of praising God for His goodness and enduring faithfulness. How can you cultivate a spirit of gratitude and worship, acknowledging God's blessings and sovereignty in your life?

Mark 16

Reflection: Mark 16 records the resurrection of Jesus and His commission to the disciples to preach the gospel to all creation. Reflect on the significance of Jesus' resurrection and the call to proclaim the good news. How does the resurrection impact your understanding of Jesus' identity and mission, and how does it inspire you to share His message of salvation with others?

Day 93: Deuteronomy 4-5, Psalm 93, Luke 1:1-38

Deuteronomy 4-5

Reflection: These chapters contain Moses' exhortations to Israel to obey God's commandments and warnings against idolatry and disobedience. Reflect on the importance of obedience and faithfulness to God's word. How can you heed God's commands and avoid the pitfalls of spiritual compromise and disobedience?

Psalm 93

Reflection: Psalm 93 celebrates the sovereignty and majesty of God, especially over creation and the forces of chaos. Reflect on the themes of God's kingship and steadfastness. How does recognizing God's sovereignty bring you comfort and assurance in times of uncertainty and turmoil?

Luke 1:1-38

Reflection: Luke 1 recounts the birth announcements of John the Baptist and Jesus, as well as Mary's response to the angel Gabriel. Reflect on the themes of faith, obedience, and God's miraculous intervention in human affairs. How does Mary's example of faith and submission challenge you to trust in God's promises and respond obediently to His calling in your own life?

Day 94: Deuteronomy 6-8, Psalm 94, Luke 1:39-80

Deuteronomy 6-8

Reflection: These chapters contain Moses' instructions to Israel to love and obey God wholeheartedly, as well as warnings against forgetfulness and pride. Reflect on the importance of wholehearted devotion to God and the dangers of spiritual complacency. How can you cultivate a deeper love for God and guard against the distractions and temptations that lead you away from Him?

Psalm 94

Reflection: Psalm 94 is a prayer for God's vengeance against the wicked and His comfort for the righteous. Reflect on the tension between justice and mercy, especially in the face of injustice and oppression. How can you trust in God's ultimate justice and find solace in His promises of vindication and deliverance?

Luke 1:39-80

Reflection: Luke 1 continues with Mary's visit to Elizabeth, the birth of John the Baptist, and Zechariah's prophecy. Reflect on the themes of joy, humility, and the fulfillment of God's promises. How do these accounts of miraculous births and divine intervention inspire you to rejoice in God's faithfulness and anticipate the fulfillment of His purposes in your own life?

Day 95: Deuteronomy 9-11, Psalm 95, Luke 2:1-21

Deuteronomy 9-11

Reflection: These chapters recount Moses' warnings to Israel against pride and rebellion, as well as reminders of God's faithfulness and the importance of obedience. Reflect on the consequences of disobedience and the blessings of obedience. How can you learn from Israel's mistakes and choose obedience to God's commands in your own life?

Psalm 95

Reflection: Psalm 95 is a call to worship and obedience, emphasizing the greatness of God as Creator and Shepherd. Reflect on the invitation to worship God with reverence and gratitude. How can you respond to God's invitation to enter His presence with thanksgiving and praise, acknowledging His sovereignty and care over your life?

Luke 2:1-21

Reflection: Luke 2 describes the birth of Jesus in Bethlehem, the announcement to the shepherds, and their response of worship. Reflect on the significance of Jesus' birth as the fulfillment of prophecy and the arrival of God's salvation for humanity. How does the birth of Jesus inspire you to worship Him as Savior and Lord, and how can you share the good news of His arrival with others?

Day 96: Deuteronomy 12-14, Psalm 96, Luke 2:22-52

Deuteronomy 12-14

Reflection: These chapters contain instructions to Israel regarding worship, dietary laws, and tithes. Reflect on the importance of reverence and obedience in worshiping God. How can you honor God with your offerings and live in accordance with His commands, both in your worship practices and daily life?

Psalm 96

Reflection: Psalm 96 is a song of praise for God's reign and righteousness, calling on all creation to worship Him. Reflect on the universal scope of God's sovereignty and the call to proclaim His glory among the nations. How can you join in the chorus of creation in declaring God's greatness and inviting others to worship Him?

Luke 2:22-52

Reflection: Luke 2 recounts Jesus' presentation at the temple, Simeon's prophecy, and Jesus' visit to Jerusalem as a boy. Reflect on the themes of dedication, prophecy, and growth. How does Jesus' early life demonstrate His identity as the promised Messiah and challenge you to grow in wisdom and favor with God and others?

Day 97: Deuteronomy 15-17, Psalm 97, Luke 3:1-22

Deuteronomy 15-17

Reflection: These chapters contain laws concerning the Sabbatical year, debt cancellation, and the appointment of judges and kings. Reflect on the principles of justice, compassion, and governance outlined in these laws. How can you advocate for economic justice, extend mercy to those in need, and support leaders who uphold righteousness and integrity?

Psalm 97

Reflection: Psalm 97 celebrates the reign of God as King over all the earth, exalted above all idols and powers. Reflect on the themes of sovereignty, holiness, and worship. How does acknowledging God's kingship inspire you to live in awe and reverence of Him, and how can you honor Him as the Supreme Ruler of your life?

Luke 3:1-22

Reflection: Luke 3 describes the ministry of John the Baptist, his call to repentance, and the baptism of Jesus. Reflect on the themes of preparation, repentance, and identity. How does John's message of repentance prepare the way for Jesus' ministry, and how does Jesus' baptism affirm His identity as the Son of God? How can you respond to the call to repentance and prepare your heart for the coming of Christ in your life?

Day 98: Deuteronomy 18-20, Psalm 98, Luke 3:23-38

Deuteronomy 18-20

Reflection: These chapters contain laws concerning the Levitical priesthood, false prophets, and rules of warfare. Reflect on the importance of spiritual discernment and obedience to God's commands in matters of worship and justice. How can you discern between true and false prophets and remain faithful to God's guidance in the midst of conflict and uncertainty?

Psalm 98

Reflection: Psalm 98 is a hymn of praise for God's salvation and victory. Reflect on the themes of praise, joy, and redemption. How does God's salvation inspire you to worship Him with gladness and thanksgiving, and how can you share the message of His victory with others?

Luke 3:23-38

Reflection: Luke 3 provides the genealogy of Jesus, tracing His lineage back to Adam. Reflect on the significance of Jesus' ancestry and His identification with humanity. How does Jesus' genealogy affirm His role as the promised Messiah and Savior of the world, and how does it remind you of the universality of God's love and redemption?

WEEK 15: The Great Women of the Exodus

Welcome back, Faithful and Fierce women! As we continue our faith-enriching journey, we turn our hearts to the epic story of the Exodus – the Israelites' liberation from slavery in Egypt. This pivotal narrative, chronicled in the Book of Exodus, is not just a story of male heroes; women played crucial roles in this act of liberation. This week, we celebrate the courage, faith, and leadership of these great women.

Beyond Moses: A Journey of Heroines

While Moses is undoubtedly the central figure in the Exodus story, his journey to freedom wouldn't have been possible without the contributions of exceptional women. Let's meet some of these heroines:

- **Jochebed (Moses' Mother):** Driven by love and a fierce desire to protect her son, Jochebed defied Pharaoh's decree by hiding the baby Moses for three months. Her courage and resourcefulness were the first steps on the path to liberation (Exodus 2:1-4).

- **Miriam (Moses' Sister):** Miriam's unwavering faith and quick thinking played a vital role. She watched over the baby Moses in the Nile bulrushes, and after Pharaoh's daughter found him, Miriam cleverly offered to find a Hebrew nurse – her own mother, Jochebed! (Exodus 2:4-8). Later, as the Israelites crossed the Red Sea, Miriam led the women in a celebratory song of praise (Exodus 15:20-21).

- **Shiphrah and Puah (The Midwives):** These courageous women, entrusted with the horrific task of killing newborn Hebrew boys, chose to disobey Pharaoh's command. Their defiance saved countless lives, including Moses' (Exodus 1:15-17).

- **Zipporah (Moses' Wife):** Zipporah's story showcases bravery and loyalty. During the journey out of Egypt, she intervened on Moses' behalf when an angel threatened his life (Exodus 4:24-26). Throughout their journey, she provided unwavering support to Moses.

Strength in the Face of Adversity

The women of the Exodus defied societal norms and risked their lives to fight for freedom. Their stories offer valuable lessons for us today:

- **Courage in the Face of Injustice:** These women stood up to an oppressive regime, demonstrating that even seemingly ordinary people can make a difference.

- **Faith as a Guiding Force:** Their unwavering faith in God empowered them to act with courage and defiance.

- **The Power of Collaboration:** The women of the Exodus didn't act in isolation; they supported each other and worked together towards a common goal.

- **The Importance of Maternal Strength:** The stories of Jochebed and Zipporah highlight the crucial role of mothers in protecting, nurturing, and empowering their children.

Discussion Starter: Celebrating Heroines

Let's delve deeper into the stories of these remarkable women:

- Discuss the specific actions of Miriam, Shiphrah, and Puah that contributed to the Israelites' liberation. What qualities do these actions reveal about their character?

- Explore the challenges faced by women in ancient Egyptian society. How did these women defy societal expectations in their pursuit of freedom?

- How can we celebrate and learn from the courage and faith of the women of the Exodus in our own lives today?

- Consider contemporary women who exhibit similar qualities of courage, faith, and leadership. Share their stories and how they inspire you.

Remember, dear sisters, the story of the Exodus is not just a historical account; it's a testament to the power of faith, courage, and the unwavering spirit of women. May the stories of these heroines inspire you to find your own voice, challenge injustice, and embrace your role in creating a more just and compassionate world.

As we conclude this week's enriching learning journey, remember that your faith is a powerful force. Carry the lessons learned throughout these weeks close to your heart, allowing them to guide you on your path of faith. Go forth, Faithful and Fierce women, and continue to shine your light brightly!

Day 99: Deuteronomy 21-23, Psalm 99, Luke 4:1-13

Deuteronomy 21-23

Reflection: These chapters cover various laws concerning justice, purification, and warfare. Reflect on the principles of compassion, integrity, and obedience found in these laws. How can you apply these principles in your own life and relationships, seeking justice and mercy as you walk in obedience to God?

Psalm 99

Reflection: Psalm 99 exalts the Lord as a holy and just king, worthy of praise and reverence. Reflect on the themes of holiness, sovereignty, and worship. How does recognizing God's holiness and kingship inspire you to worship Him with reverence and awe in your daily life?

Luke 4:1-13

Reflection: Luke 4 recounts Jesus' temptation in the wilderness by the devil. Reflect on the themes of temptation, obedience, and spiritual warfare. How does Jesus' response to temptation serve as an example for you in resisting temptation and remaining faithful to God's will?

Day 100: Deuteronomy 24-26, Psalm 100, Luke 4:14-44

Deuteronomy 24-26

Reflection: These chapters contain laws concerning marriage, justice, and social responsibility. Reflect on the principles of compassion, generosity, and righteousness outlined in these laws. How can you live out these principles in your interactions with others and contribute to the well-being of your community?

Psalm 100

Reflection: Psalm 100 is a joyful hymn of praise and thanksgiving to God. Reflect on the themes of worship, gratitude, and God's faithfulness. How can you cultivate a heart of thanksgiving and worship, acknowledging God's goodness and mercy in your life?

Luke 4:14-44

Reflection: Luke 4 continues with Jesus' ministry in Galilee, including His teaching in the synagogue at Nazareth and various acts of healing and deliverance. Reflect on the themes of proclamation, compassion, and authority. How does Jesus' ministry demonstrate His identity as the Messiah and the fulfillment of God's promises, and how can you participate in His mission of proclaiming the good news and bringing healing to the broken?

Day 101: Deuteronomy 27-28, Psalm 101, Luke 5:1-26

Deuteronomy 27-28

Reflection: These chapters contain blessings and curses pronounced upon Israel for obedience or disobedience to God's law. Reflect on the importance of obedience and the consequences of disobedience. How does the concept of blessings and curses challenge you to take seriously your commitment to following God's commands?

Psalm 101

Reflection: This psalm is a prayer for integrity and righteousness in leadership. Reflect on the themes of integrity, justice, and accountability. How can you strive for integrity and righteousness in your own life and leadership roles, seeking to honor God in all your decisions and actions?

Luke 5:1-26

Reflection: Luke 5 includes Jesus' miraculous catch of fish and the healing of a paralyzed man. Reflect on the themes of faith, obedience, and compassion. How does Jesus' response to Peter's obedience challenge you to step out in faith and trust His guidance in your own life? How can you demonstrate compassion and bring healing to those in need around you?

Day 102: Deuteronomy 29-30, Psalm 102, Luke 5:27-39

Deuteronomy 29-30

Reflection: These chapters contain Moses' exhortation to Israel to choose obedience and life, rather than disobedience and death. Reflect on the importance of repentance and renewal of covenant commitment. How can you respond to God's call to wholehearted devotion and choose life by walking in obedience to His commands?

Psalm 102

Reflection: This psalm is a prayer for deliverance and restoration, especially in times of distress and affliction. Reflect on the themes of lament, hope, and trust in God's faithfulness. How does the psalmist's cry for help resonate with your own experiences of suffering, and how does it encourage you to trust in God's promises of deliverance and renewal?

Luke 5:27-39

Reflection: Luke 5 describes Jesus' call of Levi (Matthew) and His response to the Pharisees' criticism of His association with sinners. Reflect on the themes of grace, repentance, and spiritual renewal. How does Jesus' call of Levi demonstrate His compassion for the lost and His invitation to all to follow Him? How can you respond to Jesus' call to repentance and experience the transformative power of His grace in your own life?

Day 103: Deuteronomy 31-32, Psalm 103, Luke 6:1-26

Deuteronomy 31-32

Reflection: These chapters contain Moses' final words to the Israelites before his death, including a song of praise and warning. Reflect on the themes of trust in God's faithfulness and the consequences of disobedience. How does Moses' message challenge you to trust in God's promises and walk in obedience?

Psalm 103

Reflection: Psalm 103 is a psalm of praise for God's mercy, forgiveness, and compassion. Reflect on the themes of God's love and grace. How does meditating on God's character and blessings in your life lead you to worship and thanksgiving?

Luke 6:1-26

Reflection: Luke 6 records Jesus' teachings on Sabbath observance, the Beatitudes, and love for enemies. Reflect on the themes of obedience, humility, and righteousness. How does Jesus' call to a life of radical discipleship challenge you to live out your faith in practical ways?

Day 104: Deuteronomy 33-34, Psalm 104, Luke 6:27-49

Deuteronomy 33-34

Reflection: These chapters contain Moses' blessings upon the tribes of Israel and his final ascent to Mount Nebo, where he views the promised land before his death. Reflect on the themes of legacy and faithfulness. How can Moses' example of faithful leadership inspire you to live a life of purpose and devotion to God?

Psalm 104

Reflection: Psalm 104 praises God as the creator and sustainer of the universe. Reflect on the themes of God's sovereignty, provision, and majesty in creation. How does contemplating the beauty and order of creation deepen your awe and reverence for God?

Luke 6:27-49

Reflection: Luke 6 continues with Jesus' teachings on love for enemies, judging others, and building a foundation on His words. Reflect on the themes of love, forgiveness, and wisdom. How does Jesus' teaching challenge you to embody His love and wisdom in your relationships and daily choices?

Day 105: Galatians 1-3, Psalm 105, Luke 7:1-28

Galatians 1-3

Reflection: These chapters contain Paul's defense of his apostleship and his teachings on justification by faith. Reflect on the themes of grace, freedom, and faithfulness. How does Paul's emphasis on salvation by faith apart from works challenge you to rely more fully on God's grace and trust in His promises?

Psalm 105

Reflection: Psalm 105 recounts God's faithfulness to His covenant promises and His deliverance of Israel from Egypt. Reflect on the themes of remembrance, gratitude, and providence. How does remembering God's faithfulness in the past strengthen your faith and trust in His provision and guidance for the future?

Luke 7:1-28

Reflection: Luke 7 includes the healing of the centurion's servant and Jesus' testimony about John the Baptist. Reflect on the themes of faith, compassion, and humility. How does the centurion's faith and Jesus' affirmation of John's ministry challenge you to trust in God's power and respond with humility and compassion to those in need around you?

WEEK 16: Faith and Resourcefulness in Difficult Times

Welcome back, Faithful and Fierce women! This week, we delve into the captivating story of Judith, a heroine from the deuterocanonical Book of Judith. This narrative, filled with intrigue, bravery, and unwavering faith, offers valuable lessons for navigating difficult times in our own lives.

A Story of Courage and Cunning

The Book of Judith unfolds during a time of Assyrian dominance. The city of Bethulia faces imminent destruction by the ruthless General Holofernes. Enter Judith, a beautiful and resourceful widow, who devises a daring plan to save her people. Disguised as a wealthy woman seeking refuge, she enters Holofernes' camp, using her wit and charm to gain his trust. Culminating in a dramatic act of bravery, Judith ultimately liberates Bethulia from the clutches of the Assyrian army.

Faith and Resourcefulness: A Powerful Combination

Judith's story is not just about a cunning woman outsmarting a villain; it's a testament to the power of faith and resourcefulness in overcoming seemingly insurmountable challenges. Here's a closer look:

- **Faith as a Guiding Force:** Judith's actions are driven by her unwavering faith in God. She enters this perilous situation with a prayer on her lips, trusting in God's guidance and protection.

- **Resourcefulness in the Face of Adversity:** Judith doesn't rely solely on faith; she uses her intelligence, charm, and resourcefulness to outwit Holofernes. Her story reminds us that faith and practical action go hand-in-hand.

- **Discernment in Decision Making:** Judith doesn't rush into action; she carefully discerns God's will and devises a plan based on her strengths and the situation at hand.

- **Courage in the Face of Fear:** Judith's actions require immense courage. She ventures into enemy territory, risking her life for the sake of her people. Her story reminds us that even in the face of fear, faith can empower us to act with courage.

Self-Reflection: A Journey of Faith and Resourcefulness

Take some quiet time for reflection:

- **Recall a challenging time in your life.** This could be anything from a job loss to a personal conflict or a health scare.

- **How did your faith sustain you during this difficult period?** Did you find comfort in prayer, scripture, or the support of your faith community?

- **Did you have to rely on your resourcefulness to overcome this challenge?** Perhaps you had to develop new skills, seek out support networks, or find creative solutions to problems.

- **Reflect on how your faith and resourcefulness worked together.** Did your faith inspire you to find creative solutions? Did your resourcefulness help you maintain your faith during challenging times?

Remember, dear sisters, life throws curveballs, and we all face challenges. The Book of Judith reminds us that by drawing strength from our faith and employing our God-given resourcefulness, we can overcome adversity and emerge stronger.

Day 106: Galatians 4-6, Psalm 106, Luke 7:29-50

Galatians 4-6

Reflection: These chapters contain Paul's teachings on freedom in Christ, the works of the flesh versus the fruit of the Spirit, and instructions for Christian living. Reflect on the themes of freedom, grace, and spiritual growth. How does Paul's message challenge you to live a life characterized by love, humility, and obedience to God's Word?

Psalm 106

Reflection: Psalm 106 is a prayer of confession and praise, recounting Israel's history of rebellion and God's faithfulness. Reflect on the themes of repentance, mercy, and covenant love. How does reflecting on God's mercy and forgiveness in the face of human sinfulness inspire you to turn to Him in repentance and praise?

Luke 7:29-50

Reflection: Luke 7 continues with Jesus' teachings on John the Baptist and His interactions with various individuals, including the sinful woman who anoints His feet. Reflect on the themes of repentance, forgiveness, and grace. How does Jesus' response to the sinful woman challenge you to embrace humility, repentance, and gratitude for God's forgiveness in your own life?

Day 107: Joshua 1-3, Psalm 107, Luke 8:1-25

Joshua 1-3

Reflection: These chapters mark the beginning of Joshua's leadership as he leads the Israelites across the Jordan River into the promised land. Reflect on the themes of courage, obedience, and God's faithfulness. How does Joshua's example of courage and trust in God's promises encourage you to step out in faith and obedience to God's calling in your own life?

Psalm 107

Reflection: Psalm 107 is a song of thanksgiving for God's deliverance and provision in various circumstances. Reflect on the themes of praise, gratitude, and God's redeeming love. How does remembering God's faithfulness in times of trouble inspire you to trust Him in every circumstance and give thanks for His goodness?

Luke 8:1-25

Reflection: Luke 8 records Jesus' ministry, including His teachings, parables, and miracles. Reflect on the themes of faith, healing, and spiritual growth. How do the examples of faith and perseverance in the midst of trials challenge you to deepen your trust in Jesus and grow in your relationship with Him?

Day 108: Joshua 4-6, Psalm 108, Luke 8:26-56

Joshua 4-6

Reflection: These chapters narrate the crossing of the Jordan River and the conquest of Jericho. Reflect on the themes of faith, obedience, and God's power. How does the miraculous victory at Jericho serve as a reminder of God's faithfulness and His ability to fulfill His promises?

Psalm 108

Reflection: Psalm 108 is a prayer for God's victory and vindication. Reflect on the themes of trust, praise, and reliance on God's strength. How does the psalmist's confidence in God's help and deliverance inspire you to trust in God's sovereignty and seek His guidance in your own life?

Luke 8:26-56

Reflection: Luke 8 continues with Jesus' ministry, including His healing of the demon-possessed man and the raising of Jairus' daughter. Reflect on the themes of deliverance, faith, and compassion. How do these miraculous acts of Jesus demonstrate His power over evil and His compassion for the marginalized and suffering?

Day 109: Joshua 7-9, Psalm 109, Luke 9:1-27

Joshua 7-9

Reflection: These chapters recount the defeat at Ai due to Achan's sin, the deception of the Gibeonites, and the alliance against Israel. Reflect on the themes of sin, deception, and consequences. How does the story of Achan's sin and its consequences serve as a warning against disobedience and the importance of integrity before God?

Psalm 109

Reflection: Psalm 109 is a lament and imprecation against enemies. Reflect on the themes of justice, vindication, and mercy. How does the psalmist's cry for justice and deliverance from enemies challenge you to trust in God's righteous judgment and to extend mercy and forgiveness even to those who wrong you?

Luke 9:1-27

Reflection: Luke 9 records Jesus' commissioning of the twelve apostles and Peter's confession of Christ. Reflect on the themes of discipleship, mission, and identity in Christ. How does Jesus' call to take up the cross and follow Him challenge you to prioritize your allegiance to Him above all else and to embrace His mission of proclaiming the kingdom of God?

Day 110: Joshua 10-12, Psalm 110, Luke 9:28-50

Joshua 10-12

Reflection: These chapters describe the conquest of the southern and northern kings of Canaan by Joshua and the Israelites. Reflect on the themes of victory, sovereignty, and fulfillment of God's promises. How do the victories of Joshua and the Israelites demonstrate God's faithfulness and His power to accomplish His purposes?

Psalm 110

Reflection: Psalm 110 is a Messianic psalm that speaks of the exaltation and reign of the Messiah. Reflect on the themes of kingship, victory, and divine authority. How does the psalmist's portrayal of the Messiah as both king and priest foreshadow the ministry of Jesus Christ and His ultimate triumph over sin and death?

Luke 9:28-50

Reflection: Luke 9 recounts the transfiguration of Jesus, His teaching on discipleship, and His rebuke of the disciples' pride. Reflect on the themes of glory, humility, and servanthood. How does the transfiguration reveal Jesus' divine nature and His fulfillment of the Law and the Prophets? How does Jesus' teaching on humility challenge you to prioritize service and selflessness in your own life?

Day 111: Joshua 13-16, Psalm 111, Luke 10:1-24

Joshua 13-16

Reflection: These chapters detail the division of the land among the tribes of Israel and the inheritance of the Levites. Reflect on the themes of provision, inheritance, and God's faithfulness. How does the distribution of the land among the tribes remind you of God's promises fulfilled and His provision for His people?

Psalm 111

Reflection: Psalm 111 is a hymn of praise for God's wonderful works and His faithfulness to His covenant. Reflect on the themes of praise, remembrance, and wisdom. How does reflecting on God's mighty deeds and His righteous character inspire you to praise Him and to seek His wisdom in your daily life?

Luke 10:1-24

Reflection: Luke 10 records Jesus sending out the seventy-two disciples and their return with joy over their successful ministry. Reflect on the themes of mission, empowerment, and spiritual warfare. How does Jesus' commission to the seventy-two disciples challenge you to embrace your role as a laborer in God's harvest and to rely on His power and authority in your ministry?

Day 112: Joshua 17-19, Psalm 112, Luke 10:25-42

Joshua 17-19

Reflection: These chapters continue the distribution of the land among the tribes of Israel, including the inheritance of Ephraim, Manasseh, and the remaining tribes. Reflect on the themes of blessings, stewardship, and community. How does the allocation of land among the tribes emphasize the importance of unity and cooperation among God's people?

Psalm 112

Reflection: Psalm 112 is a psalm celebrating the blessings of the righteous and their trust in God. Reflect on the themes of righteousness, generosity, and trust in God's provision. How does the psalmist's description of the righteous person challenge you to live a life characterized by faithfulness, generosity, and trust in God's promises?

Luke 10:25-42

Reflection: Luke 10 includes the parable of the Good Samaritan and Jesus' visit to the home of Mary and Martha. Reflect on the themes of compassion, hospitality, and devotion. How do these stories challenge you to show love and compassion to your neighbors, to prioritize spending time with Jesus, and to find balance between service and devotion in your life?

WEEK 17: Women and Forgiveness: Letting Go and Moving Forward

Welcome back, Faithful and Fierce women! We continue our exploration of faith with a crucial yet challenging topic – **forgiveness.** Letting go of resentment and hurt can be a tall order, but the Bible offers powerful stories and teachings that can guide us on this path to healing and freedom.

The Power of Forgiveness: A Biblical Journey

The Bible overflows with stories of forgiveness, both human and divine. Here are a few examples that illuminate the transformative power of letting go:

- **Joseph and His Brothers:** In the Book of Genesis, Joseph is betrayed by his own brothers, sold into slavery, and endures years of hardship. Yet, upon reuniting with them, he chooses forgiveness, demonstrating the power of love over resentment (Genesis 45).

- **The Woman Caught in Adultery:** In the Gospel of John, a woman caught in adultery is brought before Jesus. Instead of condemning her, Jesus offers her forgiveness and a chance to start anew (John 8:3-11).

- **The Parable of the Unforgiving Servant:** This parable in Matthew 18:21-35 teaches a powerful lesson. A king forgives his servant a massive debt, yet the servant refuses to forgive a fellow servant who owes him a small sum. The parable highlights the importance of extending forgiveness to others, just as God forgives us.

Letting Go for Your Own Sake

Forgiveness isn't about condoning wrongdoing; it's about releasing ourselves from the burden of anger and resentment. Here's why forgiveness is crucial for your well-being:

- **Promotes Healing:** Holding onto anger can be emotionally and spiritually toxic. Forgiveness allows us to heal from past hurts and move forward with our lives.

- **Breaks the Cycle of negativity:** Resentment can breed bitterness and negativity. Forgiveness frees us from this cycle and allows us to embrace joy and peace.

- **Strengthens Relationships:** Even the closest relationships hit bumps. Forgiveness allows us to mend broken bridges and rebuild trust.

- **Empowers You:** Choosing forgiveness puts you back in control of your emotions. You refuse to let someone else's actions define your present or future.

Challenge: The Power of Letting Go

Forgiveness can be a difficult journey, but this week, I challenge you to take a step towards letting go:

- **Identify someone who has hurt you.** This could be a friend, family member, or even a stranger who has wronged you.

- **Write a letter of forgiveness (optional):** Putting your thoughts and emotions on paper can be a powerful tool for healing. You don't have to send the letter, but use it as a vehicle to express your hurt and ultimately, your choice to forgive.

- **Pray for their well-being:** Sending positive thoughts and prayers, even for those who have hurt you, can be a transformative act of forgiveness.

- **Seek support:** If you're struggling to forgive, talking to a trusted friend, spiritual advisor, or therapist can provide guidance and support.

Remember, dear sisters, forgiveness is a process, not a one-time event. Be patient with yourself, and trust that with time and God's grace, you can find the strength to let go and move forward in peace.

BIBLE READING: Week 17

Day 113: Joshua 20-22, Psalm 113, Luke 10:25-42

Joshua 20-22

Reflection: These chapters detail the establishment of cities of refuge, the return of the eastern tribes to their inheritance, and their construction of an altar. Reflect on the themes of justice, unity, and worship. How do these events demonstrate the importance of seeking justice, maintaining unity among believers, and worshiping God in sincerity and truth?

Psalm 113

Reflection: Psalm 113 is a hymn of praise for God's sovereignty and compassion, especially towards the lowly. Reflect on the themes of praise, humility, and God's care for the vulnerable. How does meditating on God's character inspire you to praise Him and trust in His provision and protection?

Luke 10:25-42

Reflection: Luke 10 includes the parable of the Good Samaritan and Jesus' visit to the home of Mary and Martha. Reflect on the themes of compassion, hospitality, and devotion. How do these stories challenge you to show love and compassion to your neighbors, to prioritize spending time with Jesus, and to find balance between service and devotion in your life?

Day 114: Joshua 23-24, Psalm 114, Luke 11:1-28

Joshua 23-24

Reflection: These chapters contain Joshua's farewell address to Israel and the renewal of the covenant at Shechem. Reflect on the themes of faithfulness, covenant, and commitment. How does Joshua's call to choose whom to serve and his own commitment to serving the Lord challenge you to prioritize your allegiance to God and to live faithfully according to His Word?

Psalm 114

Reflection: Psalm 114 celebrates God's power in delivering Israel from Egypt and leading them through the wilderness. Reflect on the themes of deliverance, awe, and trust in God's providence. How does remembering God's past acts of deliverance inspire you to trust Him in times of difficulty and uncertainty?

Luke 11:1-28

Reflection: Luke 11 includes Jesus' teaching on prayer, His response to accusations of casting out demons by Beelzebul, and His teaching on the sign of Jonah. Reflect on the themes of prayer, spiritual warfare, and repentance. How do Jesus' teachings on prayer and spiritual discernment challenge you to deepen your prayer life and to seek God's kingdom above all else?

Day 115: Ephesians 1:1-3:24, Psalm 115, Luke 11:29-54

Ephesians 1:1-3:24

Reflection: These chapters contain Paul's letter to the Ephesians, which emphasizes the believers' identity in Christ, God's plan of redemption, and instructions for Christian living. Reflect on the themes of spiritual blessings, unity in Christ, and the mystery of the gospel. How does Paul's teaching on these topics deepen your understanding of your identity and purpose in Christ?

Psalm 115

Reflection: Psalm 115 contrasts the sovereignty of God with the idols of the nations and calls for trust in the Lord. Reflect on the themes of worship, trust, and the futility of idolatry. How does the psalmist's declaration of trust in the living God challenge you to place your confidence in Him alone and to worship Him wholeheartedly?

Luke 11:29-54

Reflection: Luke 11 includes Jesus' rebuke of the crowds seeking a sign, His condemnation of the Pharisees and lawyers, and His warnings against hypocrisy. Reflect on the themes of faith, repentance, and judgment. How do Jesus' words challenge you to examine your own heart, to seek genuine faith and repentance, and to live with integrity before God and others?

Day 116: Ephesians 3:25-6:24, Psalm 116-117, Luke 12:1-34

Ephesians 3:25-6:24

Reflection: These chapters contain Paul's exhortations on Christian living, including instructions for relationships, spiritual warfare, and the armor of God. Reflect on the themes of unity, spiritual maturity, and standing firm in faith. How does Paul's guidance on these matters equip you to live out your faith in a manner worthy of your calling as a follower of Christ?

Psalm 116-117

Reflection: Psalm 116 is a song of thanksgiving for deliverance from death, while Psalm 117 is a brief hymn of praise. Reflect on the themes of gratitude, praise, and God's faithfulness. How do these psalms encourage you to express thankfulness to God for His deliverance and to praise Him for His steadfast love and faithfulness?

Luke 12:1-34

Reflection: Luke 12 includes Jesus' warnings against hypocrisy, His teaching on fearlessness in the face of persecution, and His exhortation to seek the kingdom of God above all else. Reflect on the themes of trust, stewardship, and the pursuit of God's kingdom. How do Jesus' words challenge you to prioritize eternal values over temporal concerns and to trust in God's provision for your needs?

Day 117: Judges 1-3, Psalm 118, Luke 12:35-59

Judges 1-3

Reflection: These chapters depict Israel's initial struggles to conquer the Promised Land and their subsequent cycles of disobedience, oppression, repentance, and deliverance under various judges. Reflect on the themes of obedience, consequences, and God's faithfulness. How do the events in these chapters illustrate the importance of faithfulness to God's commands and the cycle of repentance and restoration in the life of God's people?

Psalm 118

Reflection: Psalm 118 is a hymn of praise for God's steadfast love and deliverance. Reflect on the themes of salvation, victory, and trust in God's goodness. How does the psalmist's declaration of God's faithfulness and salvation inspire you to trust in God's providence and to give Him thanks and praise in all circumstances?

Luke 12:35-59

Reflection: Luke 12 includes Jesus' teaching on readiness for His return, the need for faithful stewardship, and the call to interpret the signs of the times. Reflect on the themes of vigilance, readiness, and accountability. How do Jesus' words challenge you to live with a sense of urgency, to faithfully steward the resources entrusted to you, and to be prepared for His coming?

Day 118: Judges 4-5, Psalm 119:1-48, Luke 13:1-17

Judges 4-5

Reflection: These chapters recount the stories of Deborah and Barak, the defeat of Sisera, and the song of Deborah and Barak. Reflect on the themes of leadership, courage, and God's deliverance. How do the actions of Deborah, Barak, and Jael demonstrate the importance of courageously obeying God's call and trusting in His power to deliver His people from oppression?

Psalm 119:1-48

Reflection: Psalm 119 extols the virtues of God's law and the blessings of obedience. Reflect on the themes of love for God's word, obedience, and the pursuit of righteousness. How does the psalmist's devotion to God's law inspire you to seek after God's ways and to align your life with His commands?

Luke 13:1-17

Reflection: Luke 13 includes Jesus' warnings about repentance and the parable of the fig tree, as well as His healing of a crippled woman on the Sabbath. Reflect on the themes of repentance, compassion, and the kingdom of God. How do these passages challenge you to examine your own heart, to show compassion to those in need, and to prioritize the things of God in your life?

Day 119: Judges 6-9, Psalm 119:49-88, Luke 13:18-35

Judges 6-9

Reflection: These chapters narrate the stories of Gideon, his call to deliver Israel from the Midianites, and the subsequent events including the destruction of Baal's altar and Gideon's victories. Reflect on the themes of faith, obedience, and God's empowerment. How does Gideon's journey from doubt to faith and his reliance on God's strength challenge you to trust in God's power and step out in obedience to His call, even in the face of overwhelming odds?

Psalm 119:49-88

Reflection: Psalm 119 is an acrostic poem celebrating the beauty and value of God's word. Reflect on the themes of meditation, obedience, and the sufficiency of God's word. How does the psalmist's deep love and reverence for God's law inspire you to meditate on Scripture, to obey God's commands, and to find guidance and comfort in His word?

Luke 13:18-35

Reflection: Luke 13 includes Jesus' parables of the mustard seed and the yeast, as well as His lament over Jerusalem. Reflect on the themes of growth, the kingdom of God, and repentance. How do these parables challenge you to recognize the transformative power of God's kingdom, to repent and turn to God, and to embrace His invitation to participate in His redemptive work in the world?

WEEK 18: The Fruits of the Holy Spirit: Cultivating Christ-like Qualities

Welcome back, Faithful and Fierce women! As we continue this transformative journey of faith, we delve into a vital aspect of Christian living – cultivating the Fruits of the Holy Spirit. In Galatians 5:22-23, the apostle Paul outlines these precious fruits as: love, joy, peace, patience, kindness, goodness, faithfulness, gentleness, and self-control. These qualities, nurtured by the Holy Spirit within us, empower us to live Christ-like lives, radiating God's love and grace in the world.

A Journey of Spiritual Virtues

The Fruits of the Holy Spirit aren't mere ideals; they are practical qualities that can be cultivated in our daily lives. Let's explore some of these fruits:

- **Love:** This foundational fruit encompasses a deep love for God, others, and ourselves. It manifests in compassion, empathy, and acts of selfless service.

- **Joy:** This isn't fleeting happiness based on external circumstances; it's a deep-seated joy rooted in faith and a connection with God. It's the ability to find joy even in difficult times.

- **Peace:** This fruit offers a sense of inner calm and tranquility, even amidst life's storms. It's the peace that comes from knowing God's presence and trusting in His plan.

- **Patience:** This fruit equips us to endure challenges and setbacks with grace and perseverance. It allows us to wait on God's timing without complaining.

- **Kindness:** This extends beyond mere politeness; it involves showing genuine care and compassion for others, expressed in our words and actions.

- **Goodness:** This fruit highlights the importance of living a morally upright life, doing what is right, and choosing actions that reflect God's character.

- **Faithfulness:** This embodies loyalty and trustworthiness. It's about being reliable and keeping our promises, both to God and others.

- **Gentleness:** This fruit emphasizes humility, meekness, and treating others with respect and sensitivity.

- **Self-Control:** The ability to manage our emotions, desires, and impulses is crucial for living a Christ-centered life. It allows us to make wise choices and avoid destructive behaviors.

From Knowledge to Action: Cultivating the Fruits

The Fruits of the Holy Spirit aren't bestowed upon us magically; they are cultivated through intentional effort and cooperation with the Holy Spirit. Here are some ways to cultivate these precious fruits:

- **Prayer:** Regular prayer invites the Holy Spirit to work within you. Ask God to help you cultivate specific fruits in your life.

- **Scripture Study:** The Bible is filled with wisdom on living a Christ-like life. Seek verses that speak to the fruits you want to cultivate.

- **Reflection and Journaling:** Regular reflection and journaling allow you to assess your progress and identify areas where you can focus your growth efforts.

- **Serving Others:** Putting your faith into action by serving others is a powerful way to cultivate love, kindness, and compassion.

- **Accountability:** Share your goals with a trusted friend or mentor and ask for their support and encouragement.

Journaling: Cultivating a Fruit

Take some quiet time for reflection and journaling:

- Choose a specific Fruit of the Holy Spirit that resonates with you this week. It could be love, joy, patience, kindness, or any other fruit that you feel needs cultivation in your life.

- Reflect on how this fruit manifests in your life currently. Are there areas where you excel? Are there areas where you can improve?

- Write down specific actions you can take this week to cultivate this chosen fruit. These actions could be anything from volunteering in your community to simply practicing patience with your loved ones.

- Journal your daily experiences as you strive to cultivate this fruit. What challenges do you face? What victories do you celebrate?

Remember, dear sisters, cultivating the Fruits of the Holy Spirit is a lifelong journey. There will be times of struggle and setbacks. But with perseverance, prayer, and cooperation with the Holy Spirit, you can blossom into a woman who radiates God's love and embodies the beautiful fruits of Christ-like character.

Day 120: Judges 10-12, Psalm 119:89-136, Luke 14

Judges 10-12

Reflection: These chapters describe the judgeship of Jair and Jephthah, as well as the conflict with the Ammonites. Reflect on the themes of leadership, faithfulness, and consequences of disobedience. How do the stories of Jair and Jephthah illustrate the importance of seeking God's guidance in leadership and the consequences of turning away from Him?

Psalm 119:89-136

Reflection: Psalm 119 continues its celebration of God's word, highlighting its eternal nature, its significance for personal growth, and its power to bring understanding and guidance. Reflect on the themes of the enduring nature of God's word, its role in shaping our character, and the psalmist's longing for deeper understanding and obedience. How does the psalmist's commitment to God's word inspire you to seek greater intimacy with God through Scripture and to align your life more closely with His commands?

Luke 14

Reflection: Luke 14 contains teachings and parables by Jesus, including the parable of the great banquet and the cost of discipleship. Reflect on the themes of humility, hospitality, and commitment to follow Jesus. How do Jesus' teachings challenge you to humble yourself, to extend hospitality to others, and to count the cost of discipleship as you follow Him?

Day 121: Judges 13-16, Psalm 119:137-176, Luke 15:1-10

Judges 13-16

Reflection: These chapters recount the story of Samson, his birth, exploits, and downfall. Reflect on the themes of God's sovereignty, human weakness, and the consequences of sin. How does Samson's life serve as a cautionary tale about the dangers of disregarding God's commands and relying on one's own strength?

Psalm 119:137-176

Reflection: Psalm 119 concludes with a passionate plea for God's mercy, deliverance, and guidance. Reflect on the themes of longing for God's righteousness, commitment to His word, and dependence on His grace. How does the psalmist's heartfelt cry for God's intervention resonate with your own experiences of seeking God's guidance and deliverance in times of trial?

Luke 15:1-10

Reflection: Luke 15 contains the parables of the lost sheep and the lost coin, highlighting God's relentless pursuit of the lost. Reflect on the themes of repentance, restoration, and rejoicing in heaven over the repentance of sinners. How do these parables deepen your understanding of God's love and His desire to reconcile the lost to Himself?

Day 122: Judges 17-19, Psalm 120-121, Luke 15:11-32

Judges 17-19

Reflection: These chapters narrate the account of Micah's idolatry, the Levite and his concubine, and the subsequent civil war. Reflect on the themes of moral decline, religious syncretism, and the consequences of forsaking God's commands. How do these tragic events serve as a warning against compromising with sin and abandoning true worship of God?

Psalm 120-121

Reflection: Psalm 120 expresses the psalmist's distress over deceitful lips and longing for peace, while Psalm 121 declares trust in the Lord as the keeper and protector of Israel. Reflect on the themes of trust, deliverance, and God's faithfulness. How do these psalms speak to your own experiences of seeking God's help in times of trouble and finding refuge in His unfailing love?

Luke 15:11-32

Reflection: Luke 15 contains the parable of the prodigal son, illustrating God's extravagant love and the joy of repentance and reconciliation. Reflect on the themes of repentance, forgiveness, and restoration. How does the father's response to the prodigal son challenge you to embrace God's grace and extend forgiveness to others, even those who have wronged you?

Day 123: Judges 20-21, Psalm 122, Luke 16:1-15

Judges 20-21

Reflection: These chapters recount the tragic events following the Levite's concubine, including the civil war with the tribe of Benjamin and the aftermath. Reflect on the themes of justice, accountability, and the consequences of sin. How do these events reveal the devastating effects of moral decay and the importance of upholding God's standards of righteousness in society?

Psalm 122

Reflection: Psalm 122 celebrates the joy of worshiping in Jerusalem and the peace within its walls. Reflect on the themes of unity, worship, and longing for God's presence. How does the psalmist's love for the house of the Lord inspire you to prioritize worship and seek unity among God's people?

Luke 16:1-15

Reflection: Luke 16 includes the parable of the shrewd manager and teachings on the proper use of wealth. Reflect on the themes of stewardship, honesty, and the pursuit of eternal treasures. How do Jesus' teachings challenge you to be faithful and wise stewards of the resources entrusted to you, using them to advance God's kingdom and bless others?

Day 124: Ruth, Psalm 123, Luke 16:16-31

Ruth

Reflection: The book of Ruth tells the story of Ruth's loyalty to her mother-in-law Naomi, her relationship with Boaz, and God's providential care for them. Reflect on the themes of loyalty, kindness, and redemption. How do the actions of Ruth and Boaz demonstrate God's faithfulness in difficult circumstances and His ability to bring beauty from ashes?

Psalm 123

Reflection: Psalm 123 expresses the psalmist's plea for mercy and deliverance from scorn and contempt. Reflect on the themes of humility, dependence on God, and trusting in His mercy. How does the psalmist's posture of humility and trust challenge you to turn to God in times of difficulty and to rely on His unfailing love and faithfulness?

Luke 16:16-31

Reflection: Luke 16 includes teachings on the kingdom of God, the law and the prophets, and the parable of the rich man and Lazarus. Reflect on the themes of righteousness, judgment, and the eternal destiny of the righteous and the wicked. How do these passages prompt you to consider the fleeting nature of earthly wealth and the importance of investing in eternal treasures?

Day 125: 1 Samuel 1-4, Psalm 124, Luke 17:1-19

1 Samuel 1-4

Reflection: These chapters introduce the prophet Samuel and recount the birth of Samuel, his dedication to God's service, and the Israelites' defeat by the Philistines and the loss of the ark of the covenant. Reflect on the themes of prayer, obedience, and God's sovereignty. How do the characters in these narratives demonstrate the importance of faithful prayer and obedience to God's will, even in the face of challenges and setbacks?

Psalm 124

Reflection: Psalm 124 is a song of deliverance, praising God for His intervention and protection. Reflect on the themes of dependence on God, gratitude for His deliverance, and trust in His unfailing love. How does the psalmist's acknowledgment of God's past faithfulness encourage you to trust in God's provision and protection in your own life?

Luke 17:1-19

Reflection: Luke 17 includes teachings on forgiveness, faith, and gratitude, as well as the healing of ten lepers. Reflect on the themes of forgiveness, faithfulness, and gratitude. How do Jesus' teachings challenge you to cultivate a spirit of forgiveness, to trust in God's promises, and to express gratitude for His blessings in your life?

Day 126: 1 Samuel 5-7, Psalm 125, Luke 17:20-37

1 Samuel 5-7

Reflection: These chapters describe the capture of the ark by the Philistines, God's judgment on the Philistine idols, and the return of the ark to Israel. Reflect on the themes of God's sovereignty, holiness, and the consequences of disobedience. How do these events demonstrate God's power over false gods and His commitment to uphold His holiness among His people?

Psalm 125

Reflection: Psalm 125 expresses confidence in God's protection and security for His people. Reflect on the themes of trust in God's faithfulness, stability, and the assurance of His presence. How does the psalmist's assurance of God's protection challenge you to trust in God's provision and to find security in His presence, even in uncertain times?

Luke 17:20-37

Reflection: Luke 17 includes teachings on the kingdom of God, the coming of the Son of Man, and the need for readiness and perseverance. Reflect on the themes of the kingdom of God, eschatology, and the call to be vigilant and faithful. How do these teachings encourage you to live in anticipation of Christ's return, to prioritize the things of God, and to remain steadfast in your faith?

WEEK 19: The Parable of the Widow's Mite: Faithfulness and Generosity

Welcome back, Faithful and Fierce women! As we embark on this week of our faith-filled exploration, we turn our hearts to a powerful parable found in the Gospel of Mark – the Parable of the Widow's Mite (Mark 12:41-44). This seemingly simple story offers profound lessons on faithfulness, generosity, and the value of giving, no matter the size.

A Journey of Giving:

In this short parable, Jesus observes people depositing their offerings in the temple treasury. Wealthy individuals contribute large sums, drawing attention with their displays of generosity. Then, a poor widow quietly places two small copper coins, known as mites, into the treasury.

Beyond Appearances: True Generosity

While the rich gave generously in terms of quantity, Jesus highlights the widow's offering as the most significant. Here's why:

- **Proportionality of Giving:** Jesus emphasizes that the widow gave "out of her poverty" (Mark 12:42). Her two mites represented her entire livelihood, showcasing a level of sacrifice far exceeding the wealthy who gave from their abundance.

- **The Value of Faith:** The widow's act was an expression of her unwavering faith in God. Her trust in Him wasn't dependent on material possessions.

- **Giving from the Heart:** The widow's offering wasn't motivated by a desire for recognition; it was a heartfelt act of devotion and generosity.

The Call to Faithful Giving

The Parable of the Widow's Mite challenges us to re-evaluate our own approach to giving. Here are some key takeaways:

- **Giving Proportionately:** Our generosity should be measured by the sacrifice we make, not just the amount we give.

- **Giving from the Heart:** True generosity is rooted in love for God and a desire to help others, not self-promotion.

- **Every Contribution Matters:** Regardless of your financial situation, your willingness to give, even in small ways, holds immense value.

Action Step: Putting Faith into Action

This week, I challenge you to take a concrete step towards faithful and generous giving:

- **Donate to a Charity:** Identify a cause close to your heart and make a financial donation, no matter the size. Many charities offer online donation options, making the process easy and convenient.

- **Volunteer Your Time:** Not everyone has financial resources to spare, but everyone has time to offer. Volunteer your skills and talents at a local soup kitchen, homeless shelter, or organization that aligns with your interests.

- **Offer a Helping Hand:** Look for opportunities to extend a helping hand to those in need within your own community. This could be offering groceries to an elderly neighbor, helping a friend with childcare, or simply offering a listening ear.

Remember, dear sisters, the act of giving isn't just about financial resources; it's about giving of your time, talents, and resources in ways that honor God and contribute to a better world.

Discussion Starter:

- Reflect on your own giving habits. How can you incorporate the lessons from the Parable of the Widow's Mite into your approach to generosity?

- Share stories of women you admire who exemplify the spirit of faithful giving.

- Discuss the importance of volunteering and community service in extending God's love to others.

BIBLE READING: Week 19

Day 127:1 Samuel 8-10, Psalm 126, Luke 18:1-14

1 Samuel 8-10:

Reflection: These chapters depict Israel's request for a king and the anointing of Saul as the first king of Israel. Reflect on the themes of leadership, obedience, and the consequences of human desires over God's guidance. How can you discern between God's will and your own desires in matters of leadership and decision-making?

Psalm 126:

Reflection: Psalm 126 celebrates the restoration of Zion and God's faithfulness to His people. Reflect on the themes of joy, gratitude, and hope in times of restoration. How can you cultivate a spirit of gratitude and hopefulness, trusting in God's faithfulness even in challenging circumstances?

Luke 18:1-14:

Reflection: In this passage, Jesus teaches about the persistent widow and the humble tax collector. Reflect on the themes of prayer, humility, and faith. How can you cultivate a persistent prayer life and maintain humility before God, trusting in His justice and mercy rather than your own righteousness?

Day 128: 1 Samuel 11-12, Psalm 127, Luke 18:15-43

1 Samuel 11-12

Reflection: In these chapters, Saul consolidates his kingship over Israel, and Samuel delivers his farewell address. Reflect on the themes of leadership, obedience to God's commands, and the consequences of rejecting God as king. How do Saul's actions and Samuel's warnings serve as reminders of the importance of aligning our leadership with God's will and submitting to His authority?

Psalm 127

Reflection: Psalm 127 celebrates God's provision and the blessings of family life. Reflect on the themes of dependence on God, the importance of God's blessing in our endeavors, and the value of family. How does the psalmist's recognition of God's sovereignty in building and protecting a household challenge you to trust in God's provision and to prioritize your relationships with others?

Luke 18:15-43

Reflection: Luke 18 contains teachings on the kingdom of God and the importance of childlike faith, as well as Jesus' encounter with the rich ruler and the healing of a blind beggar. Reflect on the themes of faith, humility, and spiritual sight. How do these passages challenge you to approach God with childlike trust, to surrender everything to follow Him, and to recognize His power to bring spiritual and physical healing into your life?

Day 129: 1 Samuel 13-14, Psalm 128, Luke 19:1-27

1 Samuel 13-14

Reflection: These chapters recount Saul's disobedience and Jonathan's victory over the Philistines. Reflect on the themes of obedience, faithfulness, and the consequences of impulsive actions. How do Saul and Jonathan's contrasting responses to challenges illustrate the importance of trusting in God and obeying His commands, even in the face of difficult circumstances?

Psalm 128

Reflection: Psalm 128 is a song of blessing for those who fear the Lord and walk in His ways. Reflect on the themes of obedience, prosperity, and the fear of the Lord. How does the psalmist's portrayal of the blessed life challenge you to prioritize obedience to God's commands and to cultivate a reverent awe of His holiness in your daily life?

Luke 19:1-27

Reflection: Luke 19 includes the account of Jesus' encounter with Zacchaeus, the parable of the ten minas, and the triumphal entry into Jerusalem. Reflect on the themes of repentance, stewardship, and the kingdom of God. How do these passages challenge you to respond to Jesus' call to repentance, to faithfully steward the resources He has entrusted to you, and to eagerly anticipate His coming kingdom?

Day 130: 1 Samuel 15-16, Psalm 129, Luke 19:28-48

1 Samuel 15-16

Reflection: These chapters detail Samuel's anointing of David as the future king of Israel and Saul's continued disobedience. Reflect on the themes of obedience, humility, and the qualifications of leadership. How do Saul's downfall and David's anointing highlight the importance of a heart submitted to God's will and the qualities of a true leader who seeks after God's heart?

Psalm 129

Reflection: Psalm 129 is a prayer for deliverance from enemies and oppression. Reflect on the themes of perseverance, trust in God's deliverance, and the triumph of righteousness over evil. How does the psalmist's confidence in God's faithfulness amidst adversity inspire you to trust in God's protection and to persevere in times of trial?

Luke 19:28-48

Reflection: Luke 19 narrates Jesus' triumphal entry into Jerusalem, His weeping over the city, and His cleansing of the temple. Reflect on the themes of kingship, prophecy, and the true meaning of worship. How do these events reveal Jesus' identity as the promised Messiah and challenge you to respond to His authority with reverence and wholehearted devotion?

Day 131: 1 Samuel 17, Psalm 130, Luke 20:1-19

1 Samuel 17

Reflection: In this famous chapter, David defeats Goliath, showcasing his courage and faith in God. Reflect on the themes of courage, faith, and trusting in God's power. How does David's example inspire you to face your own giants with faith and confidence in God's ability to overcome obstacles in your life?

Psalm 130

Reflection: Psalm 130 is a cry for mercy and forgiveness, acknowledging God's abundant redemption. Reflect on the themes of repentance, hope, and waiting on the Lord. How does the psalmist's trust in God's mercy and redemption encourage you to turn to Him in repentance and to patiently wait for His deliverance in times of trouble?

Luke 20:1-19

Reflection: Luke 20 records Jesus' authority questioned by the religious leaders and His parable of the tenants. Reflect on the themes of authority, stewardship, and rejection of God's messengers. How do these passages challenge you to recognize Jesus' authority in your life, to faithfully steward the resources He has given you, and to heed His warnings against rejecting His message?

Day 132: 1 Samuel 18-20, Psalm 131, Luke 20:20-47

1 Samuel 18-20

Reflection: These chapters explore the complex relationships between David, Saul, and Jonathan, including David's rise to prominence, Saul's jealousy, and Jonathan's friendship with David. Reflect on the themes of friendship, loyalty, and jealousy. How do the dynamics between these characters offer insights into the nature of human relationships and the importance of loyalty and trust in God's plans?

Psalm 131

Reflection: Psalm 131 expresses humility and trust in God's care, likening the psalmist's soul to a weaned child with its mother. Reflect on the themes of humility, contentment, and childlike trust. How does the psalmist's example of surrendering to God's will and finding rest in His presence challenge you to cultivate a spirit of humility and trust in your own relationship with God?

Luke 20:20-47

Reflection: Luke 20 continues with Jesus' interactions with the religious leaders, including questions about paying taxes, the resurrection, and David's son. Reflect on the themes of authority, hypocrisy, and true worship. How do Jesus' responses challenge you to examine your own heart, to submit to His authority, and to worship Him in spirit and truth?

Day 133: 1 Samuel 21-23, Psalm 132, Luke 21:1-19

1 Samuel 21-23

Reflection: These chapters recount David's interactions with Saul, his flight from Saul's pursuit, and his time of hiding in the wilderness. Reflect on the themes of trust in God's protection, integrity in the face of adversity, and the testing of faith. How do David's actions during this period demonstrate his reliance on God's guidance and his commitment to righteousness even in difficult circumstances?

Psalm 132

Reflection: Psalm 132 is a song recalling God's covenant with David and the desire for the Lord's dwelling place in Jerusalem. Reflect on the themes of covenant, worship, and the longing for God's presence. How does the psalmist's passion for God's presence and the fulfillment of His promises inspire you to seek after God with wholehearted devotion and to prioritize worship as a central aspect of your life?

Luke 21:1-19

Reflection: Luke 21 records Jesus' teachings about the destruction of the temple, signs of the end times, and persecution of believers. Reflect on the themes of eschatology, perseverance, and trust in God's provision. How do Jesus' words challenge you to remain faithful and steadfast in your commitment to Him, even in the midst of trials and uncertainty about the future?

WEEK 20: Women and the Church: Finding Your Place in the Catholic Community

Welcome back, Faithful and Fierce women! We've reached the 20th week of our faith-enriching exploration. This week, we delve into the crucial role women play in the life of the Catholic Church. While the official position on ordination remains a point of discussion, there are countless ways for women to actively participate and contribute to the vibrancy of the Catholic community.

A Journey of Contributions:

Throughout history, women have played critical roles in the Church, from early patrons of the faith to pioneering theologians and religious leaders. Here's a glimpse at their ongoing contributions:

- **Leaders in Faith Formation:** Women serve as catechists, scripture study leaders, and youth group facilitators, nurturing the faith of future generations.

- **Ministers of Hospitality:** From welcoming newcomers to coordinating parish events, women create a warm and inviting atmosphere in the Church community.

- **Social Justice Advocates:** Women champion causes like social justice, education, and healthcare, embodying the Church's call to serve the marginalized.

- **Liturgical Ministers:** Women serve as lectors, cantors, and Eucharistic ministers, actively participating in worship celebrations.

- **Theologians and Scholars:** Women contribute to the intellectual life of the Church through scholarly work and theological reflection.

Beyond Tradition: Discovering Your Unique Calling

The Church needs the voices, talents, and leadership of women in all its aspects. Here are some ways to discover your place in the Church community:

- **Identify Your Gifts:** What are you passionate about? What skills and talents can you offer the Church?

- **Explore Ministries:** Research the various ministries available in your parish or diocese. Find a role that aligns with your interests and strengths.

- **Speak Up and Lead:** Don't be afraid to share your ideas and suggestions. There may be opportunities for women to take on leadership roles within the Church community.

- **Find a Mentor:** Connect with women who are already actively involved in the Church. They can offer guidance and support as you navigate your path.

Discussion Starter: Expanding Our Roles

The Church continues to evolve, and the role of women within it can too. Let's explore this topic further:

- Research Catholic theologians and advocates who are promoting greater roles for women in the Church. Share their insights and perspectives.

- Discuss specific ways your parish or diocese can create more opportunities for women to participate actively.

- Imagine an ideal future for women's roles in the Church. What changes would you like to see?

Remember, dear sisters, God has gifted you with unique talents and a passion to serve. Don't be discouraged by limitations; be empowered by the countless ways you can contribute to the Church.

Beyond This Book:

As this enriching lesson concludes, remember that your role in the Church continues to blossom! Here are some ways to stay engaged:

- **Stay Connected:** Regularly attend Mass, participate in parish activities, and connect with other Catholic women in your community.

- **Continue Learning:** Read books, articles, and attend lectures on topics related to women and the Church. Stay informed and empowered.

- **Advocate for Change:** Respecting Church teachings, be a respectful voice for change that allows women to contribute their full potential to the Church's mission.

Day 134: 1 Samuel 24-25, Psalm 133, Luke 21:20-38

1 Samuel 24-25:

Reflection: These chapters narrate David's encounter with Saul and his interactions with Nabal. Reflect on the themes of forgiveness, revenge, and reliance on God's justice. How can you emulate David's example of forgiveness and trust in God's timing when faced with injustice or mistreatment?

Psalm 133:

Reflection: Psalm 133 celebrates the beauty and blessing of unity among God's people. Reflect on the themes of unity, harmony, and brotherly love. How can you contribute to fostering unity within your community and among fellow believers?

Luke 21:20-38:

Reflection: In this passage, Jesus foretells the destruction of Jerusalem and speaks about the signs of the end times. Reflect on the themes of perseverance, watchfulness, and readiness for Christ's return. How can you live in a state of spiritual preparedness, eagerly anticipating the fulfillment of God's promises?

Day 135: 1 Samuel 26-28, Psalm 134, Luke 22:1-38

1 Samuel 26-28:

Reflection: These chapters recount David sparing Saul's life again, his interaction with the witch of Endor, and Saul's death. Reflect on the themes of mercy, trust in God's timing, and the consequences of seeking guidance outside of God's will. How can you trust in God's sovereignty even in the midst of difficult circumstances?

Psalm 134:

Reflection: Psalm 134 is a call to worship and bless the Lord. Reflect on the themes of worship, service, and reverence. How can you cultivate a lifestyle of worship and service, honoring God with your actions and attitudes?

Luke 22:1-38:

Reflection: In this passage, Jesus shares the Last Supper with His disciples and foretells Peter's denial. Reflect on the themes of betrayal, loyalty, and communion. How does this passage challenge you to examine your own loyalty to Christ and commitment to following Him, even in the face of trials?

Day 136: 1 Samuel 29-31, Psalm 135, Luke 22:39-71

1 Samuel 29-31:

Reflection: These chapters describe David's departure from the Philistine army, the death of Saul and his sons in battle, and David's lament for Saul and Jonathan. Reflect on the themes of loyalty, leadership, and the consequences of sin. How can you learn from the examples of David and Saul in navigating the challenges of leadership and remaining faithful to God?

Psalm 135:

Reflection: Psalm 135 praises God for His sovereignty and mighty acts. Reflect on the themes of worship, praise, and trust in God's power. How can you cultivate a heart of worship and praise, acknowledging God's greatness and faithfulness in your life?

Luke 22:39-71:

Reflection: In this passage, Jesus prays in Gethsemane, is betrayed by Judas, and undergoes a series of trials. Reflect on the themes of prayer, betrayal, and suffering. How can you learn from Jesus' example of prayerful submission to God's will in the face of betrayal and adversity?

Day 137: 2 Samuel 1-3, Psalm 136, Luke 23:1-32

2 Samuel 1-3:

Reflection: These chapters depict David's reaction to the news of Saul's death, his lament for Saul and Jonathan, and his rise to kingship over Judah. Reflect on the themes of grief, forgiveness, and leadership. How can you emulate David's compassion and integrity in your own responses to loss and conflict?

Psalm 136:

Reflection: Psalm 136 is a hymn of thanksgiving, recounting God's enduring love and mighty deeds. Reflect on the themes of gratitude, praise, and God's faithfulness. How can you cultivate a spirit of gratitude in your daily life, acknowledging God's steadfast love and provision?

Luke 23:1-32:

Reflection: In this passage, Jesus appears before Pilate and Herod, is mocked and beaten, and begins His journey to the cross. Reflect on the themes of injustice, suffering, and redemption. How does Jesus' willingness to endure unjust treatment and suffering challenge you to persevere in faithfulness, even in the face of adversity?

Day 138: 2 Samuel 4-6, Psalm 137, Luke 23:33-56

2 Samuel 4-6:

Reflection: These chapters describe the death of Ish-bosheth, David's kingship over all Israel, and the bringing of the ark to Jerusalem. Reflect on the themes of justice, leadership, and reverence for God's presence. How can you seek to honor God's presence in your life and leadership roles, like David did with the ark?

Psalm 137:

Reflection: Psalm 137 reflects on the Israelites' longing for Jerusalem while in exile. Reflect on the themes of longing, exile, and hope for restoration. How can you maintain hope and faithfulness to God's promises, even in times of difficulty or separation from your spiritual home?

Luke 23:33-56:

Reflection: In this passage, Jesus is crucified, dies, and is buried. Reflect on the themes of sacrifice, redemption, and mourning. How does Jesus' sacrificial death on the cross impact your understanding of God's love and salvation? How can you respond to His sacrifice with gratitude and devotion?

Day 139: 2 Samuel 7-10, Psalm 138, Luke 24:1-35

2 Samuel 7-10:

Reflection: These chapters contain God's covenant with David, David's desire to build a temple for the Lord, and his victories over various enemies. Reflect on the themes of God's faithfulness, human ambition, and the importance of seeking God's will. How can you align your ambitions with God's purposes and trust in His faithfulness to fulfill His promises?

Psalm 138:

Reflection: Psalm 138 is a song of praise for God's faithfulness and answered prayers. Reflect on the themes of gratitude, trust, and confidence in God's goodness. How can you cultivate a heart of thanksgiving and trust in God's faithfulness, even in challenging circumstances?

Luke 24:1-35:

Reflection: In this passage, the women discover Jesus' empty tomb, encounter angels who announce His resurrection, and encounter the risen Jesus on the road to Emmaus. Reflect on the themes of resurrection, doubt, and revelation. How does Jesus' resurrection give you hope and assurance in the face of doubt or uncertainty? How can you be open to encountering the risen Christ in unexpected ways?

Day 140: 2 Samuel 11-12, Psalm 139, Luke 24:36-53

2 Samuel 11-12:

Reflection: These chapters recount David's sin with Bathsheba and his confrontation by Nathan the prophet. Reflect on the themes of sin, repentance, and consequences. How can you guard against temptation and respond with humility and repentance when you fall short of God's standards?

Psalm 139:

Reflection: Psalm 139 celebrates God's intimate knowledge of and care for His people. Reflect on the themes of God's omniscience, omnipresence, and love. How does the psalmist's recognition of God's intimate involvement in every aspect of life inspire you to trust in God's guidance and care?

Luke 24:36-53:

Reflection: In this passage, Jesus appears to His disciples, shows them His wounds, and ascends into heaven. Reflect on the themes of resurrection, commissioning, and hope. How does Jesus' resurrection and ascension empower you to fulfill His commission to proclaim the gospel and make disciples? How can you live in the hope of His promised return?

WEEK 21: Strength in Humility and Service

Welcome back, Faithful and Fierce women! As we embark on this week of our exploration of faith, we return to a cornerstone of Jesus' teachings – the Beatitudes found in the Gospel of Matthew (Matthew 5:1-12). These eight blessings, seemingly paradoxical at first glance, reveal a counter-intuitive path to true happiness and fulfillment.

A Journey of Blessings:

The Beatitudes challenge societal norms and redefine what true blessedness entails. Here's a closer look at each blessing:

- **Blessed are the poor in spirit:** This doesn't refer to material poverty; it's about acknowledging our spiritual need for God and recognizing our dependence on Him.

- **Blessed are those who mourn:** Jesus acknowledges the pain of loss but suggests that mourning can lead to a deeper connection with God and an appreciation for the blessings we have.

- **Blessed are the meek:** Meekness doesn't equate weakness; it's about humility, gentleness, and a reliance on God's strength.

- **Blessed are those who hunger and thirst for righteousness:** This speaks to a longing for a just and compassionate world and a desire to live according to God's will.

- **Blessed are the merciful:** True happiness lies in showing compassion and forgiveness to others, just as God shows mercy to us.

- **Blessed are the pure in heart:** This emphasizes the importance of moral purity and living a life free from hypocrisy and deceit.

- **Blessed are the peacemakers:** Actively working for peace and reconciliation brings true blessedness.

- **Blessed are those who are persecuted for righteousness:** Jesus acknowledges the challenges faced by those who live faithfully, but promises ultimate reward in heaven.

Strength in Humility and Service

The Beatitudes are more than just blessings; they are a call to action. They urge us to:

- **Embrace Humility:** True strength lies in recognizing our limitations and dependence on God.

- **Focus on Service:** Happiness comes from serving others and working for a more just and compassionate world.

- **Live with Integrity:** Purity of heart and righteous living are essential components of a blessed life.

- **Embrace Challenges:** Following Jesus' teachings may not always be easy, but it leads to ultimate fulfillment.

Challenge: Embracing a Beatitude

This week, I challenge you to choose a specific Beatitude that resonates with you and actively strive to live it out:

- **Practice compassion:** Volunteer at a homeless shelter, visit a sick neighbor, or donate to a charity that supports those in need.

- **Seek peace:** Meditate on forgiveness, mend a broken relationship, or initiate dialogue in a conflict situation.

- **Hunger for righteousness:** Study scripture or theology, advocate for social justice issues, or live with integrity in your daily interactions.

- **Embrace meekness:** Listen attentively to others, offer help without seeking recognition, and prioritize humility in your interactions.

Journaling: Reflection and Growth

Take some quiet time for reflection and journaling:

- Reflect on the Beatitude you chose for this week. What does it mean to you in the context of your life?

- Identify specific actions you can take this week to live out this Beatitude.

- Journal your daily experiences as you strive to embody this Beatitude. What challenges do you face? What victories do you experience?

Remember, dear sisters, the Beatitudes aren't a checklist to achieve happiness; they are a roadmap for living a life of purpose, service, and ultimately, true blessedness.

Beyond This Book:

As we continue this faith-enriching experience, remember that your learning journey also continues! Here are some ways to keep the spirit of the Beatitudes alive:

- **Memorize the Beatitudes:** Having them readily available will serve as a constant reminder of the values they represent.

- **Live by Example:** Let your faith be evident in your actions, embodying the values of compassion, peacemaking, and service.

- **Share the Message:** Spread the teachings of the Beatitudes with others, inspiring them to embrace this path of true happiness.

BIBLE READING: Week 21

Day 141: 2 Samuel 13-14, Psalm 140, John 1:1-18

2 Samuel 13-14:

Reflection: These chapters narrate the tragic events in David's family, including Amnon's assault on Tamar and Absalom's revenge. Reflect on the themes of sin, justice, and family dynamics. How can you strive to promote healthy relationships and confront injustice within your own family and community?

Psalm 140:

Reflection: Psalm 140 is a prayer for deliverance from enemies. Reflect on the themes of protection, trust, and reliance on God in times of trouble. How can you turn to God for refuge and strength when facing opposition or adversity in your life?

John 1:1-18:

Reflection: In this passage, John proclaims the identity and significance of Jesus as the Word made flesh. Reflect on the themes of incarnation, revelation, and grace. How does the incarnation of Jesus Christ deepen your understanding of God's love and purpose for humanity? How can you share the message of Jesus as the Light of the world with others?

Day 142: 2 Samuel 15-17, Psalm 141, John 1:19-51

2 Samuel 15-17:

Reflection: These chapters detail Absalom's conspiracy against David and David's flight from Jerusalem. Reflect on the themes of betrayal, loyalty, and trust in God's sovereignty. How can you respond with faith and trust in God's providence when faced with betrayal or opposition?

Psalm 141:

Reflection: Psalm 141 is a prayer for protection and guidance in righteous living. Reflect on the themes of prayer, righteousness, and dependence on God. How can you cultivate a lifestyle of prayer and seek God's guidance to walk in integrity and righteousness in your daily life?

John 1:19-51:

Reflection: In this passage, John the Baptist testifies about Jesus, who is revealed as the Lamb of God and the Son of God. Reflect on the themes of witness, revelation, and discipleship. How does John's testimony about Jesus inspire you to bear witness to Christ in your own life? How can you respond to Jesus' invitation to follow Him and become His disciple?

Day 143: 2 Samuel 18-20, Psalm 142, John 2:1-12

2 Samuel 18-20:

Reflection: These chapters describe the aftermath of Absalom's rebellion and David's restoration as king. Reflect on the themes of justice, forgiveness, and the consequences of rebellion. How can you learn from David's example of seeking reconciliation and restoration after experiencing conflict or betrayal?

Psalm 142:

Reflection: Psalm 142 is a prayer of lament and trust in God's deliverance. Reflect on the themes of distress, trust, and refuge in God. How can you follow the psalmist's example of pouring out your heart to God in times of trouble and finding refuge in His presence?

John 2:1-12:

Reflection: In this passage, Jesus performs His first miracle at the wedding in Cana, turning water into wine. Reflect on the themes of divine power, provision, and faith. How does Jesus' miracle at Cana demonstrate His authority and ability to meet human needs? How can you trust in Jesus' provision and exercise faith in His promises in your own life?

Day 144: 2 Samuel 21-22, Psalm 143, John 2:13-25

2 Samuel 21-22:

Reflection: These chapters recount various battles and victories during David's reign. Reflect on the themes of justice, redemption, and God's faithfulness in times of trouble. How can you trust in God's deliverance and seek His guidance when facing challenges or conflicts in your life?

Psalm 143:

Reflection: Psalm 143 is a prayer for deliverance and guidance in times of trouble. Reflect on the themes of desperation, trust, and surrender to God's will. How can you emulate the psalmist's posture of humility and reliance on God's mercy and righteousness in your own prayers?

John 2:13-25:

Reflection: In this passage, Jesus cleanses the temple and confronts the religious leaders. Reflect on the themes of zeal for God's house, true worship, and the authority of Jesus. How does Jesus' actions in the temple challenge you to examine your own attitudes toward worship and devotion? How can you ensure that your worship is genuine and honors God's holiness?

Day 145: 2 Samuel 23-24, Psalm 144, John 3:1-21

2 Samuel 23-24:

Reflection: These chapters contain David's last words and his sin in numbering the people, resulting in judgment. Reflect on the themes of leadership, accountability, and repentance. How can you learn from David's example of acknowledging sin, seeking forgiveness, and submitting to God's discipline in your own life?

Psalm 144:

Reflection: Psalm 144 is a song of praise for God's deliverance and victory. Reflect on the themes of praise, dependence, and trust in God's protection. How can you cultivate a heart of gratitude and praise, acknowledging God's power and faithfulness in your life?

John 3:1-21:

Reflection: In this passage, Jesus teaches Nicodemus about the necessity of being born again to enter the kingdom of God. Reflect on the themes of spiritual rebirth, salvation, and belief in Jesus Christ. How does Jesus' conversation with Nicodemus challenge you to examine your own understanding of salvation and commitment to following Jesus? How can you share the message of new life in Christ with others?

Day 146: Colossians 1-2, Psalm 145, John 3:22-36

Colossians 1-2:

Reflection: These chapters contain Paul's greeting to the Colossian church and his exhortation to remain rooted in Christ. Reflect on the themes of Christ's supremacy, reconciliation, and spiritual maturity. How can you deepen your understanding of Christ's preeminence in your life and grow in spiritual maturity through your relationship with Him?

Psalm 145:

> *Reflection:* Psalm 145 is a song of praise for God's greatness and goodness. Reflect on the themes of praise, thanksgiving, and God's faithfulness. How can you cultivate a lifestyle of praise and thanksgiving, recognizing God's abundant blessings and steadfast love in your life?

John 3:22-36:

> *Reflection:* In this passage, John the Baptist testifies about Jesus and emphasizes His authority and superiority. Reflect on the themes of humility, witness, and belief in Jesus. How does John's example of humility and single-minded devotion to Jesus inspire you to bear witness to Christ in your own life? How can you reflect Jesus' supremacy and bring glory to His name through your words and actions?

Day 147: Colossians 3-4, Psalm 146, John 4:1-42

Colossians 3-4:

> *Reflection:* These chapters instruct believers to set their minds on heavenly things and live in accordance with the new life in Christ. Reflect on the themes of spiritual transformation, unity in Christ, and living out the Christian virtues. How can you apply the principles of putting off the old self and putting on the new self in your daily life and relationships?

Psalm 146:

> *Reflection:* Psalm 146 praises God as the trustworthy helper of the oppressed and the needy. Reflect on the themes of trust, justice, and God's sovereignty. How can you trust in God's provision and care for those who are marginalized or in need? How can you advocate for justice and righteousness in your community, reflecting God's heart for the vulnerable?

John 4:1-42:

> *Reflection:* In this passage, Jesus encounters the Samaritan woman at the well and reveals Himself as the Messiah. Reflect on the themes of spiritual thirst, revelation, and evangelism. How does Jesus' interaction with the Samaritan woman challenge you to engage in meaningful conversations about faith with others? How can you share the message of living water and lead others to encounter Jesus in their lives?

WEEK 22: The Woman at the Well: Finding Faith and Acceptance

Welcome back, Faithful and Fierce women! We continue our exploration of faith with a beautiful story from the Gospel of John – the encounter between Jesus and the Samaritan woman at the well (John 4:4-26). This powerful narrative highlights the transformative power of God's love, acceptance, and the importance of extending similar kindness to others.

A Wellspring of Compassion

In this story, Jesus, weary from his journey, sits by a well in Samaria, a region with a history of tension with the Jews. A Samaritan woman arrives to draw water, and Jesus initiates a conversation, a surprising act in itself considering the social norms of the time.

Breaking Barriers:

Jesus' interaction with the woman shatters several societal barriers:

- **Ethnic Division:** Jesus, a Jew, engages with a Samaritan woman, defying social and religious boundaries.

- **Gender Stereotypes:** In that era, men rarely engaged in extended conversation with women in public.

- **Moral Judgment:** The woman's past relationships were likely known, yet Jesus avoids condemnation and offers her acceptance.

The Power of Respectful Dialogue

Jesus' approach throughout the conversation is one of respect and understanding. He:

- **Listens attentively:** Jesus shows genuine interest in the woman's life and experiences.

- **Challenges gently:** He subtly pushes the woman to consider her spiritual needs.

- **Offers living water:** Jesus goes beyond physical needs and speaks of a deeper spiritual thirst that only He can quench.

The Transformation of a Soul

The woman's initial skepticism gradually melts away as Jesus reveals his true identity as the Messiah. She becomes an evangelist, rushing back to her village to share the good news of her encounter with Jesus.

Self-Reflection: Extending Kindness and Acceptance

The story of the woman at the well offers a powerful lesson on how to extend kindness and acceptance to others, just as Jesus did:

- **Challenge Preconceptions:** We all have biases. Be mindful of preconceived notions you may have about people based on their background or circumstances.

- **Practice Active Listening:** Give others your full attention, showing genuine interest in their stories and perspectives.

- **Offer Compassion:** Extend kindness and understanding, even to those who may have made mistakes or hold different beliefs.

- **Seek Common Ground:** Look beyond differences to find areas of common humanity and shared values.

Imagine this:

Think about someone in your life who you may struggle to accept fully. Perhaps it's a neighbor with opposing political views, a coworker with a difficult personality, or a family member who has hurt you in the past.

- How can you approach this person with more respect and understanding, even if you disagree with their beliefs or actions?

- Can you find a common ground or shared experience that allows you to connect on a deeper level?

- How can you offer compassion instead of judgment?

Remember, dear sisters, extending kindness and acceptance doesn't require condoning wrongdoing. It's about recognizing the inherent dignity in every person, just as Jesus saw the worth in the Samaritan woman.

Beyond This Book:

As we close this empowering lesson, let's carry the lessons learned forward:

- **Be a bridge-builder:** Seek opportunities to connect with people from different backgrounds and perspectives.

- **Practice empathy:** Put yourself in others' shoes and try to understand their experiences.

- **Radiate God's love:** Let your faith motivate you to extend kindness and acceptance to all you encounter.

Day 148: 1 Kings 1-2, Psalm 147, John 4:43-54

1 Kings 1-2:

Reflection: These chapters depict the transition of leadership from David to Solomon and the beginning of Solomon's reign as king. Reflect on the themes of succession, wisdom, and obedience to God. How can you learn from Solomon's example of seeking wisdom and following God's guidance in your own life, especially in times of transition or leadership roles?

Psalm 147:

Reflection: Psalm 147 celebrates God's care for Jerusalem and His power over creation. Reflect on the themes of praise, provision, and divine sovereignty. How can you cultivate a heart of praise and thanksgiving, acknowledging God's power and goodness in your life and in the world around you?

John 4:43-54:

Reflection: In this passage, Jesus performs a miraculous healing from a distance, demonstrating His authority over sickness and disease. Reflect on the themes of faith, miracles, and spiritual healing. How does the official's response to Jesus' words challenge you to deepen your faith and trust in Jesus' power to bring healing and restoration to your life and the lives of others?

Day 149: 1 Kings 3-5, Psalm 148, John 5:1-30

1 Kings 3-5:

Reflection: These chapters detail Solomon's wisdom, his prayer for wisdom, and the construction of the temple and other important structures in Israel. Reflect on the themes of wisdom, prayer, and God's provision. How can you emulate Solomon's desire for wisdom and dependence on God in your own life, seeking His guidance and provision in all circumstances?

Psalm 148:

Reflection: Psalm 148 calls upon all creation to praise the Lord, from the heavens to the earth. Reflect on the themes of praise, worship, and God's sovereignty over all creation. How can you join with creation in offering praise and worship to God, recognizing His greatness and majesty in every aspect of your life?

John 5:1-30:

Reflection: In this passage, Jesus heals a man at the pool of Bethesda and teaches about His authority and relationship with the Father. Reflect on the themes of healing, authority, and divine sonship. How does Jesus' interaction with the man at the pool challenge your understanding of Jesus' authority and His identity as the Son of God? How can you respond to Jesus' invitation to believe in Him and receive eternal life?

Day 150: 1 Kings 6-8, Psalm 149, John 5:31-47

1 Kings 6-8:

Reflection: These chapters describe the construction and dedication of the temple in Jerusalem during Solomon's reign. Reflect on the themes of worship, God's presence, and covenant fulfillment. How does the dedication of the temple remind you of God's faithfulness to His promises and His desire to dwell among His people? How can you cultivate a heart of worship and reverence in your relationship with God?

Psalm 149:

Reflection: Psalm 149 calls for praise and worship to God for His victory and protection over His people. Reflect on the themes of praise, victory, and spiritual warfare. How can you engage in spiritual warfare through praise and worship, trusting in God's power to overcome all enemies and obstacles in your life?

John 5:31-47:

Reflection: In this passage, Jesus presents various witnesses to testify about His identity and mission. Reflect on the themes of testimony, belief, and eternal life. How does Jesus' invitation to believe in Him challenge you to examine your own faith and understanding of who Jesus is? How can you bear witness to Jesus' identity and share the message of eternal life with others?

Day 151: 1 Kings 9-11, Psalm 150, John 6:1-24

1 Kings 9-11:

Reflection: These chapters narrate God's response to Solomon's prayer and the blessings and warnings associated with the building of the temple. Reflect on the themes of obedience, covenant fidelity, and consequences of disobedience. How can Solomon's experience serve as a lesson for your own life, encouraging you to remain faithful to God's commands and heed His warnings?

Psalm 150:

Reflection: Psalm 150 is a hymn of praise that calls for everything that has breath to praise the Lord. Reflect on the themes of praise, worship, and celebration. How can you cultivate a lifestyle of praise and worship, offering your whole being as a living sacrifice to glorify God in every aspect of your life?

John 6:1-24:

Reflection: In this passage, Jesus miraculously feeds the multitude and walks on water, demonstrating His power over nature and His ability to satisfy spiritual hunger. Reflect on the themes of provision, faith, and spiritual hunger. How does Jesus' provision for physical and spiritual needs challenge you to trust in His sufficiency and seek satisfaction in Him alone?

Day 152: 1 Kings 12-14, Proverbs 1, John 6:25-59

1 Kings 12-14:

Reflection: These chapters describe the reigns of Rehoboam and Jeroboam, highlighting the division and decline of the kingdom of Israel. Reflect on the themes of leadership, disobedience, and consequences. How can the mistakes and actions of these kings serve as lessons for leaders today, emphasizing the importance of seeking God's wisdom and following His commands?

Proverbs 1:

Reflection: Proverbs 1 introduces the purpose and benefits of the book of Proverbs, emphasizing the fear of the Lord as the beginning of wisdom. Reflect on the themes of wisdom, instruction, and the fear of the Lord. How can you pursue wisdom and understanding in your own life, recognizing the importance of aligning your heart with God's ways?

John 6:25-59:

Reflection: In this passage, Jesus declares Himself as the bread of life and invites people to partake of Him for eternal life. Reflect on the themes of spiritual nourishment, faith, and communion with Christ. How does Jesus' offer of Himself challenge you to deepen your relationship with Him and find true satisfaction and sustenance in Him alone?

Day 153: 1 Kings 15-16, Proverbs 2, John 6:60-71

1 Kings 15-16:

Reflection: These chapters detail the reigns of various kings of Judah and Israel, highlighting their obedience or disobedience to God's commands. Reflect on the themes of leadership, faithfulness, and idolatry. How do the actions of these kings illustrate the consequences of aligning with or turning away from God's ways? How can you apply these lessons to your own life and leadership responsibilities?

Proverbs 2:

Reflection: Proverbs 2 emphasizes the pursuit of wisdom and understanding as essential for living a life pleasing to God. Reflect on the themes of wisdom, righteousness, and protection. How can you actively seek after wisdom and understanding in your daily life, trusting in God to guide you and protect you from the snares of evil?

John 6:60-71:

Reflection: In this passage, many of Jesus' disciples struggle to accept His teaching about eating His flesh and drinking His blood, which symbolizes partaking of His sacrifice for eternal life. Reflect on the themes of faith, commitment, and rejection. How does Jesus' call to radical discipleship challenge you to wholeheartedly trust in Him and follow Him, even when His teachings seem difficult to understand or accept?

Day 154: 1 Kings 17-18, Proverbs 3, John 7:1-13

1 Kings 17-18:

Reflection: These chapters depict the ministries of Elijah during a time of drought and famine, highlighting God's provision and power. Reflect on the themes of faithfulness, obedience, and miracles. How do Elijah's experiences reveal God's faithfulness to His promises and His ability to work through His faithful servants even in the midst of challenging circumstances?

Proverbs 3:

Reflection: Proverbs 3 emphasizes the importance of trusting in the Lord and acknowledging Him in all aspects of life. Reflect on the themes of trust, wisdom, and guidance. How can you cultivate a deeper trust in God and seek His wisdom in decision-making, knowing that He will direct your paths and lead you in the way of righteousness?

John 7:1-13:

Reflection: In this passage, Jesus faces opposition and skepticism from His own brothers as He prepares to attend the Feast of Tabernacles. Reflect on the themes of misunderstanding, rejection, and perseverance in faith. How does Jesus' response to skepticism and opposition encourage you to remain steadfast in your faith and trust in Him, even when others may doubt or misunderstand you?

WEEK 23: Women and Prayer: Developing a Strong Prayer Life

Welcome back, Faithful and Fierce women! As we continue this remarkable exploration of faith, we delve into the cornerstone of a vibrant spiritual life – prayer. Prayer is the vital dialogue between you and God, a space for expressing gratitude, seeking guidance, and deepening your connection with the Divine. This week, we'll explore different prayer styles and practices to help you cultivate a personalized and fulfilling prayer life.

A Journey of Prayer:

There's no one-size-fits-all approach to prayer. Just as we are all unique, our prayer styles can be diverse as well. Here are some popular methods:

- **Contemplative Prayer:** This practice involves quiet reflection, focusing on God's presence and cultivating inner peace. Techniques like Lectio Divina (prayerful reading of scripture) and centering prayer can be incorporated here.

- **Journaling Prayer:** Putting your thoughts and feelings on paper can be a powerful way to connect with God. Journal your worries, praises, and questions, allowing them to flow freely.

- **Petitionary Prayer:** In this form of prayer, you directly petition God for your needs and the needs of others. This can include prayers for healing, guidance, and strength.

- **Intercessory Prayer:** Here, you intercede on behalf of others, lifting their needs before God and praying for their well-being.

- **Prayers of Praise and Thanksgiving:** Expressing gratitude for God's blessings and praising His goodness is an essential aspect of prayer.

- **Liturgical Prayer:** Participating in formal prayers, such as the Rosary or Mass prayers, fosters a sense of community and connection with the wider Church.

Finding Your Prayer Style:

The key to developing a strong prayer life lies in finding a method or combination of methods that resonates with you. Here are some tips:

- **Experiment with Different Styles:** Try out various forms of prayer and see what feels most natural and fulfilling for you.

- **Create a Prayer Routine:** Set aside dedicated time for prayer each day, even if it's just for a few minutes. Consistency is key!

- **Find a Quiet Space:** Create a dedicated prayer space where you can minimize distractions and focus on connecting with God.

- **Incorporate Prayer Throughout Your Day:** Weave short prayers of gratitude, petition, or praise throughout your daily activities.

- **Pray with Others:** Consider joining a prayer group or finding a partner for prayer accountability. Sharing your faith journey with others can be deeply enriching.

Action Step: Embracing a New Prayer Method

This week, I challenge you to step outside your comfort zone and try a new prayer method:

- **Lectio Divina:** Choose a passage from scripture and follow these steps – read, reflect, respond, and rest. Allow the passage to speak to you and deepen your understanding.

- **Journaling Prayer:** Grab a pen and paper and write freely about what's on your heart. Express your gratitude, worries, and questions directly to God.

- **Praying the Rosary:** This beautiful Catholic devotion focuses on meditating on the mysteries of Jesus' life and Mary's role. Many resources are available online or in prayer books to guide you.

Remember, dear sisters, prayer is a conversation, not a monologue. Be open to listening for God's voice through scripture, nature, or simply a quiet sense of knowing. Trust in the power of prayer to transform your life and deepen your connection with the Divine.

Beyond This Book:

As we close this faith-filled adventure, remember that your prayer journey continues! Here are some ways to keep a vibrant prayer life:

- **Find a Prayer App:** Several mobile apps offer daily prayer prompts, scripture readings, and guided meditations.

- **Explore Spiritual Books:** Read books on prayer practices written by theologians, spiritual leaders, or everyday women who share their prayer journeys.

- **Join a Prayer Group:** Seek out a prayer group in your church or community for shared prayer experiences and support.

Day 155: 1 Kings 19, Proverbs 4, John 7:14-36

1 Kings 19:

Reflection: This chapter details Elijah's flight from Jezebel and his encounter with God at Mount Horeb. Reflect on the themes of fear, divine encounter, and renewal. How does God's gentle whisper to Elijah in his time of despair encourage you to seek God's presence and listen for His guidance when facing your own fears and challenges?

Proverbs 4:

Reflection: Proverbs 4 emphasizes the importance of acquiring wisdom and guarding one's heart. Reflect on the themes of wisdom, discipline, and guidance. How can you prioritize seeking wisdom in your daily life and protect your heart from influences that lead you away from God's path?

John 7:14-36:

Reflection: In this passage, Jesus teaches at the Feast of Tabernacles and faces mixed reactions from the crowd. Reflect on the themes of teaching, belief, and divine timing. How does Jesus' confidence in His mission and His teachings challenge you to remain committed to sharing and living out your faith, even when faced with misunderstanding or opposition?

Day 156: 1 Kings 20-22, Proverbs 5, John 7:37-52

1 Kings 20-22:

Reflection: These chapters narrate various events including battles between Israel and Aram, and the downfall of King Ahab. Reflect on the themes of obedience, judgment, and divine justice. How do these stories illustrate the consequences of disobedience and the importance of aligning oneself with God's will?

Proverbs 5:

Reflection: Proverbs 5 warns against adultery and promotes faithfulness in marriage. Reflect on the themes of purity, fidelity, and integrity. How can you cultivate faithfulness and integrity in your relationships, and guard against temptations that threaten to undermine them?

John 7:37-52:

Reflection: In this passage, Jesus speaks about living water and the division among the people regarding His identity. Reflect on the themes of spiritual thirst, belief, and division. How does Jesus' invitation to receive living water speak to your own spiritual needs, and how can you respond to His call amidst the differing opinions and beliefs around you?

Day 157: 1 Thessalonians 1-3, Proverbs 6, John 7:53-8:11

1 Thessalonians 1-3:

Reflection: These chapters contain Paul's thanksgiving, encouragement, and concern for the Thessalonians' faith. Reflect on the themes of faith, love, and encouragement. How can you be a source of encouragement to others in their faith journey, and how does Paul's care for the Thessalonians inspire you to build up and support your faith community?

Proverbs 6:

Reflection: Proverbs 6 offers warnings against folly, laziness, and wickedness. Reflect on the themes of diligence, wisdom, and caution. How can you apply these warnings to avoid pitfalls and live a life marked by diligence, wisdom, and righteousness?

John 7:53-8:11:

Reflection: This passage recounts the story of the woman caught in adultery and Jesus' response to her accusers. Reflect on the themes of mercy, judgment, and repentance. How does Jesus' merciful response challenge you to extend grace to others, and how can you embrace His call to "go and sin no more" in your own life?

Day 158: 1 Thessalonians 4-5, Proverbs 7, John 8:12-30

1 Thessalonians 4-5:

Reflection: These chapters focus on living a holy life and the hope of Christ's return. Reflect on the themes of sanctification, hope, and encouragement. How can you live a life that pleases God while eagerly awaiting Jesus' return, and how can you encourage others in their faith journey?

Proverbs 7:

Reflection: Proverbs 7 warns against the seduction of folly and highlights the importance of wisdom. Reflect on the themes of temptation and wisdom. How can you guard your heart and mind against temptation and pursue a life of wisdom and integrity?

John 8:12-30:

Reflection: In this passage, Jesus declares Himself as the Light of the World and speaks about His relationship with the Father. Reflect on the themes of light, truth, and relationship with God. How does recognizing Jesus as the Light of the World influence the way you live and the choices you make?

Day 159: 2 Kings 1-2, Proverbs 8, John 8:31-59

2 Kings 1-2:

Reflection: These chapters recount Elijah's final acts and Elisha's succession. Reflect on the themes of legacy, faithfulness, and divine power. How can you remain faithful in your calling and mentor others to continue God's work?

Proverbs 8:

Reflection: Proverbs 8 personifies wisdom, describing its role in creation and its value. Reflect on the themes of wisdom and creation. How can you seek and apply wisdom in your daily life, recognizing its divine origin and importance?

John 8:31-59:

Reflection: Jesus speaks about the truth setting people free and declares His eternal existence. Reflect on the themes of truth, freedom, and identity. How does understanding the truth of Jesus' words impact your sense of freedom and identity in Him?

Day 160: 2 Kings 3-4, Proverbs 9, John 9

2 Kings 3-4:

Reflection: These chapters describe Elisha's miracles and his ministry. Reflect on the themes of faith, miracles, and God's provision. How can you trust in God's miraculous power and provision in your own life?

Proverbs 9:

Reflection: Proverbs 9 contrasts the invitations of wisdom and folly. Reflect on the themes of choice and consequence. How can you discern between wisdom and folly in your decisions and choose the path that leads to life?

John 9:

Reflection: This chapter narrates the healing of a man born blind and the resulting controversy. Reflect on the themes of spiritual blindness, sight, and testimony. How can you share your own testimony of how Jesus has opened your eyes to the truth?

Day 161: 2 Kings 5-6, Proverbs 10, John 10:1-21

2 Kings 5-6:

Reflection: These chapters include the healing of Naaman and the protection of Elisha. Reflect on the themes of healing, obedience, and divine protection. How can you obey God's instructions and trust in His protection and healing power in your life?

Proverbs 10:

Reflection: Proverbs 10 contrasts the righteous and the wicked, emphasizing the outcomes of their actions. Reflect on the themes of righteousness and consequences. How can you pursue righteousness in your actions and trust in God's justice?

John 10:1-21:

Reflection: In this passage, Jesus describes Himself as the Good Shepherd who lays down His life for the sheep. Reflect on the themes of leadership, sacrifice, and relationship. How can you follow Jesus, the Good Shepherd, and lead others with the same sacrificial love and care?

WEEK 24: The Power of Community: Catholic Women's Groups

Welcome back, Faithful and Fierce women! As we continue this transformative exploration of faith, we turn our hearts towards the power of community. No woman walks the path of faith alone. Catholic women's groups offer a vital space for connection, support, fellowship, and shared growth in your faith journey.

A Journey of Sisterhood:

Catholic women's groups come in all shapes and sizes, catering to diverse interests and life stages. Here's a glimpse into the enriching benefits they offer:

- **Spiritual Growth:** Groups provide a platform for Bible study, faith discussions, and sharing prayer experiences, fostering deeper understanding and strengthening your connection to God.

- **Support Network:** Life throws challenges; Catholic women's groups offer a safe space to share burdens, receive encouragement, and pray for each other.

- **Friendship and Fellowship:** Connecting with women who share your faith values can create lasting friendships and a sense of belonging.

- **Mentorship and Inspiration:** More experienced members can offer guidance and support to newer members, fostering a cycle of learning and growth.

- **Service and Advocacy:** Many groups work on social justice initiatives or volunteer together, providing opportunities to put your faith into action.

Finding Your Perfect Fit:

With so many groups available, finding the one that aligns with your needs is key. Here are some ways to navigate the options:

- **Explore Your Parish:** Most parishes offer various women's groups, from Bible study circles to young adult ministries.

- **Research Online:** Catholic women's organizations like the National Council of Catholic Women (NCCW) or the Catholic Daughters of the Americas have online directories to search for groups in your area.

- **Consider Your Interests:** Do you enjoy social events, volunteering, or in-depth theological discussions? Look for a group that aligns with your interests and preferences.

Challenge: Embracing Sisterhood

This week, I challenge you to explore the power of Catholic women's groups:

- **Research Local Groups:** Search online or talk to your parish priest or women's ministry coordinator about available groups.

- **Attend a Meeting:** Step outside your comfort zone and attend a meeting of a group that interests you. See if it feels like a good fit.

- **Consider Starting Your Own:** If you can't find the perfect group, consider starting your own! Gather a few like-minded women and create a space for fellowship and faith sharing.

Remember, dear sisters, finding your Catholic women's group can be a transformative experience. The support, encouragement, and shared faith journey of other women can empower you to live your faith more fully.

Beyond This Book:

As we continue this enriching journey, remember that the power of community continues to be a source of strength! Here are some ways to stay connected:

- **Become an Active Member:** Once you find your group, be an active participant. Share your thoughts, contribute to discussions, and be a source of support for others.

- **Invite Others:** Spread the word about your group and invite other women to join the empowering experience of Catholic women's community.

- **Connect Online:** Many Catholic women's groups have online platforms for continued engagement and support beyond regular meetings.

Day 162: 2 Kings 7-8, Proverbs 11, John 10:22-42

2 Kings 7-8:

Reflection: These chapters recount Elisha's prophecies and the subsequent events, including miraculous provisions and the rise and fall of kings. Reflect on the themes of prophecy, provision, and leadership. How can you trust in God's prophetic word and provision in your life and exercise godly leadership in your spheres of influence?

Proverbs 11:

Reflection: Proverbs 11 contrasts the rewards of righteousness and the consequences of wickedness. Reflect on the themes of integrity, generosity, and righteousness. How can you cultivate these qualities in your life and relationships, knowing that they lead to God's blessings?

John 10:22-42:

Reflection: In this passage, Jesus speaks of His unity with the Father and His role as the shepherd of His sheep. Reflect on the themes of unity, identity, and faith. How does understanding Jesus' relationship with the Father strengthen your faith and sense of belonging in God's family?

Day 163: 2 Kings 9-10, Proverbs 12, John 11:1-54

2 Kings 9-10:

Reflection: These chapters describe Jehu's anointing as king and his mission to eradicate Baal worship from Israel. Reflect on the themes of zeal, judgment, and reform. How can you be zealous for God's purposes and work towards reforming your own life and community according to His will?

Proverbs 12:

Reflection: Proverbs 12 highlights the contrast between the wise and the foolish, the diligent and the lazy. Reflect on the themes of wisdom, diligence, and truth. How can you apply these principles to your daily life and strive to live wisely and diligently in all you do?

John 11:1-54:

Reflection: This passage recounts the raising of Lazarus and the reactions of those who witnessed it. Reflect on the themes of resurrection, belief, and God's glory. How does Jesus' power over death strengthen your faith and inspire you to live for His glory?

Day 164: 2 Kings 11-13, Proverbs 13, John 11:55-12:36

2 Kings 11-13:

Reflection: These chapters cover the reigns of various kings and the prophetic ministry of Elisha. Reflect on the themes of restoration, faithfulness, and God's intervention. How can you remain faithful to God amidst challenges and trust in His power to restore and intervene in your life?

Proverbs 13:

Reflection: Proverbs 13 discusses the value of discipline, wisdom, and righteous living. Reflect on the themes of discipline, wisdom, and hope. How can you embrace discipline and wisdom to guide your actions and decisions, fostering hope and positive outcomes?

John 11:55-12:36:

Reflection: This passage includes Jesus' triumphal entry into Jerusalem and His teaching about His impending death. Reflect on the themes of sacrifice, kingship, and eternal life. How does Jesus' example of sacrifice and His kingship inspire you to live a life devoted to Him and His eternal purposes?

Day 165: 2 Kings 14-15, Proverbs 14, John 12:37-50

2 Kings 14-15:

Reflection: These chapters narrate the reigns of several kings in Judah and Israel, highlighting their faithfulness or unfaithfulness to God. Reflect on the themes of leadership, faithfulness, and legacy. How can you lead a life of faithfulness to God, leaving a legacy that honors Him?

Proverbs 14:

Reflection: Proverbs 14 contrasts wisdom and folly, touching on various aspects of life. Reflect on the themes of wisdom, prudence, and fear of the Lord. How can you seek wisdom in your daily life and cultivate a healthy fear of the Lord in your decisions and actions?

John 12:37-50:

Reflection: This passage reflects on the unbelief of the people despite Jesus' miracles and His final public teaching. Reflect on the themes of belief, judgment, and revelation. How can you strengthen your belief in Jesus and share the light of His revelation with others?

Day 166: 2 Kings 16-17, Hosea 1, John 13:1-20

2 Kings 16-17:

Reflection: These chapters describe the reign of Ahaz and the fall of Israel due to their unfaithfulness to God. Reflect on the themes of idolatry, judgment, and the consequences of forsaking God. How can you guard your heart against idolatry and stay faithful to God in your life?

Hosea 1:

Reflection: Hosea 1 introduces Hosea's marriage to Gomer as a symbol of Israel's unfaithfulness to God. Reflect on the themes of unfaithfulness, judgment, and redemption. How does this story illustrate God's unwavering love and the possibility of redemption despite unfaithfulness?

John 13:1-20:

Reflection: This passage recounts Jesus washing His disciples' feet, demonstrating servant leadership. Reflect on the themes of humility, service, and love. How can you emulate Jesus' example of servant leadership in your relationships and community?

Day 167: 2 Kings 18-19, Hosea 2, John 13:21-38

2 Kings 18-19:

Reflection: These chapters narrate King Hezekiah's trust in God during the Assyrian threat and God's deliverance. Reflect on the themes of trust, deliverance, and faith. How can Hezekiah's example inspire you to trust in God's power and faithfulness during difficult times?

Hosea 2:

Reflection: Hosea 2 depicts God's judgment on Israel for their unfaithfulness but also His promise of restoration. Reflect on the themes of judgment, mercy, and restoration. How can you find hope in God's promise of restoration and renewal, even when facing the consequences of sin?

John 13:21-38:

Reflection: This passage includes Jesus predicting His betrayal and Peter's denial, and giving a new commandment to love one another. Reflect on the themes of betrayal, love, and faithfulness. How can you live out Jesus' commandment to love others as He has loved you?

Day 168: 2 Kings 20-21, Hosea 3, John 14

2 Kings 20-21

Reflection: These chapters recount Hezekiah's illness and recovery, and the reign and sins of Manasseh. Reflect on the themes of repentance, mercy, and the long-term consequences of sin. How does Hezekiah's prayer life and Manasseh's reign challenge you to seek God's mercy and avoid sinful patterns?

Hosea 3:

Reflection: Hosea 3 describes Hosea's reconciliation with Gomer, symbolizing God's love and forgiveness towards Israel. Reflect on the themes of love, forgiveness, and redemption. How can you embrace and extend God's forgiveness and love in your own relationships?

John 14:

Reflection: In this chapter, Jesus comforts His disciples and promises the Holy Spirit. Reflect on the themes of comfort, guidance, and peace. How can you rely on the Holy Spirit for comfort and guidance in your daily life, trusting in Jesus' promise of peace?

WEEK 25: Women and Work: Balancing Faith and Career

Welcome back, Faithful and Fierce women! As we continue this inspiring exploration of faith, we delve into a topic close to many hearts – balancing faith and career. Being a dedicated employee and a woman of faith can sometimes feel like navigating a tightrope. However, the Bible offers valuable insights on work and calling that can empower you to integrate your faith seamlessly into your professional life.

A Journey of Work Ethic:

The Bible doesn't shy away from the importance of work. Here are some key themes regarding work ethic:

- **Work as a Calling:** Genesis 2:15 tells us that God placed humanity in the Garden of Eden "to work it and take care of it." Work is not a curse; it's an integral part of God's plan and allows us to use our gifts and talents.

- **Excellence and Diligence:** Colossians 3:23-24 urges us to "work at it with all your heart, as working for the Lord, not for human masters." Our work, regardless of its nature, should be done with excellence and dedication, honoring God through our efforts.

- **Integrity and Fairness:** Proverbs 11:1 states, "The Lord detests dishonest scales, but accurate weights find favor with him." Honesty, integrity, and fairness must guide our work ethic and decision-making in the workplace.

- **Respect and Dignity:** Leviticus 19:13 reminds us, "Do not defraud or rob a neighbor. Do not hold back the wages of a hired worker overnight." Treating colleagues and employees with respect and ensuring fair compensation are core principles.

Walking Your Faith at Work:

Integrating your faith into your work goes beyond simply praying before starting your workday. Here are some ways to live out your faith in a professional setting:

- **Demonstrate Strong Work Ethic:** Be reliable, hardworking, and dedicated to exceeding expectations. Let your commitment and integrity shine through.

- **Advocate for Just Practices:** Speak up against unethical behavior or unfair treatment of colleagues. Be a voice for fairness and compassion within the workplace.

- **Offer Help and Support:** Be a source of encouragement and support for your colleagues. Extend a helping hand whenever possible.

- **Balance Work and Life:** Maintain healthy boundaries to avoid burnout. Prioritize time for prayer, reflection, and family to nurture your spiritual well-being.

- **Share Your Faith Openly (if appropriate):** While respecting workplace boundaries, you can subtly integrate your faith through your actions and words.

Discussion Starter: Faith in Action

Integrating faith into the professional world presents unique challenges and opportunities. Let's explore this further:

- Share specific examples of how you've witnessed someone living out their faith at work. What impact did it have?

- Discuss practical ways to advocate for fair treatment and ethical practices within the workplace. How can we use our voices to make a difference?

- Brainstorm ways to prioritize both professional success and spiritual growth. How can we create a healthy balance?

Remember, dear sisters, finding harmony between faith and career is a continuous journey. Trust that your work has value and purpose, and use your talents to glorify God while making a positive contribution in your professional sphere.

Beyond This Book:

Remember that your commitment to integrating faith and work ethic continues! Here are some ways to stay inspired:

- **Seek Mentorship:** Connect with women who have successfully navigated faith and career challenges. Learn from their experiences and wisdom.

- **Read Uplifting Books:** Several books focus on the intersection of faith and work. Explore these resources for guidance and inspiration.

- **Join a Faith-Based Professional Network:** Connect with other women who are passionate about integrating their faith into their careers. Find support and encouragement through these networks.

BIBLE READING: Week 25

Day 169: 2 Kings 22-23, Hosea 4, John 15:1-10

2 Kings 22-23:

Reflection: These chapters describe King Josiah's reforms and the discovery of the Book of the Law. Reflect on the themes of repentance, renewal, and obedience to God's word. How can Josiah's dedication to reform and obedience to God's law inspire you to seek spiritual renewal and adherence to God's commands in your own life?

Hosea 4:

Reflection: Hosea 4 details Israel's unfaithfulness and the resulting judgment. Reflect on the themes of knowledge of God, sin, and consequences. How can you prioritize knowing God and living according to His ways to avoid the consequences of straying from His path?

John 15:1-10:

Reflection: Jesus speaks about the vine and the branches, emphasizing the importance of remaining in Him. Reflect on the themes of connection, fruitfulness, and obedience. How can you ensure you remain connected to Jesus, allowing His life to flow through you and produce spiritual fruit?

Day 170: 2 Kings 24-25, Hosea 5:1-14, John 15:11-17

2 Kings 24-25:

Reflection: These chapters recount the fall of Jerusalem and the end of the kingdom of Judah. Reflect on the themes of judgment, exile, and hope. How does the fall of Jerusalem challenge you to remain faithful to God amidst trials, and where can you find hope even in dire circumstances?

Hosea 5:1-14:

Reflection: Hosea 5:1-14 continues the theme of Israel's unfaithfulness and impending judgment. Reflect on the themes of accountability, repentance, and divine judgment. How can you take responsibility for your actions, seek repentance, and turn back to God to avoid spiritual downfall?

John 15:11-17:

Reflection: Jesus speaks about love and friendship, urging His disciples to love one another as He has loved them. Reflect on the themes of love, joy, and friendship with Jesus. How can you embody Christ-like love in your relationships, fostering joy and deepening your friendship with Jesus?

Day 171: 2 Thessalonians, Hosea 5:15-7:2, John 15:18-16:4a

2 Thessalonians:

Reflection: Paul's second letter to the Thessalonians addresses persecution, the return of Christ, and encouragement to stand firm. Reflect on the themes of hope, endurance, and faithfulness. How can you stand firm in your faith during times of trial, holding onto the hope of Christ's return?

Hosea 5:15-7:2:

Reflection: These verses highlight Israel's unrepentance and God's call for them to return. Reflect on the themes of repentance, return, and God's healing. How can you respond to God's call to return to Him, experiencing His healing and restoration in areas of your life where you have strayed?

John 15:18-16:4a:

Reflection: Jesus warns about the world's hatred towards His followers. Reflect on the themes of persecution, perseverance, and the cost of discipleship. How can you prepare for and endure persecution for your faith, remaining steadfast in your commitment to Jesus?

Day 172: Amos 1-3, Hosea 7:3-12, John 16:4b-15

Amos 1-3:

Reflection: These chapters contain prophecies against Israel and its neighbors for their injustices and sins. Reflect on the themes of justice, judgment, and righteousness. How can you pursue justice and righteousness in your community, standing against injustices that dishonor God?

Hosea 7:3-12:

Reflection: Hosea continues to denounce Israel's unfaithfulness. Reflect on the themes of deceit, waywardness, and divine judgment. How can you recognize and correct any deceit or waywardness in your life, seeking God's guidance and correction?

John 16:4b-15:

Reflection: Jesus speaks about the work of the Holy Spirit. Reflect on the themes of guidance, truth, and the Holy Spirit's role. How can you be more attuned to the Holy Spirit's guidance in your daily life, allowing Him to lead you into all truth?

Day 173: Amos 4-6, Hosea 7:12-8:14, John 16:16-33

Amos 4-6:

Reflection: These chapters focus on Israel's failure to return to God and the coming judgment. Reflect on the themes of repentance, social justice, and divine judgment. How can you ensure you are living justly and seeking God wholeheartedly, avoiding complacency and spiritual neglect?

Hosea 7:12-8:14:

Reflection: Hosea addresses Israel's idolatry and alliances with foreign nations. Reflect on the themes of idolatry, misplaced trust, and consequences. How can you identify and remove idols in your life, placing your trust fully in God?

John 16:16-33:

Reflection: Jesus speaks about His departure, the coming joy, and overcoming the world. Reflect on the themes of sorrow, joy, and victory in Christ. How can you find joy in Jesus' promises and strength in His victory over the world, especially during difficult times?

Day 174: Amos 7-9, Hosea 9, John 17

Amos 7-9:

Reflection: Amos concludes with visions of judgment and a promise of restoration. Reflect on the themes of divine judgment, repentance, and restoration. How can you remain hopeful in God's promise of restoration despite the reality of judgment for unfaithfulness?

Hosea 9:

Reflection: Hosea 9 continues to depict Israel's impending judgment due to their sins. Reflect on the themes of judgment, consequences, and sorrow. How can you understand and respond to the serious consequences of sin, seeking God's mercy and repentance?

John 17:

Reflection: Jesus prays for Himself, His disciples, and all believers. Reflect on the themes of unity, sanctification, and eternal life. How can you join in Jesus' prayer for unity and sanctification, striving to live a life that glorifies God?

Day 175: Micah 1-3, Hosea 10, John 18:1-27

Micah 1-3:

Reflection: Micah pronounces judgment on Israel and Judah for their injustices and sins. Reflect on the themes of justice, judgment, and true worship. How can you advocate for justice and live a life of genuine worship that honors God?

Hosea 10:

Reflection: Hosea 10 continues to describe Israel's sins and the resulting judgment. Reflect on the themes of unfaithfulness, consequences, and repentance. How can you recognize areas of unfaithfulness in your life and turn back to God in sincere repentance?

John 18:1-27:

Reflection: This passage details Jesus' arrest and Peter's denial. Reflect on the themes of betrayal, courage, and loyalty. How can you remain loyal to Jesus in the face of challenges, and how can you find courage to stand firm in your faith?

WEEK 26: Mary Magdalene: A Story of Redemption and Second Chances

Welcome back, Faithful and Fierce women! As we continue this remarkable exploration of faith, we turn our hearts to the powerful story of Mary Magdalene, a woman often misunderstood and misrepresented. Through the lens of the Gospels, we discover a narrative of redemption, transformation, and the unwavering grace of God who offers second chances to all.

A Journey of Transformation:

While the Gospels offer varying details, they paint a compelling portrait of Mary Magdalene:

- **A Woman of Faith:** Several Gospel accounts mention Mary Magdalene as a follower of Jesus, present during His teachings and miracles. Mark 15:40-41 describes her as one of the women who witnessed the Crucifixion and remained faithful.

- **Beyond Stereotypes:** Despite historical misinterpretations, there's no evidence to suggest Mary Magdalene was a prostitute. The Gospels highlight her association with Jesus and the transformative power of His love.

- **Witness to the Resurrection:** All four Gospels emphasize Mary Magdalene's crucial role in the Resurrection narrative. She is often the first to encounter the risen Christ, becoming a vital witness to His victory over death.

The Power of God's Forgiveness

While details and interpretations may vary, one thing remains clear – Mary Magdalene's story is a testament to God's boundless forgiveness and the transformative power of faith. Here's why:

- **From Follower to Devoted Disciple:** Mary Magdalene's journey demonstrates how encountering Jesus can spark a transformative change of heart, leading to a life dedicated to Him.

- **Second Chances and Redemption:** Regardless of her past, Jesus offered Mary Magdalene acceptance and the opportunity to start afresh. His message of forgiveness is available to all.

- **A Beacon of Hope:** Mary Magdalene's story offers hope and encouragement to those who feel burdened by past mistakes or societal judgment. God's grace can lead to a fresh start.

Self-Reflection: The Gift of Forgiveness

Mary Magdalene's story invites us to reflect on the transformative power of forgiveness, both from God and from ourselves:

- **Consider a time when you felt God's forgiveness.** How did it impact your life?

- **Have you forgiven yourself for past mistakes?** If not, how can you begin the process of self-forgiveness?

- **Think of someone you may need to forgive.** Is there a way to mend the relationship and offer forgiveness?

Remember, dear sisters, God's love and forgiveness are boundless. Just as He embraced Mary Magdalene, He extends the same grace to you. Let go of burdens and embrace the hope of a new beginning.

Beyond This Book:

As we continue this enriching adventure in faith, remember that the lessons learned stay with you:

- **Spread the Message of Forgiveness:** Share the story of Mary Magdalene and the message of God's forgiveness with others.

- **Seek Reconciliation:** If you have strained relationships, consider reaching out in a spirit of forgiveness and reconciliation.

- **Live with Unconditional Love:** Emulate the love of Christ by extending unconditional love and acceptance to all.

BIBLE READING: Week 26

Day 176: Micah 4-5, Hosea 11, John 18:27-40

Micah 4-5

Reflection: These chapters speak of future hope and the coming ruler from Bethlehem. Reflect on the themes of hope, restoration, and the messianic promise. How can you hold onto hope in God's promises and look forward to the ultimate restoration brought by Christ?

Hosea 11

Reflection: Hosea 11 portrays God's enduring love for Israel despite their unfaithfulness. Reflect on the themes of divine love, compassion, and forgiveness. How can you experience and share God's enduring love and compassion in your daily interactions?

John 18:27-40

Reflection: This passage details Jesus' trial before Pilate and the choice between Jesus and Barabbas. Reflect on the themes of truth, justice, and sacrifice. How can you stand for truth and justice in a world that often chooses otherwise, following Jesus' example of sacrificial love?

Day 177: Micah 6-7, Hosea 12:1-13:1, John 19:1-30

Micah 6-7

Reflection: These chapters contain a call to repentance and a message of hope. Reflect on the themes of repentance, justice, and God's faithfulness. How can you act justly, love mercy, and walk humbly with your God in response to His faithfulness?

Hosea 12:1-13:1

Reflection: Hosea addresses Israel's continued unfaithfulness and reliance on false gods. Reflect on the themes of idolatry, repentance, and divine judgment. How can you identify and turn away from modern-day idols, fully trusting in God's provision and guidance?

John 19:1-30

Reflection: This passage details Jesus' crucifixion. Reflect on the themes of sacrifice, redemption, and love. How can you live in gratitude for Jesus' sacrifice, allowing His love to transform and guide your life?

Day 178: 1 Timothy 1-3, Hosea 13:2-14:1, John 19:31-42

1 Timothy 1-3

Reflection: Paul provides instructions on sound doctrine, prayer, and leadership. Reflect on the themes of faithfulness, sound teaching, and godly leadership. How can you uphold sound doctrine and contribute to your community's spiritual growth through prayer and leadership?

Hosea 13:2-14:1

Reflection: Hosea continues to call Israel to repentance and return to God. Reflect on the themes of repentance, divine love, and restoration. How can you return to God in areas of your life where you have strayed, experiencing His love and restoration?

John 19:31-42

Reflection: This passage describes Jesus' burial. Reflect on the themes of death, fulfillment of prophecy, and hope. How does Jesus' burial and the fulfillment of prophecy strengthen your faith in God's plan and give you hope for the future?

Day 179: 1 Timothy 4-6, Hosea 14:2-10, John 20:1-18

1 Timothy 4-6

Reflection: Paul gives further instructions on godliness, contentment, and pastoral duties. Reflect on the themes of perseverance, godliness, and stewardship. How can you pursue godliness and contentment, faithfully stewarding your resources and responsibilities?

Hosea 14:2-10

Reflection: Hosea concludes with a call to repentance and a promise of healing. Reflect on the themes of repentance, healing, and divine love. How can you embrace God's invitation to return to Him, experiencing His healing and love?

John 20:1-18

Reflection: This passage details the resurrection of Jesus and His appearance to Mary Magdalene. Reflect on the themes of resurrection, hope, and personal encounter with Jesus. How can the reality of the resurrection bring you hope and inspire a deeper personal relationship with Jesus?

Day 180: 1 Chronicles 1-3, Proverbs 15, John 20:19-31

1 Chronicles 1-3

Reflection: These chapters provide genealogies from Adam to David. Reflect on the themes of heritage, legacy, and God's faithfulness through generations. How can you honor your spiritual heritage and contribute to a legacy of faith for future generations?

Proverbs 15

Reflection: Proverbs 15 offers wisdom on various aspects of life. Reflect on the themes of wisdom, discipline, and righteous living. How can you apply the wisdom found in Proverbs to live a life that honors God and benefits others?

John 20:19-31

Reflection: This passage describes Jesus' appearance to the disciples and Thomas' encounter with Him. Reflect on the themes of faith, doubt, and peace. How can you move from doubt to faith, experiencing the peace that comes from believing in the risen Christ?

Day 181: 1 Chronicles 4-6, Proverbs 16, John 21:1-14

1 Chronicles 4-6

Reflection: These chapters continue the genealogies and include the descendants of Judah and Levi. Reflect on the themes of identity, purpose, and God's plan. How can understanding your identity in Christ and your spiritual heritage shape your purpose and actions?

Proverbs 16

Reflection: Proverbs 16 focuses on God's sovereignty and human plans. Reflect on the themes of humility, trust, and divine guidance. How can you submit your plans to God, trusting in His sovereign will and guidance for your life?

John 21:1-14

Reflection: This passage recounts Jesus' post-resurrection appearance to His disciples by the Sea of Galilee. Reflect on the themes of provision, recognition, and mission. How can you recognize Jesus' presence and provision in your life, and respond to His call to mission?

Day 182: 1 Chronicles 7:1-9:34, Proverbs 17, John 21:15-25

1 Chronicles 7:1-9:34

Reflection: These chapters continue with genealogies, focusing on the tribes of Israel. Reflect on the themes of belonging, purpose, and God's plan. How can understanding your place in God's family and His plan for your life give you a sense of belonging and purpose?

Proverbs 17

Reflection: Proverbs 17 offers wisdom on relationships and personal conduct. Reflect on the themes of integrity, relationships, and godly living. How can you cultivate integrity and godly character in your relationships and daily interactions?

John 21:15-25

Reflection: This passage describes Jesus' reinstatement of Peter and His final words to him. Reflect on the themes of restoration, love, and following Jesus. How can you experience Jesus' restoration in areas where you have failed, and how can you follow Him more closely in your daily life?

WEEK 27: The Catholic Woman and Social Justice: Living Out Your Faith in Action

Welcome back, Faithful and Fierce women! As we continue this impactful exploration of faith, we delve into a cornerstone of Catholic life – social justice. Your faith compels you to not only nurture your personal relationship with God, but also to actively work towards a more just and compassionate world. This week, we'll explore the Catholic Church's teachings on social justice and how you can translate them into meaningful action.

A Journey of Compassion:

Catholic social justice isn't just about charity; it's about advocating for systemic change. Here are some core principles that guide this call to action:

- **The Dignity of Every Person:** Every human being, regardless of race, ethnicity, nationality, or socioeconomic status, is created in the image and likeness of God and deserves to be treated with dignity and respect.

- **The Common Good:** We are all interconnected, and the well-being of each member is essential for the well-being of society as a whole. We must work towards a just system that benefits everyone.

- **Solidarity:** We are called to stand in solidarity with the marginalized and oppressed, using our voices and resources to advocate for their rights and needs.

- **Rights and Responsibilities:** Every person has a fundamental right to basic necessities like food, shelter, and healthcare. However, this right comes with a responsibility to contribute positively to society.

- **Option for the Poor and Vulnerable:** The Church prioritizes the needs of the most vulnerable members of society, advocating for policies and actions that alleviate poverty, injustice, and oppression.

Faith in Action: Embracing Your Role

Living out your faith through social justice involves translating these principles into concrete actions. Here's how you can get involved:

- **Identify Your Passion:** What social issues ignite a fire within you? Poverty, human trafficking, environmental degradation? Focus your efforts on a cause that resonates deeply.

- **Learn and Advocate:** Educate yourself about the issues and learn about Catholic teachings related to them. Use your voice to raise awareness and advocate for policy changes.

- **Volunteer Your Time and Resources:** Donate your time and skills to organizations working towards social justice. Contribute financially or volunteer your expertise, even if it's a few hours a week.

- **Live Justly:** Beyond external actions, embody social justice values in your daily life. Support fair-trade businesses, treat others with compassion, and strive to leave a positive impact on your community.

Challenge: Embracing the Call

This week, I challenge you to take a concrete step towards social justice:

- **Research Local Organizations:** Seek out local organizations working on issues that align with your passion. Consider homeless shelters, refugee resettlement programs, or social justice advocacy groups.

- **Volunteer Your Time:** Contact these organizations and inquire about volunteer opportunities. Offer your time and talents to make a tangible difference.

- **Advocate for Change:** Participate in awareness campaigns, write letters to your local representatives, or join peaceful protests to advocate for policies that promote social justice.

Remember, dear sisters, even small actions can create a ripple effect. Your commitment to social justice, however you choose to express it, can contribute to a more just and compassionate world.

Beyond This Book:

As we continue this transformative journey, remember that your commitment to social justice continues! Here are some ways to stay engaged:

- **Stay Informed:** Follow reputable news sources on social justice issues and subscribe to newsletters from advocacy groups.

- **Connect with Others:** Join social justice groups or online communities to share resources, ideas, and support for your ongoing efforts.

- **Lead by Example:** Inspire others by openly discussing your passion for social justice and encouraging them to get involved.

BIBLE READING: Week 27

Day 183: 1 Chronicles 9:35-11:47, Proverbs 18, Matthew 1:1-17

1 Chronicles 9:35-11:47

Reflection: These chapters recount genealogies and David's early exploits. Reflect on the themes of heritage, leadership, and God's guidance. How can understanding your spiritual heritage and recognizing God's guidance in your life enhance your leadership and faith journey?

Proverbs 18

Reflection: Proverbs 18 offers wisdom on communication, relationships, and integrity. Reflect on the themes of wise speech, conflict resolution, and integrity. How can you practice wise and gracious communication in your relationships, fostering peace and understanding?

Matthew 1:1-17

Reflection: This passage provides the genealogy of Jesus. Reflect on the themes of promise, fulfillment, and divine plan. How does knowing Jesus' lineage from Abraham to David and beyond deepen your appreciation of God's faithfulness and His divine plan through history?

Day 184: 1 Chronicles 12-14, Proverbs 19, Matthew 1:18-25

1 Chronicles 12-14

Reflection: These chapters describe David's mighty men and his rise to power. Reflect on the themes of loyalty, divine favor, and leadership. How can you cultivate loyalty and seek God's favor in your life, following David's example of relying on God's guidance?

Proverbs 19

Reflection: Proverbs 19 highlights the importance of wisdom, discipline, and righteousness. Reflect on the themes of wisdom, patience, and righteousness. How can you seek and apply godly wisdom in your decisions, exercising patience and living righteously?

Matthew 1:18-25

Reflection: This passage narrates the birth of Jesus from Joseph's perspective. Reflect on the themes of obedience, faith, and divine intervention. How can you respond to God's guidance with faith and obedience, even when it challenges your understanding or plans?

Day 185: 1 Chronicles 15-17, Proverbs 20, Matthew 2:1-12

1 Chronicles 15-17

Reflection: These chapters describe the return of the Ark and God's covenant with David. Reflect on the themes of worship, covenant, and divine promise. How can you prioritize worship and trust in God's promises, following David's example of reverence and faith?

Proverbs 20

Reflection: Proverbs 20 offers wisdom on conduct, integrity, and diligence. Reflect on the themes of integrity, diligence, and godly living. How can you cultivate integrity and diligence in your daily activities, honoring God with your actions and choices?

Matthew 2:1-12

Reflection: This passage tells the story of the Magi visiting Jesus. Reflect on the themes of seeking, worship, and divine revelation. How can you seek Jesus with the same fervor as the Magi, offering your worship and being open to divine revelations in your life?

Day 186: 1 Chronicles 18-20, Proverbs 21, Matthew 2:13-23

1 Chronicles 18-20

Reflection: These chapters recount David's military victories. Reflect on the themes of victory, divine support, and justice. How can you rely on God's support in your battles, striving for justice and righteousness in all your endeavors?

Proverbs 21

Reflection: Proverbs 21 emphasizes the sovereignty of God, righteousness, and wisdom. Reflect on the themes of divine sovereignty, righteousness, and wise living. How can you align your life with God's will, seeking righteousness and wisdom in your actions?

Matthew 2:13-23

Reflection: This passage details the flight to Egypt and return to Nazareth. Reflect on the themes of protection, obedience, and fulfillment of prophecy. How can you trust in God's protection and guidance, responding with obedience and recognizing the fulfillment of His promises?

Day 187: 1 Chronicles 21-22, Proverbs 22, Matthew 3

1 Chronicles 21-22

Reflection: These chapters describe David's census and preparation for the temple. Reflect on the themes of repentance, preparation, and divine purpose. How can you prepare your heart and life for God's purposes, seeking repentance and aligning with His will?

Proverbs 22

Reflection: Proverbs 22 offers wisdom on various aspects of life, including integrity, generosity, and training. Reflect on the themes of integrity, generosity, and godly upbringing. How can you practice and teach these values in your daily life and interactions?

Matthew 3

Reflection: This chapter describes John the Baptist's ministry and Jesus' baptism. Reflect on the themes of repentance, preparation, and divine approval. How can you embrace repentance and prepare the way for God's work in your life, seeking His approval and guidance?

Day 188: 1 Chronicles 23-25, Proverbs 23, Matthew 4:1-17

1 Chronicles 23-25

Reflection: These chapters outline the organization of Levites and temple musicians. Reflect on the themes of service, worship, and order. How can you offer your talents in service to God, contributing to the order and beauty of worship in your community?

Proverbs 23

Reflection: Proverbs 23 advises on discipline, wisdom, and the dangers of excess. Reflect on the themes of self-control, wisdom, and moderation. How can you apply self-discipline and seek wisdom, avoiding the pitfalls of excess and indulgence?

Matthew 4:1-17

Reflection: This passage recounts Jesus' temptation and the beginning of His ministry. Reflect on the themes of temptation, resilience, and proclamation. How can you resist temptation, rely on God's Word, and boldly proclaim His message in your life?

Day 189: 1 Chronicles 26-27, Proverbs 24, Matthew 4:18-25

1 Chronicles 26-27

Reflection: These chapters describe the divisions of gatekeepers, treasurers, and army commanders. Reflect on the themes of stewardship, responsibility, and leadership. How can you faithfully steward your responsibilities and lead with integrity in your various roles?

Proverbs 24

Reflection: Proverbs 24 offers wisdom on building a strong life, avoiding evil, and perseverance. Reflect on the themes of wisdom, resilience, and righteous living. How can you build your life on godly wisdom, persevere through challenges, and avoid evil influences?

Matthew 4:18-25

Reflection: This passage describes Jesus calling His first disciples and His early ministry. Reflect on the themes of calling, discipleship, and healing. How can you respond to Jesus' call to follow Him, embracing the journey of discipleship and participating in His healing work?

WEEK 28: Women Finding Balance Between Action and Contemplation

Welcome back, Faithful and Fierce women! As we continue this enriching exploration of faith, we delve into a timeless story from the Gospel of Luke (Luke 10:38-42) – the narrative of Martha and Mary. This seemingly simple passage offers profound insights about finding balance between a life of action (Martha) and a life of contemplation (Mary).

A Journey of Hospitality:

Jesus arrives at the home of Martha and Mary, two sisters known for their contrasting personalities. Here's a closer look at their approaches:

- **Martha, the Busy Hostess:** Martha is portrayed as diligently preparing a feast, consumed with serving Jesus and ensuring a perfect visit.

- **Mary, the Devoted Listener:** Mary, in contrast, sits at Jesus' feet, intently listening to His teachings and absorbing His wisdom.

Beyond Stereotypes:

This story isn't about portraying one sister as better than the other. It's about recognizing the importance of balance in our spiritual lives.

- **Action without Contemplation Can Lead to Emptiness:** While serving others is important, neglecting time for prayer, reflection, and connecting with God can leave us feeling spiritually drained.

- **Contemplation without Action Can Lead to Stagnation:** Faith isn't just about knowledge; it's about putting our beliefs into action through service and living out God's message in the world.

Finding Your Center: Action and Contemplation

The key takeaway from this story is the importance of finding a healthy balance between action and contemplation in your faith journey:

- **Schedule Time for Prayer and Reflection:** Carve out dedicated time each day for prayer, meditation, or simply sitting quietly in God's presence.

- **Listen Attentively to God's Voice:** Be mindful of how God speaks to you – through scripture, nature, or even in the quiet moments of contemplation.

- **Serve with a Joyful Heart:** When you engage in acts of service, do so with a spirit of love and compassion, not just out of obligation.

- **Be Present in the Moment:** Whether you're praying or serving others, be fully present in the moment, focusing on the task at hand with your whole heart.

Journaling: Embracing Balance

Take some quiet time for reflection and journaling:

- Reflect on your own tendencies. Do you naturally gravitate towards action or contemplation?

- Can you identify times when you've been overly focused on one aspect and neglected the other?

- What steps can you take to create a more balanced approach to your faith life?

Remember, dear sisters, finding balance is a lifelong journey. There will be times when you lean more towards action and other times when contemplation takes center stage. The key is to be mindful, listen to your inner voice, and strive for a rhythm that nourishes your soul and strengthens your connection with God.

Beyond This Book:

As we continue this faith-enriching journey, remember that the pursuit of balance continues! Here are some ways to maintain a balanced life:

- **Create a Daily Routine:** Develop a daily routine that incorporates both prayer/reflection and opportunities for service.

- **Find a Spiritual Mentor:** Seek guidance from a priest, spiritual director, or mentor who can offer insights on finding balance in your faith life.

- **Embrace Mindfulness Practices:** Techniques like meditation or centering prayer can help you become more present and attuned to God's presence.

BIBLE READING: Week 28

Day 190: 1 Chronicles 28-29, Proverbs 25, Matthew 5:1-12

1 Chronicles 28-29

Reflection: These chapters detail David's charge to Solomon and the people's offerings for the temple. Reflect on the themes of legacy, stewardship, and worship. How can you leave a godly legacy, faithfully stewarding what God has entrusted to you and engaging in heartfelt worship?

Proverbs 25

Reflection: Proverbs 25 offers wisdom on humility, patience, and righteous living. Reflect on the themes of humility, patience, and discretion. How can you cultivate humility and patience, exercising discretion in your interactions and relationships?

Matthew 5:1-12

Reflection: This passage contains the Beatitudes, Jesus' teachings on blessedness. Reflect on the themes of humility, righteousness, and kingdom values. How can you embody the qualities of the Beatitudes, seeking to live in alignment with God's kingdom and experiencing His blessings?

Day 191: 2 Timothy, Proverbs 26, Matthew 5:13-26

2 Timothy

Reflection: Paul's second letter to Timothy provides encouragement and instructions for ministry. Reflect on the themes of perseverance, faithfulness, and sound teaching. How can you persevere in your faith and ministry, remaining faithful to God's Word and His calling on your life?

Proverbs 26

Reflection: Proverbs 26 offers wisdom on folly, laziness, and contentiousness. Reflect on the themes of wisdom, diligence, and healthy relationships. How can you avoid folly and laziness, striving for wisdom and fostering peace in your interactions with others?

Matthew 5:13-26

Reflection: This passage includes Jesus' teachings on salt and light, as well as His instructions on anger and reconciliation. Reflect on the themes of influence, righteousness, and reconciliation. How can you be a preserving influence in the world, living righteously and seeking reconciliation in your relationships?

Day 192: 2 Chronicles 1-2, Proverbs 27, Matthew 5:27-37

2 Chronicles 1-2

Reflection: These chapters detail Solomon's reign, including his wisdom and preparations for building the temple. Reflect on the themes of wisdom, worship, and divine guidance. How can you seek God's wisdom and guidance in your endeavors, prioritizing worship and obedience to His will?

Proverbs 27

Reflection: Proverbs 27 offers wisdom on friendship, humility, and foresight. Reflect on the themes of friendship, humility, and planning. How can you cultivate meaningful friendships, practice humility, and wisely plan for the future?

Matthew 5:27-37

Reflection: This passage contains Jesus' teachings on adultery, divorce, and oaths. Reflect on the themes of purity, faithfulness, and integrity. How can you honor God's standards of purity and faithfulness in your relationships and commitments, living with integrity and sincerity?

Day 193: 2 Chronicles 3-5, Proverbs 28, Matthew 5:38-48

2 Chronicles 3-5

Reflection: These chapters describe the construction and dedication of the temple under Solomon's reign. Reflect on the themes of worship, glory, and God's presence. How can you cultivate an environment of worship and seek God's presence in your life and community?

Proverbs 28

Reflection: Proverbs 28 offers wisdom on righteousness, integrity, and justice. Reflect on the themes of righteousness, honesty, and consequences. How can you pursue righteousness and integrity in your actions, recognizing the consequences of both righteousness and wickedness?

Matthew 5:38-48

Reflection: This passage contains Jesus' teachings on retaliation, love for enemies, and perfection. Reflect on the themes of forgiveness, love, and holiness. How can you embody the principles of forgiveness and love, seeking to reflect God's perfect love and holiness in your life?

Day 194: 2 Chronicles 6-7, Proverbs 29, Matthew 6:1-18

2 Chronicles 6-7

Reflection: These chapters depict Solomon's prayer of dedication for the temple and God's response with His glory filling the temple. Reflect on the themes of prayer, dedication, and God's presence. How can you cultivate a life of prayerful dedication, inviting God's presence to dwell in your heart and life?

Proverbs 29

Reflection: Proverbs 29 offers wisdom on leadership, discipline, and righteousness. Reflect on the themes of leadership, discipline, and obedience. How can you demonstrate wise and righteous leadership in your sphere of influence, maintaining discipline and obedience to God's Word?

Matthew 6:1-18

Reflection: This passage includes Jesus' teachings on giving to the needy, prayer, and fasting. Reflect on the themes of sincerity, humility, and spiritual discipline. How can you practice acts of righteousness with sincerity and humility, engaging in prayer and fasting as spiritual disciplines to deepen your relationship with God?

Day 195: 2 Chronicles 8-9, Proverbs 30, Matthew 6:19-34

2 Chronicles 8-9

Reflection: These chapters describe Solomon's achievements and the visit of the Queen of Sheba. Reflect on the themes of prosperity, wisdom, and seeking God. How can you pursue wisdom and seek God's guidance in all areas of your life, acknowledging Him as the source of true prosperity?

Proverbs 30

Reflection: Proverbs 30 offers wisdom on humility, contentment, and reverence for God. Reflect on the themes of humility, contentment, and trust in God's provision. How can you cultivate humility and contentment in your life, trusting in God's faithfulness to provide for your needs?

Matthew 6:19-34

Reflection: This passage contains Jesus' teachings on storing up treasures in heaven, seeking God's kingdom, and trusting in His provision. Reflect on the themes of priorities, faithfulness, and trust. How can you prioritize seeking God's kingdom and righteousness, trusting in His provision and releasing anxiety about material needs?

Day 196: 2 Chronicles 10-12, Proverbs 31, Matthew 7

2 Chronicles 10-12

Reflection: These chapters depict the reigns of Rehoboam and his successors, including their disobedience and the consequences they faced. Reflect on the themes of leadership, obedience, and consequences. How can you learn from the mistakes of Rehoboam and seek to lead with obedience to God's commands?

Proverbs 31

Reflection: Proverbs 31 describes the virtuous woman, highlighting her wisdom, industry, and godly character. Reflect on the themes of wisdom, diligence, and virtue. How can you embody the characteristics of the virtuous woman, pursuing wisdom, working diligently, and cultivating godly character in your life?

Matthew 7

Reflection: This chapter contains Jesus' teachings on judging others, asking, seeking, and knocking, and the narrow and wide gates. Reflect on the themes of discernment, prayer, and the path to eternal life. How can you exercise discernment without being judgmental, persist in prayer, and choose the narrow path that leads to life?

WEEK 29: Women and Body Image: Embracing Your God-Given Beauty

Welcome back, Faithful and Fierce women! As we continue this empowering exploration of faith, we turn our hearts towards a vital topic – body image. In a world obsessed with external appearances, it's easy to lose sight of your true beauty, the one that radiates from within. This week, we'll explore the Bible's perspective on inner beauty and self-worth, empowering you to embrace your God-given gifts with confidence.

A Journey of True Beauty:

The Bible offers a refreshing perspective on beauty, emphasizing the importance of inner qualities over superficial appearances. Here are some key themes:

- **The Value of Inner Beauty:** Proverbs 31:30 describes a woman of valor whose "charm is deceptive, and beauty is fleeting; but a woman who fears the Lord is to be praised." True beauty lies in character, faith, and strength.

- **Worth Beyond Appearance:** 1 Samuel 16:7 tells us, "The Lord does not look at the things people look at. People look at the outward appearance, but the Lord looks at the heart." God sees beyond our physical bodies and values our inner qualities.

- **We Are All Created in God's Image:** Genesis 1:27 states, "So God created mankind in his own image, in the image of God he created them; male and female he created them." Being created in God's image imbues us with inherent worth and dignity, regardless of physical appearance.

Shifting Your Focus: From External to Internal

The journey towards healthy body image involves shifting your focus from external validation to appreciating your God-given beauty:

- **Challenge Negative Self-Talk:** Identify and replace negative thoughts about your body with affirmations that celebrate your strengths and unique qualities.

- **Focus on Gratitude:** Cultivate gratitude for your body's abilities – the strength it gives you to move, the senses that allow you to experience the world, the resilience it possesses.

- **Nurture Your Temple:** Treat your body with respect by nourishing it with healthy food, getting adequate rest, and engaging in activities that promote physical and mental well-being.

- **Surround Yourself with Positivity:** Seek out media, friends, and role models who celebrate diversity and inner beauty.

Challenge: Embracing Your Value

This week, I challenge you to actively cultivate body positivity and appreciation for your body as a temple of the Holy Spirit:

- **Practice Body Positivity Affirmations:** Start your day with affirmations that highlight your worth and beauty beyond appearance. Repeat statements like "I am a strong and capable woman," "My body is worthy of love and respect," or "I am loved by God just as I am."

- **Engage in Self-Care Activities:** Schedule time for activities that promote self-care and appreciation for your body. Try a pampering spa day, take a relaxing bath, or go for a walk in nature to reconnect with your body.

- **Celebrate Diversity:** Seek out media and role models who challenge traditional beauty standards and celebrate the beauty of all body types and ethnicities.

Remember, dear sisters, true beauty radiates from within. Your faith, strength, compassion, and unique gifts are what truly make you beautiful. Embrace your God-given essence and allow your inner light to shine through.

Beyond This Book:

As we close this empowering week, remember that your journey towards positive body image is continuous! Here are some ways to stay on track:

- **Create a Support System:** Surround yourself with positive people who celebrate you for who you are, not just how you look.

- **Practice Mindfulness:** Meditation or mindfulness exercises can help you become more accepting of your body and present in the moment.

- **Seek Professional Help:** If you struggle with negative body image that significantly impacts your life, consider seeking help from a therapist or counselor.

Day 197: 2 Chronicles 13-15, Isaiah 1, Matthew 8:1-17

2 Chronicles 13-15

Reflection: These chapters narrate the reign of Abijah and Asa, highlighting their faithfulness and reforms in Judah. Reflect on the themes of faithfulness, repentance, and revival. How can you learn from the examples of Abijah and Asa to remain faithful to God and lead others in repentance and revival?

Isaiah 1

Reflection: Isaiah 1 contains a message of rebuke and calls for repentance from the sinful nation of Israel. Reflect on the themes of justice, rebellion, and restoration. How does this passage challenge you to confront injustice, turn away from rebellion, and embrace God's offer of restoration through repentance?

Matthew 8:1-17

Reflection: In this passage, Jesus heals the leper, the centurion's servant, Peter's mother-in-law, and many others, demonstrating His authority over sickness and disease. Reflect on the themes of faith, compassion, and authority. How can you exercise faith in Jesus' authority to bring healing and restoration to those in need around you?

Day 198: 2 Chronicles 16-18, Isaiah 2, Matthew 8:18-34

2 Chronicles 16-18

Reflection: These chapters describe the reigns of Asa, Jehoshaphat, and Jehoram, highlighting their victories and defeats. Reflect on the themes of trust, compromise, and consequences. How can you learn from the successes and failures of these kings to trust in God wholeheartedly and avoid compromising your faith?

Isaiah 2

Reflection: Isaiah 2 contains a vision of the future glory of Jerusalem and God's judgment on the proud and arrogant. Reflect on the themes of humility, worship, and judgment. How does this vision challenge you to humble yourself before God, worship Him in spirit and truth, and live in anticipation of His righteous judgment?

Matthew 8:18-34

Reflection: This passage includes Jesus' teachings on the cost of discipleship and His authority over nature and demons. Reflect on the themes of discipleship, trust, and obedience. How can you count the cost of following Jesus, trust in His authority in every aspect of your life, and obediently follow Him wherever He leads?

Day 199: 2 Chronicles 19-21, Isaiah 3, Matthew 9:1-17

2 Chronicles 19-21

Reflection: These chapters depict the reigns of Jehoshaphat and his descendants, focusing on their adherence to or departure from God's commands. Reflect on the themes of leadership, judgment, and restoration. How can you cultivate godly leadership and remain faithful to God's Word, knowing that His judgment brings both discipline and restoration?

Isaiah 3

Reflection: Isaiah 3 contains a prophecy of judgment against Judah for their rebellion and idolatry. Reflect on the themes of rebellion, accountability, and consequence. How does this passage prompt you to examine your own life for areas of rebellion against God's authority and prepare for the consequences of disobedience?

Matthew 9:1-17

Reflection: In this passage, Jesus heals a paralytic, calls Matthew as a disciple, and responds to questions about fasting. Reflect on the themes of healing, calling, and renewal. How can you respond to Jesus' invitation to follow Him, experience His healing and renewal, and embrace the new life He offers through faith?

Day 200: 2 Chronicles 22-23, Isaiah 4, Matthew 9:18-38

2 Chronicles 22-23

Reflection: These chapters narrate the reigns of Ahaziah and Athaliah, along with the righteous reign of Joash. Reflect on the themes of leadership, loyalty, and restoration. How can you learn from the examples of Ahaziah, Athaliah, and Joash to lead with integrity, remain loyal to God's commands, and participate in His work of restoration?

Isaiah 4

Reflection: Isaiah 4 describes a vision of restoration and purification for Jerusalem. Reflect on the themes of redemption, holiness, and protection. How does this vision of God's presence as a shelter and refuge inspire you to seek His purification and protection in your own life?

Matthew 9:18-38

Reflection: In this passage, Jesus heals a woman with a hemorrhage, raises a girl from the dead, and continues His ministry of healing and teaching. Reflect on the themes of faith, compassion, and mission. How can you demonstrate faith in Jesus' power to bring healing and restoration, show compassion to those in need, and join in His mission of proclaiming the kingdom of God?

Day 201: 2 Chronicles 24-25, Isaiah 5, Matthew 10:1-15

2 Chronicles 24-25

Reflection: These chapters depict the reigns of Joash and Amaziah, highlighting both their faithfulness and their eventual downfall. Reflect on the themes of faithfulness, pride, and consequences. How can you learn from the successes and failures of Joash and Amaziah to remain steadfast in your faith and humble before God?

Isaiah 5

Reflection: Isaiah 5 presents a parable of the vineyard, portraying God's judgment upon Israel for their unfaithfulness. Reflect on the themes of justice, judgment, and accountability. How does this parable challenge you to examine your own life and actions in light of God's standards, and how can you align yourself more closely with His will?

Matthew 10:1-15

Reflection: In this passage, Jesus commissions the twelve disciples and instructs them on their mission. Reflect on the themes of discipleship, authority, and hospitality. How can you embrace the call to discipleship, recognizing the authority given by Christ, and demonstrate hospitality and openness as you share the message of the kingdom?

Day 202: 2 Chronicles 26-27, Isaiah 6, Matthew 10:16-33

2 Chronicles 26-27

Reflection: These chapters narrate the reigns of Uzziah and Jotham, highlighting their successes and failures as kings of Judah. Reflect on the themes of pride, obedience, and dependence on God. How can you learn from the experiences of Uzziah and Jotham to cultivate humility, obedience, and reliance on God in your own life?

Isaiah 6

Reflection: Isaiah 6 records Isaiah's vision of God's glory in the temple, which leads to his commissioning as a prophet. Reflect on the themes of holiness, surrender, and mission. How does Isaiah's encounter with God inspire you to surrender yourself completely to His will and embrace the mission of proclaiming His message to the world?

Matthew 10:16-33

Reflection: Jesus warns His disciples of the challenges they will face in their ministry, yet reassures them of God's provision and care. Reflect on the themes of persecution, courage, and trust. How can you find courage and trust in God's promises even in the face of opposition or hardship, knowing that He is faithful to sustain you?

Day 203: 2 Chr 28-29, Isa 7, Mt 10:34-11:1

2 Chronicles 28-29

Reflection: These chapters recount the reigns of Ahaz and Hezekiah, two kings of Judah with contrasting attitudes toward God. Reflect on the consequences of faithfulness and disobedience in leadership. How can the examples of Ahaz and Hezekiah guide you in your own leadership roles, whether in your family, community, or workplace?

Isaiah 7

Reflection: Isaiah 7 depicts the prophecy of the sign of Immanuel, a child to be born of a virgin, and offers assurance of God's presence and protection. Reflect on the themes of faith, prophecy, and divine intervention. How does the prophecy of Immanuel encourage you to trust in God's promises, especially in times of uncertainty or difficulty?

Matthew 10:34-11:1

Reflection: Jesus declares that He has come not to bring peace, but a sword, and emphasizes the cost of discipleship. Reflect on the themes of commitment, division, and the call to follow Christ. How does Jesus' challenging words prompt you to reevaluate your priorities and commitment to Him as a disciple?

WEEK 30: Women Facing Challenges: Finding Hope in Difficult Times

Welcome back, Faithful and Fierce women! As we continue this remarkable journey of faith, we delve into a topic close to many hearts – navigating challenges and finding hope in difficult times. Life throws curveballs, and women are often on the frontlines, facing adversity with courage and resilience. This week, we'll explore stories of strong women in the Bible who overcame hardship, drawing inspiration from their unwavering faith.

A Journey of Resilience:

The Bible is a treasure trove of stories about women who faced immense challenges, from social injustice to emotional turmoil. Here are a few examples:

- **Ruth:** A foreigner who faced poverty and loss, Ruth demonstrated unwavering loyalty and faith. Through her resilience and resourcefulness, she built a new life and secured a place in the lineage of Jesus.

- **Esther:** An orphan who became queen in a foreign land, Esther faced a life-or-death decision. Her courage and faith in God empowered her to advocate for her people and save them from destruction.

- **Job's Wife:** Throughout Job's unimaginable suffering, his wife is mentioned only briefly, yet her story speaks volumes. She endured immense personal loss while facing societal pressure to blame God.

Lessons from Strength:

These narratives offer valuable lessons about navigating challenges with faith and hope:

- **Faith as a Source of Strength:** While facing adversity, these women found solace and strength in their faith in God. Their connection to God kept them grounded and provided the courage to persevere.

- **The Power of Community:** Though facing hardship, these women weren't alone. Ruth found support in her mother-in-law Naomi, Esther relied on her advisor Mordecai, and Job's wife, though unnamed, likely found strength in her husband or community.

- **Hope Amidst Darkness:** Despite their struggles, these women never lost hope. They clung to the promise of a better future and trusted in God's plan even when they couldn't understand it.

Discussion Starter: Strength in the Scriptures

The Bible offers a wealth of stories about women who overcame adversity. Let's delve deeper:

- Share a story from the Bible (or another source) of a woman who faced hardship with faith and resilience. What qualities did she display?

- How can we find strength and hope in our faith communities when facing challenges?

- Discuss practical ways to cultivate hope and maintain a positive outlook even during difficult times.

Remember, dear sisters, life's trials may test you, but you don't have to face them alone. Draw inspiration from the stories of strong women in the Bible and beyond. Remember, your faith can be a source of strength, and your community can provide the support you need to navigate challenges and emerge stronger than ever.

Beyond This Book:

As we continue this enriching adventure in faith, remember that the lessons learned stay with you:

- **Become a Beacon of Hope:** Share stories of resilient women with others facing challenges. Be a source of inspiration and encouragement.

- **Build Your Support System:** Cultivate strong connections with friends, family, and faith communities. Knowing you're not alone will strengthen your ability to face difficulties.

- **Develop Your Faith:** Nurture your relationship with God through prayer, reflection, and studying the Bible. A strong spiritual foundation will serve as a source of comfort and guidance during challenging times.

BIBLE READING: Week 30

Day 204: 2 Chr 30-31, Isaiah 8, Matthew 11:2-19

2 Chronicles 30-31

Reflection: These chapters detail King Hezekiah's revival and restoration of worship in Judah. Reflect on the themes of repentance, renewal, and worship. How can Hezekiah's actions inspire you to pursue spiritual renewal and restoration in your own life and community?

Isaiah 8

Reflection: Isaiah 8 prophesies the Assyrian invasion and warns against fearing man instead of God. Reflect on the themes of trust, fear, and divine sovereignty. How can you cultivate a trust in God that surpasses worldly fears and anxieties, especially in times of uncertainty or adversity?

Matthew 11:2-19

Reflection: John the Baptist sends messengers to Jesus to confirm if He is the Messiah. Reflect on Jesus' response and His affirmation of John's role as the forerunner. How does this interaction deepen your understanding of Jesus' identity and the importance of recognizing Him as the promised Savior?

Day 205: 2 Chr 32-33, Isaiah 9, Matthew 11:20-30

2 Chronicles 32-33

Reflection: These chapters recount King Hezekiah's reign and the spiritual reforms he implemented. Reflect on the themes of faithfulness, obedience, and dependence on God. How can Hezekiah's example inspire you to trust in God's faithfulness and seek obedience to His commands in your own life?

Isaiah 9

Reflection: Isaiah 9 prophesies the birth of a child who will bring light to a darkened world. Reflect on the themes of hope, salvation, and the promise of Immanuel. How does the promise of a coming Savior bring hope and light to your life, especially in times of darkness and despair?

Matthew 11:20-30

Reflection: Jesus denounces the unrepentant cities and invites all who are weary to find rest in Him. Reflect on the themes of repentance, rest, and grace. How does Jesus' invitation to find rest in Him resonate with you, and how can you respond with humility and trust in His promise of rest for your soul?

Day 206: 2 Chronicles 34-36, Isaiah 10, Matthew 12:1-14

2 Chronicles 34-36

Reflection: These chapters narrate the reign of King Josiah and the final days of the Kingdom of Judah before the Babylonian exile. Reflect on the consequences of disobedience and the importance of repentance and renewal. How can you learn from the mistakes of the past and prioritize obedience to God's commands in your own life?

Isaiah 10

Reflection: Isaiah 10 depicts God's judgment on Assyria for their arrogance and oppression. Reflect on the themes of justice and righteousness. How does this passage illustrate God's sovereignty and His concern for the oppressed? How can you advocate for justice and stand against oppression in your community?

Matthew 12:1-14

Reflection: In this passage, Jesus challenges the Pharisees' legalism and emphasizes the importance of mercy and compassion over religious rules. Reflect on the balance between law and love in your own life. How can you emulate Jesus' example of showing mercy and kindness to others, even when it challenges conventional norms?

Day 207: Zephaniah, Isaiah 11, Matthew 12:15-37

Zephaniah

Reflection: Zephaniah prophesies about the coming judgment on Judah and other nations, as well as the restoration of the remnant. Reflect on the themes of judgment, restoration, and hope. How does the promise of restoration offer hope even in times of judgment? How can you trust in God's faithfulness and look forward to His restoration in your life?

Isaiah 11

Reflection: Isaiah 11 prophesies about the righteous reign of the Messiah and the peace that His kingdom will bring. Reflect on the characteristics of the Messiah's kingdom, such as righteousness, justice, and harmony. How does this passage inspire you to seek after these qualities in your own life and contribute to God's kingdom of peace?

Matthew 12:15-37

Reflection: In this passage, Jesus continues to confront the Pharisees and teaches about the nature of the kingdom of God. Reflect on Jesus' response to the Pharisees' accusations and His teachings on blasphemy against the Holy Spirit. How can you ensure that your words and actions reflect a heart aligned with God's kingdom values?

Day 208: Titus, Isaiah 12, Matthew 12:38-50

Titus

Reflection: Titus contains instructions from Paul to Titus regarding leadership in the church and the conduct of believers. Reflect on the qualities of sound doctrine, godly leadership, and righteous living emphasized in this letter. How can you apply these principles to your own life and leadership roles within your community?

Isaiah 12

Reflection: Isaiah 12 is a hymn of praise and thanksgiving for God's salvation and His faithfulness to His people. Reflect on the themes of salvation, joy, and trust in God's deliverance. How can you cultivate a spirit of gratitude and praise, even in the midst of challenges and uncertainties?

Matthew 12:38-50

Reflection: Jesus responds to the demand for a sign with a rebuke and teaches about true kinship in the kingdom of God. Reflect on Jesus' words about the importance of obedience and spiritual kinship. How can you ensure that your relationship with God is characterized by genuine obedience and alignment with His will?

Day 209: Nahum, Isaiah 13, Matthew 13:1-30

Nahum

Reflection: Nahum prophesies about the impending judgment on Nineveh, the capital of Assyria. Reflect on the themes of God's justice and His sovereignty over the nations. How does Nahum's message remind you of the consequences of pride and injustice, and the assurance of God's righteous judgment?

Isaiah 13

Reflection: Isaiah 13 describes the judgment on Babylon and the devastation that will come upon the earth in the day of the Lord. Reflect on the themes of judgment, redemption, and the sovereignty of God over history. How does this passage inspire you to trust in God's ultimate victory over evil and His faithfulness to His promises?

Matthew 13:1-30

Reflection: Jesus teaches the parable of the sower and the parable of the wheat and the weeds, illustrating the mysteries of the kingdom of heaven. Reflect on the different responses to the message of the kingdom and the significance of bearing fruit. How can you ensure that your heart is receptive to God's word and that your life produces a harvest of righteousness?

Day 210: Philemon, Isaiah 14, Matthew 13:31-53

Philemon

Reflection: Philemon is a letter from Paul to Philemon, urging him to forgive his runaway slave, Onesimus, and receive him as a brother in Christ. Reflect on the themes of forgiveness, reconciliation, and Christian love. How does this letter challenge you to extend forgiveness and reconciliation to those who have wronged you, even when it's difficult? How can you embody the spirit of reconciliation and demonstrate Christ-like love in your relationships?

Isaiah 14

Reflection: Isaiah 14 describes the downfall of the king of Babylon and the triumph of God's sovereignty over the nations. Reflect on the dangers of pride and arrogance, as well as the assurance of God's justice. How does this passage encourage you to trust in God's ultimate victory over the forces of evil and injustice in the world?

Matthew 13:31-53

Reflection: In these parables, Jesus illustrates the growth of the kingdom of heaven from small beginnings to a global impact. Reflect on the themes of growth, faith, and judgment. How can you actively participate in the expansion of God's kingdom and contribute to the spread of His message of love and salvation to all people?

WEEK 31: The Women at the Cross: Faithfulness and Strength in Suffering

Welcome back, Faithful and Fierce women! As we continue this deeply moving exploration of faith, we turn our hearts towards a pivotal scene in the Gospels – the Crucifixion. Standing amidst unimaginable suffering, a group of women displayed unwavering faith and strength. This week, we delve into their story, drawing inspiration from their courage and unwavering devotion to Jesus.

A Journey of Witness:

While the Gospels differ slightly in details, they consistently portray a group of women present at the Crucifixion. Here's what we know about these remarkable women:

- **Identified Women:** The Gospels mention Mary, the mother of Jesus; Mary Magdalene; Salome, the wife of Zebedee; and Mary, the wife of Cleophas. These are just a few; there were likely many other unnamed women present.

- **Their Significance:** Unlike most men who fled in fear, these women chose to stand by Jesus during his most agonizing moments. Their presence speaks volumes about their unwavering devotion and courage.

- **Witnessing the Unthinkable:** These women bore witness to the brutal torture and crucifixion of Jesus. They experienced immense grief and emotional turmoil, yet their faith remained unshaken.

Beyond Witnessing: Acts of Comfort and Commitment

The presence of these women at the cross goes beyond mere observation. Here's how they displayed faith and love in action:

- **Offering Comfort:** While details are limited, it's likely these women attempted to offer comfort and support to Jesus, even during his unimaginable suffering.

- **Undeterred by Fear:** The presence of Roman guards and a hostile crowd wouldn't have deterred these women. Their love for Jesus outweighed any fear.

- **Following Through with Commitment:** These women had likely followed Jesus during his ministry, witnessed his miracles, and believed in his message. They remained loyal even in the face of tragedy.

Self-Reflection: The Strength to Endure

The women at the cross offer a powerful example of faith and resilience in the face of suffering. Consider this:

- Reflect on a time in your life when you experienced immense pain or loss. How did you cope with these difficulties?

- Can you identify moments when your faith has been a source of strength and comfort during hardship?

- How can you cultivate the kind of unwavering faith displayed by the women at the cross to face future challenges?

Remember, dear sisters, life comes with inevitable hardships. However, the story of the women at the cross reminds us that even in the darkest moments, faith can be a source of strength, comfort, and unwavering commitment.

Beyond This Book:

As we draw this inspiring weekly journey to a close, remember that your faith empowers you to navigate challenges:

- **Share Your Story:** By sharing your own experiences of faith and resilience, you can become a source of inspiration for others facing difficulties.

- **Seek Strength in Community:** Lean on your faith community for support and encouragement during challenging times.

- **Nurture Your Faith:** Regular prayer, reflection, and studying scripture can strengthen your spiritual foundation and prepare you to face life's storms with courage and faith.

Day 211: Habakkuk 2:1-20 Isaiah 15 Matthew 13:54-14:21

Habakkuk

Reflection: Habakkuk wrestles with God over the problem of evil and the apparent silence of God in the face of injustice. Reflect on the prophet's journey from doubt to trust and his commitment to wait on God's timing. How can you cultivate a similar faith that perseveres in seeking God's purposes even in times of uncertainty?

Isaiah 15

Reflection: Isaiah prophesies against Moab, describing the devastation that will come upon the land. Reflect on the consequences of pride and rebellion against God's authority. How does Moab's downfall serve as a warning against relying on human strength and worldly power rather than trusting in God?

Matthew 13:54-14:21

Reflection: In these passages, Jesus returns to His hometown of Nazareth, performs miracles, and feeds the five thousand. Reflect on the themes of faith, rejection, and provision. How do the responses of the people to Jesus' miracles reveal their attitudes toward Him, and what lessons can you learn from these encounters?

Day 212: James 1-3 Isaiah 16 Matthew 14:22-36

James 1-3

Reflection: James addresses various aspects of Christian living, including trials, wisdom, and the power of the tongue. Reflect on the practical wisdom and ethical teachings found in these chapters. How can you apply James' exhortations to be doers of the word and live out your faith in daily actions and speech?

Isaiah 16

Reflection: Isaiah prophesies against Moab, urging them to seek refuge in God amidst impending judgment. Reflect on the themes of trust, humility, and God's mercy. How does Moab's plight serve as a reminder of the importance of turning to God for refuge and salvation in times of trouble?

Matthew 14:22-36

Reflection: These passages include Jesus walking on water and Peter's attempt to do the same, as well as the healing of many who touched Jesus' garment. Reflect on the themes of faith, doubt, and Jesus' authority over nature and sickness. How can you trust in Jesus' power and presence even in the midst of life's storms?

Day 213: James 4-5 Isaiah 17 Matthew 15:1-20

James 4-5

Reflection: James continues his exhortations on living a godly life, addressing issues such as pride, conflicts, and the importance of prayer. Reflect on the call to humility, repentance, and reliance on God's grace in these chapters. How can you cultivate a humble and prayerful attitude in your relationship with God and others?

Isaiah 17

Reflection: Isaiah prophesies against Damascus, warning of its impending destruction. Reflect on the consequences of relying on human alliances rather than trusting in God. How does the fall of Damascus serve as a reminder of the fleeting nature of worldly power and the importance of seeking refuge in God alone?

Matthew 15:1-20

Reflection: Jesus confronts the Pharisees and teaches about true defilement and the importance of inner purity. Reflect on the difference between outward religion and genuine faith from the heart. How can you ensure that your worship and devotion to God are not merely external rituals but expressions of true love and obedience?

Day 214: Jeremiah 1-2 Isaiah 18 Matthew 15:21-39

Jeremiah 1-2

Reflection: Jeremiah is called as a prophet to the nations, tasked with delivering God's messages of judgment and restoration. Reflect on Jeremiah's response to his calling and the parallels with your own journey of faith and obedience. How can you respond faithfully to God's call on your life, despite challenges and opposition?

Isaiah 18

Reflection: Isaiah prophesies against Cush, describing God's watchfulness over the nations and His call to repentance. Reflect on the themes of divine judgment and mercy. How does

God's concern for all peoples challenge you to pray for and share the message of salvation with those who have not yet heard?

Matthew 15:21-39

Reflection: Jesus demonstrates His compassion and power through the healing of a Canaanite woman's daughter and the feeding of the four thousand. Reflect on the themes of faith, compassion, and provision. How do these miracles reveal Jesus' heart for the marginalized and His ability to meet the needs of His people?

Day 215: Jeremiah 3-4 Isaiah 19 Matthew 16:1-12

Jeremiah 3-4

Reflection: Jeremiah calls Israel back to repentance and warns of the consequences of their unfaithfulness. Reflect on God's enduring love and His call to His people to return to Him. How can you respond to God's call to repentance in your own life and turn away from anything that hinders your relationship with Him?

Isaiah 19

Reflection: Isaiah prophesies about Egypt and its eventual restoration by the Lord. Reflect on the theme of God's sovereignty over all nations and His desire for their redemption. How does God's plan for Egypt reflect His mercy and grace even toward those outside of Israel?

Matthew 16:1-12

Reflection: Jesus warns the disciples about the leaven of the Pharisees and the Sadducees, highlighting the importance of spiritual discernment. Reflect on the significance of recognizing false teachings and maintaining a pure faith. How can you guard against spiritual deception and cultivate discernment in your walk with Christ?

Day 216: Jeremiah 5-6 Isaiah 20 Matthew 16:13-28

Jeremiah 5-6

Reflection: Jeremiah confronts the people of Jerusalem for their rebellion and unfaithfulness to God. Reflect on the consequences of rejecting God's word and refusing to repent. How can you heed Jeremiah's warning and turn back to God with sincere repentance and obedience?

Isaiah 20

Reflection: Isaiah's symbolic actions concerning Egypt and Cush serve as a warning of the consequences of relying on human alliances instead of trusting in the Lord. Reflect on the dangers of placing our trust in worldly powers rather than in God's strength and faithfulness. How can you ensure that your confidence is firmly anchored in God alone?

Matthew 16:13-28

Reflection: Jesus asks His disciples who they say He is, and Peter confesses Him as the Christ, the Son of the living God. Reflect on the significance of Peter's confession and Jesus' subsequent teachings about His death and resurrection. How does understanding Jesus' identity impact your own discipleship and willingness to take up your cross and follow Him?

Day 217: Jeremiah 7-8 Isaiah 21 Matthew 17

Jeremiah 7-8

Reflection: Jeremiah delivers a message at the temple, warning the people against their false sense of security and their disregard for God's law. Reflect on the dangers of religious hypocrisy and outward rituals devoid of true faith. How can you ensure that your worship is genuine and pleasing to God, characterized by obedience and devotion from the heart?

Isaiah 21

Reflection: Isaiah prophesies about the fall of Babylon, describing the devastation that will come upon the city. Reflect on the certainty of God's judgments against the nations and His faithfulness to fulfill His word. How does the fall of Babylon remind you of God's sovereignty over human affairs and His justice in dealing with sin?

Matthew 17

Reflection: The Transfiguration reveals Jesus' glory to Peter, James, and John, foreshadowing His ultimate victory over sin and death. Reflect on the significance of this event and its confirmation of Jesus' identity as the beloved Son of God. How does the Transfiguration strengthen your faith and hope in Jesus as the promised Messiah and Savior of the world?

WEEK 32: The Unexpected Heroine - A Hidden Legacy in Jesus' Family Tree

Welcome back, Sisters! This week, we delve into the fascinating story of Rahab, a woman from the Canaanite city of Jericho. Often portrayed as a prostitute, Rahab's story challenges assumptions and reveals the surprising ways God works in our lives. Let's explore how this unlikely heroine became an ancestor of Jesus, showcasing God's grace and the power of redemption.

A City on the Brink:

The Book of Joshua tells the story of the Israelites preparing to enter the Promised Land. Jericho, a fortified city, stood in their way. Joshua sent two spies to scout the city, and they encountered Rahab, a woman who lived on the city wall.

An Act of Faith:

Fearing the Israelites and knowing Jericho's fate was sealed, Rahab made a daring decision. She hid the spies and promised to protect them in exchange for her family's safety when the Israelites conquered the city (Joshua 2:1-13). Rahab's actions were motivated by her belief in the God of the Israelites, a God far mightier than the Canaanite gods.

A Scarlet Cord of Salvation:

Rahab instructed the spies to hang a scarlet cord from her window as a signal to spare her and her family. This scarlet cord foreshadows the blood of Jesus Christ, shed for the salvation of humanity (Joshua 2:18).

Walls Crumble, Faith Endures:

The Israelites conquered Jericho, but the city walls crumbled, leaving Rahab's house on the fortified wall intact. The Israelites honored their promise, saving Rahab and her family (Joshua 6:22-25). Rahab joined the Israelites, embracing their faith and becoming part of their community.

An Unexpected Lineage:

Rahab's story doesn't end there. The Book of Ruth reveals that Rahab married Salmon, an Israelite, and they had a son named Boaz. Boaz, in turn, married Ruth, a

Moabite woman, and their son was Obed, the grandfather of King David (Ruth 4:13-22). Through this lineage, Rahab becomes an unexpected ancestor of Jesus Christ!

Lessons from Rahab's Story:

Rahab's story offers valuable lessons for our own lives:

- **God's Grace Extends to All:** Rahab, a foreigner and a woman with a past, is embraced by God's grace. Her story reminds us that God's love and forgiveness are available to everyone, regardless of background or past mistakes.

- **Faith Can Bloom in Unexpected Places:** Rahab's faith emerged amidst challenging circumstances. Her story reminds us that faith can blossom even in the most unlikely places.

- **Courage to Choose the Right Path:** Rahab made a courageous choice to protect the Israelites and embrace their God. Her story reminds us to have the courage to stand up for what we believe in, even when it's difficult.

Remember:

Rahab's story is a powerful reminder that God's plans are vast and his grace knows no bounds. Even the most unlikely individuals can play a role in God's grand design.

Activity:

Discuss the challenges Rahab faced and how her faith led her to make courageous choices. Explore the family tree of Jesus and highlight Rahab's unexpected role in his lineage.

Remember, God sees the potential for good in everyone. By learning from Rahab's story, we can open our hearts to God's grace and allow him to work in our lives in unexpected ways. May your family journey be filled with faith, hope, and the knowledge that God's love extends to all!

BIBLE READING: Week 32

Day 218: Jeremiah 9-10 Isaiah 22 Matthew 18:1-20

Jeremiah 9-10

Reflection: Jeremiah mourns over the sins of Judah and the impending judgment from God. Reflect on the prophet's lament and his call to repentance. How can you cultivate a heart of humility and genuine repentance in response to God's call for His people to turn back to Him?

Isaiah 22

Reflection: Isaiah pronounces judgment on Jerusalem and Shebna, the steward of the palace. Reflect on the consequences of pride and self-reliance, contrasted with the blessing of trusting in God's strength. How can you avoid the pitfalls of self-sufficiency and instead place your trust in the Lord for your security and salvation?

Matthew 18:1-20

Reflection: Jesus teaches about humility, forgiveness, and the importance of community in the kingdom of God. Reflect on the principles of reconciliation and restoration outlined in this passage. How can you embody the spirit of humility and forgiveness in your relationships with others, seeking reconciliation and unity within the body of Christ?

Day 219: Jeremiah 11-12 Isaiah 23 Matthew 18:21-35

Jeremiah 11-12

Reflection: Jeremiah confronts the people of Judah for their covenant unfaithfulness and warns of the consequences of disobedience. Reflect on the importance of honoring our commitments to God and the blessings that come from obedience. How can you renew your commitment to follow God wholeheartedly and trust in His promises?

Isaiah 23

Reflection: Isaiah prophesies judgment against Tyre, a powerful commercial center. Reflect on the dangers of pursuing wealth and material gain at the expense of righteousness. How can you prioritize spiritual values over worldly success and invest in treasures that have eternal significance?

Matthew 18:21-35

Reflection: Peter asks Jesus about forgiveness, and Jesus responds with the parable of the unforgiving servant. Reflect on the challenge of forgiving others as we have been forgiven by God. How can you cultivate a heart of forgiveness and extend grace to those who have wronged you, reflecting God's mercy and love?

Day 220: Jeremiah 13-14 Isaiah 24 Matthew 19:1-15

Jeremiah 13-14

Reflection: Jeremiah uses visual aids to illustrate God's judgment on Judah's pride and idolatry. Reflect on the symbolism of the ruined waistband and the drought as warnings of spiritual decay and barrenness. How can you guard against spiritual pride and cultivate a fruitful relationship with God?

Isaiah 24

Reflection: Isaiah prophesies about the judgment on the earth and the restoration that will follow. Reflect on the contrast between God's judgment on sin and His promise of redemption for His people. How does the hope of restoration encourage you to persevere in faithfulness amid the challenges of life?

Matthew 19:1-15

Reflection: Jesus teaches about marriage, divorce, and the importance of childlike faith. Reflect on the significance of Jesus' teachings for relationships and the value of childlike trust in God. How can you honor God's design for marriage and approach Him with childlike faith in all aspects of your life?

Day 221: Jeremiah 15-16 Isaiah 25 Matthew 19:16-30

Jeremiah 15-16

Reflection: Jeremiah expresses his anguish over the judgment that will come upon Judah, lamenting their stubbornness and refusal to repent. Reflect on Jeremiah's emotional response to the people's rebellion and his unwavering commitment to proclaim God's word. How can you cultivate a similar passion for truth and righteousness in your own life?

Isaiah 25

Reflection: Isaiah praises God for His salvation and His promises of restoration for His people. Reflect on the themes of redemption, deliverance, and the triumph of God's kingdom. How does the hope of God's ultimate victory over sin and death inspire you to worship Him with gratitude and trust?

Matthew 19:16-30

Reflection: Jesus engages with a rich young man who asks about eternal life and teaches about the challenges of wealth and the rewards of discipleship. Reflect on the cost of following Jesus and the blessings of surrendering everything for the sake of the kingdom. How can you align your priorities with the values of God's kingdom and find true treasure in Him?

Day 222: Jeremiah 17-18 Isaiah 26 Matthew 20:1-16

Jeremiah 17-18

Reflection: Jeremiah contrasts the fate of those who trust in man with those who trust in the Lord, emphasizing the importance of faithfulness and obedience. Reflect on the imagery of the tree planted by the water and the potter and the clay, representing God's sovereignty and His desire for His people to yield to His molding. How can you ensure that your trust is firmly rooted in God alone, allowing Him to shape and guide your life according to His perfect will?

Isaiah 26

Reflection: Isaiah celebrates the security and salvation found in God, contrasting it with the fate of the wicked. Reflect on the themes of trust, peace, and righteousness portrayed in this passage. How can you cultivate a lifestyle of trust in God's unfailing promises and experience His peace in the midst of life's uncertainties?

Matthew 20:1-16

Reflection: Jesus tells the parable of the laborers in the vineyard, highlighting God's generosity and the principle of grace. Reflect on the grace of God extended to all who respond to His call, regardless of their background or merit. How can you embrace God's grace in your own life and extend it to others without prejudice or favoritism?

Day 223: Jeremiah 19-20 Isaiah 27 Matthew 20:17-34

Jeremiah 19-20

Reflection: Jeremiah is persecuted for delivering God's message of judgment, yet he remains faithful to his calling despite opposition and personal suffering. Reflect on the challenges and rewards of proclaiming God's truth in a world hostile to His word. How can you stand firm in your convictions and boldly declare God's message of redemption, even in the face of adversity?

Isaiah 27

Reflection: Isaiah prophesies about the restoration of Israel and the defeat of their enemies, symbolized by the vineyard and the removal of thorns and briers. Reflect on the themes of restoration, protection, and judgment found in this passage. How does the imagery of the vineyard convey God's commitment to His people and His ultimate victory over evil? How can you trust in God's promises of restoration and find hope in His faithfulness, even in times of trial and uncertainty?

Matthew 20:17-34

Reflection: Jesus predicts His death and resurrection for the third time, and then demonstrates His compassion through healing the blind men near Jericho. Reflect on the humility and sacrificial love of Jesus, who willingly laid down His life for others. How can you follow Jesus' example of selflessness and compassion in serving those in need and sharing the message of salvation with others?

Day 224: Jeremiah 21-22 Isaiah 28 Matthew 21:1-17

Jeremiah 21-22

Reflection: Jeremiah delivers God's message of judgment against the kings of Judah for their unrighteousness and oppression of the poor. Reflect on the responsibilities of leadership and the consequences of failing to govern with justice and integrity. How can you advocate for justice and righteousness in your sphere of influence, reflecting God's heart for the marginalized and oppressed?

Isaiah 28

Reflection: Isaiah rebukes the leaders of Ephraim for their pride and drunkenness, warning of impending judgment. Reflect on the dangers of spiritual intoxication and the importance of spiritual discernment. How can you cultivate a sober-mindedness and discernment in your walk with God, avoiding the allure of worldly pleasures and remaining steadfast in His truth?

Matthew 21:1-17

Reflection: Jesus enters Jerusalem triumphantly, fulfilling the prophecy of Zechariah, and cleanses the temple of those who were buying and selling. Reflect on the significance of Jesus' actions as the Messiah and King, bringing both judgment and salvation. How can you welcome Jesus as the rightful King of your life and worship Him with reverence and sincerity, offering Him the praise and honor He deserves?

WEEK 33: Women and Discernment: Making Faith-Based Decisions for Relationships

Welcome back, Faithful and Fierce women! As we delve deeper into navigating faith in our lives, this week we turn to a crucial aspect – discernment in relationships. Making choices about dating and marriage can be complex, and your faith can be a powerful guiding force. This week, we'll explore the importance of discernment and how to incorporate it into your relationship decisions.

A Journey of Choice:

Discernment, in a spiritual context, refers to the process of seeking God's guidance in making important decisions. When it comes to relationships, discernment empowers you to choose partners who share your values and create a foundation for a fulfilling and faith-centered union.

- **Beyond Emotions:** While emotions are important, discernment encourages you to look beyond initial attraction and consider the long-term compatibility and alignment of values.

- **Seeking God's Will:** Through prayer, reflection, and potentially spiritual guidance, discernment allows you to discern if a potential partner aligns with God's plan for your life.

- **Building a Strong Foundation:** Relationships built on faith and shared values tend to be more resilient and offer greater potential for long-term happiness.

The Discernment Toolkit: Guiding Your Choices

Here are practical tools you can utilize to navigate discernment in your relationships:

- **Clarify Your Values:** Reflect on your core values – faith, communication, respect, family life – and how they translate into what you seek in a partner.

- **Seek Guidance:** Talk to trusted friends, mentors, or spiritual leaders for guidance and support as you make decisions about your relationships.

- **Honest Communication:** Open and honest communication is vital in discernment. Express your needs and desires to potential partners and listen attentively to theirs.

- **Prayer and Reflection:** Carve out dedicated time for prayer and reflection. Ask God for wisdom and guidance in discerning the right path for your relationships.

Journaling: Values and Faith

Take some quiet time for reflection and journaling:

- Reflect on your core values and how they are intertwined with your faith.

- What qualities would you like to see in a potential partner who shares your beliefs?

- How can you integrate prayer and reflection into your discernment process when it comes to relationships?

Remember, dear sisters, discernment is a journey, not a destination. It requires patience, self-reflection, and a willingness to listen to your inner voice and God's guidance.

Beyond This Book:

As we continue on this empowering journey, remember that discernment is a lifelong practice:

- **Maintain Open Communication:** Continue to have open and honest conversations with your partner about your values and goals.

- **Nurture Your Faith:** A strong and vibrant faith life provides a solid foundation for making wise decisions, including those related to relationships.

- **Trust Your Intuition:** While discernment involves seeking guidance, ultimately, trust your gut feeling and intuition when making decisions about your relationships.

BIBLE READING: Week 33

Day 225: Jeremiah 23-24, Isaiah 29, Matthew 21:18-32

Jeremiah 23-24

Reflection: Jeremiah speaks of the righteous Branch, a prophecy of the coming Messiah, and contrasts the good figs with the bad figs, representing the fate of the exiles. Reflect on the hope and restoration promised through Jesus, the righteous Branch. How can you live in a way that aligns with the good figs, bearing fruit in keeping with repentance and righteousness?

Isaiah 29

Reflection: Isaiah warns of woe to Ariel (Jerusalem) and speaks of the blindness and deafness of the people, followed by a promise of deliverance. Reflect on the themes of spiritual blindness and God's power to restore and redeem. How can you seek to open your eyes and ears to God's truth, allowing His word to transform and guide you?

Matthew 21:18-32

Reflection: Jesus curses the fig tree and teaches on faith, and then tells the parable of the two sons, highlighting the importance of obedience. Reflect on the significance of genuine faith and obedience to God's will. How can you ensure that your faith is not merely superficial but is evidenced by actions that align with God's commands?

Day 226: Jeremiah 25-26, Isaiah 30, Matthew 21:33-46

Jeremiah 25-26

Reflection: Jeremiah prophesies the seventy-year exile and faces opposition for his messages of judgment. Reflect on the endurance and faithfulness required to speak God's truth in the face of opposition. How can you remain steadfast in sharing God's word and living according to His will, even when it is unpopular or met with resistance?

Isaiah 30

Reflection: Isaiah rebukes the rebellious children of Israel for seeking help from Egypt instead of trusting in God. Reflect on the futility of relying on human solutions instead of God's guidance and provision. How can you cultivate a deeper trust in God's plans and timing, seeking His direction in all areas of your life?

Matthew 21:33-46

Reflection: Jesus tells the parable of the tenants, illustrating the rejection of the prophets and the Son. Reflect on the consequences of rejecting God's messengers and His Son. How can you ensure that you are receptive to God's messages and honor Jesus as the cornerstone of your life?

Day 227: Jeremiah 27-29, Isaiah 31, Matthew 22:1-14

Jeremiah 27-29

Reflection: Jeremiah delivers messages about submitting to Babylon and the false prophets, including Hananiah. Reflect on the importance of discerning true prophetic voices from false ones. How can you develop spiritual discernment to recognize and follow genuine guidance from God, avoiding deception and false teachings?

Isaiah 31

Reflection: Isaiah warns against relying on Egypt and urges trust in the Lord. Reflect on the dangers of misplaced trust and the security found in relying on God. How can you shift your reliance from worldly supports to the steadfast promises and power of God?

Matthew 22:1-14

Reflection: Jesus shares the parable of the wedding banquet, emphasizing the invitation to God's kingdom and the necessity of being properly prepared. Reflect on the inclusiveness of God's invitation and the importance of responding appropriately. How can you live in readiness for God's kingdom, clothed in the righteousness of Christ?

Day 228: Jeremiah 30-31, Isaiah 32, Matthew 22:15-33

Jeremiah 30-31

Reflection: Jeremiah prophesies about the restoration of Israel and the new covenant. Reflect on the hope and promise of restoration and a new relationship with God through the new covenant. How can you embrace the transformative power of the new covenant in your life, living out the law written on your heart?

Isaiah 32

Reflection: Isaiah speaks of a righteous kingdom and the outpouring of the Spirit. Reflect on the vision of a just and peaceful kingdom under God's rule. How can you contribute to bringing God's justice and peace into your community, living by the Spirit's guidance?

Matthew 22:15-33

Reflection: Jesus responds to questions about paying taxes and the resurrection, demonstrating His wisdom and authority. Reflect on the wisdom and authority of Jesus in addressing complex issues. How can you seek to understand and apply Jesus' teachings in your life, trusting His wisdom in all matters?

Day 229: Jeremiah 32-33, Isaiah 33, Matthew 22:34-46

Jeremiah 32-33

Reflection: Jeremiah buys a field as a sign of hope and restoration, and God promises a future of peace and prosperity. Reflect on the hope and assurance of God's plans for restoration. How can you hold onto hope and trust in God's promises, even in seemingly hopeless situations?

Isaiah 33

Reflection: Isaiah prays for deliverance from enemies and describes the future glory of Zion. Reflect on the assurance of God's deliverance and the promise of future glory. How can you find strength and confidence in God's promises of protection and ultimate victory?

Matthew 22:34-46

Reflection: Jesus teaches about the greatest commandment and silences His opponents with His wisdom. Reflect on the centrality of love for God and others as the greatest commandments. How can you prioritize these commandments in your daily life, allowing love to guide your actions and relationships?

Day 230: Jeremiah 34-35, Isaiah 34, Matthew 23

Jeremiah 34-35

Reflection: Jeremiah conveys God's judgment on King Zedekiah and the people for their disobedience, and the faithfulness of the Rechabites is highlighted. Reflect on the contrast between disobedience and faithfulness. How can you strive for faithfulness in your commitment to God's commands, even when surrounded by disobedience?

Isaiah 34

Reflection: Isaiah describes the Lord's wrath against the nations and the desolation that will follow. Reflect on the seriousness of God's judgment against sin and the call to righteousness. How can you live with an awareness of God's holiness and justice, striving to align your life with His righteous standards?

Matthew 23

Reflection: Jesus pronounces woes on the scribes and Pharisees for their hypocrisy and lack of genuine faith. Reflect on the dangers of religious hypocrisy and the importance of authentic faith. How can you examine your own life for any traces of hypocrisy and seek to live authentically according to Jesus' teachings?

Day 231: Jeremiah 36-37, Isaiah 35, Matthew 24:1-28

Jeremiah 36-37

Reflection: Jeremiah's scroll is read to the king, who burns it, and Jeremiah faces imprisonment for his prophecies. Reflect on the persistence and courage required to proclaim God's truth. How can you remain faithful in sharing God's word, even when faced with opposition or indifference?

Isaiah 35

Reflection: Isaiah prophesies about the future glory and joy of the redeemed. Reflect on the hope and joy that come from God's promises of restoration and renewal. How can you hold onto this hope and let it inspire you to live joyfully and confidently in God's promises?

Matthew 24:1-28

Reflection: Jesus speaks about the signs of the end times and the need for vigilance. Reflect on the call to be watchful and prepared for Jesus' return. How can you live with a sense of urgency and readiness, staying faithful to Jesus and His mission as you anticipate His return?

WEEK 34: Women and Communication: Using Your Voice for Good

Welcome back, Faithful and Fierce women! As we navigate the complexities of life guided by faith, this week we delve into a powerful tool – communication. The ability to express yourself clearly, respectfully, and assertively is essential for building strong relationships, advocating for your needs, and ultimately, using your voice for good. This week, we'll explore the importance of communication in a Christian woman's life and equip you with practical skills to enhance your voice.

A Journey of Connection:

Communication is the cornerstone of human connection. Through words, we build relationships, share ideas, and navigate life's complexities. For women of faith, effective communication empowers you to:

- **Deepen Relationships:** Clear communication fosters understanding and strengthens bonds with loved ones, friends, and faith communities.

- **Advocate for Yourself:** Being able to articulate your needs and desires empowers you to advocate for yourself in various aspects of life.

- **Spread Your Faith:** Effective communication allows you to share your faith journey and inspire others with your message of love, hope, and compassion.

Beyond Words: Building a Communication Toolbox

Effective communication goes beyond simply expressing words. Let's explore some key tools:

- **Active Listening:** This involves truly paying attention to the speaker, acknowledging their words, and asking clarifying questions to ensure understanding.

- **Assertive Communication:** Assertiveness allows you to express your needs and opinions directly and confidently, while also respecting the rights of others.

- **Nonverbal Communication:** Body language, tone of voice, and facial expressions all play a crucial role in conveying your message. Be mindful of how your nonverbal cues complement your spoken words.

Challenge: Speak Up and Be Heard

This week, I challenge you to actively practice the skills discussed:

- **Become an Active Listener:** When someone is speaking, truly focus on their words. Ask questions and paraphrase what they've said to demonstrate understanding.

- **Practice Assertive Communication:** Think about a situation where you need to express a need or opinion. Craft a clear and confident statement, while remaining respectful of the other person.

- **Be Mindful of Your Nonverbal Cues:** Maintain eye contact, use a calm and confident tone, and open body language can project assertiveness and confidence.

Remember, dear sisters, communication is a skill that develops with practice. Don't be afraid to step outside your comfort zone and speak your truth.

Beyond This Book:

As we continue on this transformative journey, remember that communication is a lifelong practice:

- **Seek Feedback:** Ask trusted friends or mentors for feedback on your communication style. This can help you identify areas for improvement.

- **Embrace Different Communication Styles:** People communicate differently. Be patient and understanding when interacting with those who have a communication style that differs from yours.

- **Become a Role Model:** Use your communication skills to inspire others to express themselves clearly, respectfully, and with confidence.

Day 232: Jeremiah 38-39, Isaiah 36, Matthew 24:29-51

Jeremiah 38-39

Reflection: Jeremiah is thrown into a cistern but later rescued, and Jerusalem falls to Babylon. Reflect on Jeremiah's steadfastness in delivering God's message despite the danger. How can you remain faithful to God's calling in your life, even when faced with significant challenges or opposition?

Isaiah 36

Reflection: The Assyrian king Sennacherib threatens Jerusalem, mocking their faith in God. Reflect on the power of faith in the face of intimidation and threats. How can you strengthen your faith to stand firm against challenges and trust in God's protection and deliverance?

Matthew 24:29-51

Reflection: Jesus speaks about the signs of His coming and the importance of being prepared. Reflect on the urgency of being watchful and ready for Christ's return. How can you live a life of readiness and faithfulness, anticipating the return of Jesus and being diligent in your spiritual responsibilities?

Day 233: Jeremiah 40-42, Isaiah 37, Matthew 25:1-30

Jeremiah 40-42

Reflection: Jeremiah remains in Judah with the remnant, and the people seek his counsel but disobey God's command. Reflect on the importance of seeking and obeying God's guidance in your life. How can you cultivate a heart that not only seeks God's will but is also committed to following it faithfully?

Isaiah 37

Reflection: King Hezekiah prays to God for deliverance, and God miraculously saves Jerusalem. Reflect on the power of earnest prayer and God's ability to intervene in desperate situations. How can you strengthen your prayer life, trusting in God's power to deliver and provide in times of need?

Matthew 25:1-30

Reflection: Jesus teaches the parables of the ten virgins and the talents, emphasizing preparedness and faithful stewardship. Reflect on the importance of being spiritually prepared and using your gifts for God's kingdom. How can you ensure that you are ready for Christ's return and actively serving with the resources and talents God has given you?

Day 234: Jeremiah 43-44, Isaiah 38, Matthew 25:31-46

Jeremiah 43-44

Reflection: The remnant in Judah disobeys God's command and flees to Egypt, where Jeremiah prophesies against them. Reflect on the consequences of disobedience and the importance of trusting in God's instructions. How can you develop a deeper trust in God's plans and remain obedient to His commands, even when they seem difficult or counterintuitive?

Isaiah 38

Reflection: King Hezekiah prays for healing, and God extends his life. Reflect on God's compassion and the power of prayer in times of personal crisis. How can you deepen your reliance on prayer and trust in God's timing and compassion in your own life?

Matthew 25:31-46

Reflection: Jesus describes the final judgment, highlighting the importance of serving others as serving Him. Reflect on the call to compassion and service in your daily life. How can you actively seek opportunities to serve and care for others, demonstrating the love of Christ in practical ways?

Day 235: Jeremiah 45-47, Isaiah 39, Matthew 26:1-25

Jeremiah 45-47

Reflection: Jeremiah delivers messages of judgment against Egypt and other nations. Reflect on God's sovereignty over all nations and His righteous judgment. How can you live with an awareness of God's justice and sovereignty, striving to align your life with His righteous standards?

Isaiah 39

Reflection: Isaiah prophesies to King Hezekiah about the future Babylonian captivity. Reflect on the importance of humility and foresight in leadership and decision-making. How can you seek God's wisdom and maintain humility in your own decisions and leadership roles?

Matthew 26:1-25

Reflection: Jesus predicts His betrayal and begins the Passover with His disciples. Reflect on the significance of Jesus' foreknowledge of His suffering and His willingness to fulfill God's plan. How can you deepen your appreciation for Jesus' sacrifice and live in gratitude and commitment to His calling?

Day 236: Jeremiah 48-49, Lamentations 1, Matthew 26:26-56

Jeremiah 48-49

Reflection: Jeremiah prophesies against Moab, Ammon, and other nations, highlighting their pride and impending judgment. Reflect on the dangers of pride and the certainty of God's judgment. How can you cultivate humility and seek to align your actions with God's will, avoiding the pitfalls of pride and arrogance?

Lamentations 1

Reflection: Lamentations opens with a mournful reflection on the desolation of Jerusalem. Reflect on the themes of grief, loss, and the consequences of sin. How can you seek God's comfort and healing in times of personal or communal suffering, acknowledging the consequences of sin while hoping in His mercy?

Matthew 26:26-56

Reflection: Jesus institutes the Lord's Supper and prays in Gethsemane, preparing for His arrest. Reflect on the significance of the Lord's Supper and Jesus' submission to the Father's will. How can you cultivate a deeper understanding and reverence for the sacrament of communion and a willingness to submit to God's will in your life?

Day 237: Jeremiah 50-51, Lamentations 2, Matthew 26:57-75

Jeremiah 50-51

Reflection: Jeremiah prophesies the downfall of Babylon, a symbol of worldly power and arrogance. Reflect on the ultimate triumph of God's justice over worldly powers. How can you maintain a perspective of God's ultimate sovereignty and justice, trusting in His plans over human power structures?

Lamentations 2

Reflection: Lamentations continues with a vivid description of the Lord's anger and the suffering of Jerusalem. Reflect on the profound sorrow and repentance expressed in this chapter. How can you approach God with a repentant heart, seeking His forgiveness and restoration in the midst of personal or communal failures?

Matthew 26:57-75

Reflection: Jesus faces trial before the Sanhedrin, and Peter denies Him three times. Reflect on Jesus' courage and Peter's moment of weakness. How can you find strength in Jesus' example to stand firm in your faith, even when faced with fear or opposition, and seek restoration when you fall short?

Day 238: Jeremiah 52, Lamentations 3, Matthew 27:1-26

Jeremiah 52

Reflection: The final chapter recounts the fall of Jerusalem, the destruction of the temple, and the exile of the people. Reflect on the themes of loss and God's enduring faithfulness despite judgment. How can you hold onto hope and trust in God's faithfulness, even in times of great loss or hardship?

Lamentations 3

Reflection: Lamentations 3 contains expressions of deep lament but also profound hope in God's steadfast love and mercy. Reflect on the balance of grief and hope in your own life. How can you draw strength from God's unfailing love and mercy, finding hope even in the darkest times?

Matthew 27:1-26

Reflection: Jesus is handed over to Pilate, and the crowd chooses Barabbas over Jesus. Reflect on the injustice Jesus endured and His sacrificial love. How can you live in response to Jesus' sacrifice, embracing His love and seeking to live justly and compassionately in your interactions with others?

WEEK 35: Loyalty and Redemption Revisited

Welcome back, Faithful and Fierce women! As we continue this enriching exploration of faith, we revisit the beautiful story of Ruth, a Moabite woman whose unwavering loyalty and courage continue to inspire us today. This week, we delve deeper into the theme of loyalty in the Book of Ruth, exploring its relevance in women's friendships and relationships in the modern world.

A Journey of Unwavering Commitment:

The Book of Ruth is a powerful testament to the enduring strength of loyalty. Here's a glimpse into the story:

- **Ruth's unwavering loyalty:** Following the death of her husband, Ruth chooses to remain loyal to her mother-in-law, Naomi, even when it meant leaving her homeland and facing an uncertain future.

- **Naomi's unwavering faith in God:** Despite suffering immense loss, Naomi clings to her faith and hope for a better future. She encourages Ruth's loyalty and trusts in God's plan.

- **Boaz's loyalty to his family legacy:** Boaz, a distant relative of Naomi's deceased husband, fulfills his obligation to redeem the family land and provide for the women, demonstrating loyalty to tradition and family honor.

Beyond the Pages: Loyalty in Modern Relationships

The theme of loyalty in the Book of Ruth transcends time and culture. Let's explore its relevance in today's world:

- **Loyalty in Friendships:** True friends stand by each other through thick and thin, offering support, encouragement, and a listening ear in times of need. Just like Ruth and Naomi, true friendship thrives on unwavering loyalty.

- **Loyalty in Romantic Relationships:** Honesty, commitment, and prioritizing your partner's well-being are all facets of loyalty in a romantic relationship. Loyalty provides a foundation of trust and security essential for a healthy and fulfilling union.

- **Loyalty to Oneself:** Staying true to your values, beliefs, and aspirations is a form of self-loyalty. Just like Ruth remained true to her commitment to Naomi, staying true to yourself empowers you to lead a life of integrity.

Discussion Starter: The Power of Loyalty

The Book of Ruth offers a timeless message about the power of loyalty. Let's delve deeper:

- Share an example of a time when a friend or family member demonstrated unwavering loyalty to you. How did it impact your relationship?

- How can you cultivate greater loyalty in your own relationships, both personally and professionally?

- In today's world, where societal values are constantly evolving, how do you define loyalty in your own life?

Remember, dear sisters, loyalty is a cornerstone of strong and meaningful relationships. It fosters trust, creates a sense of security, and allows relationships to weather life's inevitable storms.

Beyond This Book:

As we continue this inspiring journey of faith, remember that loyalty is a continuous practice:

- **Nurture Your Relationships:** Invest time and effort in cultivating and maintaining your relationships with friends, family, and loved ones. Loyalty thrives on consistent care and connection.

- **Practice Honest Communication:** Open and honest communication is essential for building and maintaining trust, a vital component of loyalty.

- **Lead by Example:** Through your own actions, demonstrate what loyalty means to you. Be a friend, partner, and family member who others can rely on, just like Ruth was for Naomi.

Day 239: Baruch 1:1-3:8, Lamentations 4, Matthew 27:27-66

Baruch 1:1-3:8

Reflection: Baruch calls the exiles to repentance and confession, highlighting their collective sins. Reflect on the importance of acknowledging personal and communal sin before God. How can you practice sincere repentance and seek God's forgiveness in your own life and within your community?

Lamentations 4

Reflection: Lamentations 4 describes the severe suffering and devastation experienced by Jerusalem during the siege. Reflect on the consequences of turning away from God and the depth of human suffering that results. How can you develop a deeper compassion for those who suffer and a greater resolve to stay faithful to God?

Matthew 27:27-66

Reflection: This passage covers the crucifixion, death, and burial of Jesus. Reflect on the profound sacrifice Jesus made and the immense love He demonstrated. How can you live a life that honors Jesus' sacrifice, embracing His love and sharing it with others through acts of compassion and service?

Day 240: Baruch 3:9-5:9, Lamentations 5, Matthew 28

Baruch 3:9-5:9

Reflection: Baruch emphasizes the wisdom of God and calls the people to return to Him, promising restoration and hope. Reflect on the significance of God's wisdom and the hope of restoration. How can you seek God's wisdom in your daily life and hold onto the hope of His promises for restoration?

Lamentations 5

Reflection: The final chapter of Lamentations is a prayer for restoration and mercy. Reflect on the themes of lament and hope in this prayer. How can you incorporate both honest lament and hopeful expectation in your prayers, trusting in God's mercy and faithfulness?

Matthew 28

Reflection: Matthew 28 describes the resurrection of Jesus and the Great Commission. Reflect on the victory of the resurrection and the call to make disciples of all nations. How can you live out the resurrection power in your life and actively participate in the mission of sharing the Gospel with others?

Day 241: Baruch 6, Isaiah 40, Mark 1:1-13

Baruch 6

Reflection: Baruch 6, also known as the Letter of Jeremiah, warns against idolatry and urges trust in the one true God. Reflect on the dangers of idolatry and the importance of exclusive devotion to God. How can you identify and remove idols in your life, ensuring that your worship and trust are directed solely to God?

Isaiah 40

Reflection: Isaiah 40 offers comfort to God's people, emphasizing His power, majesty, and care. Reflect on the greatness of God and His tender care for His people. How can you find comfort in God's greatness and care, and how can this perspective shape your trust and reliance on Him?

Mark 1:1-13

Reflection: Mark begins with John the Baptist's ministry and Jesus' baptism and temptation. Reflect on the preparation for Jesus' ministry and His victory over temptation. How can you prepare your heart for God's work in your life and stand firm against the temptations you face?

Day 242: Tobit 1-3, Isaiah 41, Mark 1:14-31

Tobit 1-3

Reflection: Tobit and his family experience various trials, and Tobit prays for death in his despair. Reflect on Tobit's faith and perseverance amidst suffering. How can you maintain faith and hope in God during your own times of trial and distress?

Isaiah 41

Reflection: God reassures His people of His presence and support, encouraging them not to fear. Reflect on the assurance of God's presence and His call to fear not. How can you draw strength from God's promise to be with you, overcoming fear and anxiety in your life?

Mark 1:14-31

Reflection: Jesus begins His ministry, calling His first disciples and performing miracles. Reflect on the immediacy of the disciples' response and the authority of Jesus' teachings and actions. How can you respond immediately and wholeheartedly to Jesus' call in your life, and recognize His authority in all areas?

Day 243: Tobit 4-6, Isaiah 42, Mark 1:32-45

Tobit 4-6

Reflection: Tobit gives his son Tobias advice for a godly life, and Tobias sets out on his journey with Raphael. Reflect on the wisdom and guidance provided by Tobit. How can you seek and follow godly advice in your life, and trust in God's guidance and protection on your journey?

Isaiah 42

Reflection: Isaiah 42 introduces the Servant of the Lord, who will bring justice and be a light to the nations. Reflect on the mission and character of the Servant. How can you strive to embody the qualities of the Servant, seeking justice and being a light to those around you?

Mark 1:32-45

Reflection: Jesus heals many and shows compassion to a leper. Reflect on Jesus' compassion and power to heal. How can you demonstrate compassion in your daily interactions and trust in Jesus' power to heal and restore?

Day 244: Tobit 7-11, Isaiah 43, Mark 2:1-17

Tobit 7-11

Reflection: Tobias meets Sarah, and through God's intervention, they overcome demonic oppression. Reflect on the themes of divine intervention and faith. How can you trust in God's power to deliver and protect, especially when facing seemingly insurmountable challenges?

Isaiah 43

Reflection: God promises redemption and restoration, declaring His love and care for His people. Reflect on God's promises and His declaration of being with His people. How can you embrace God's promises in your life, finding assurance in His unwavering presence and love?

Mark 2:1-17

Reflection: Jesus forgives and heals a paralytic and calls Levi the tax collector. Reflect on the authority of Jesus to forgive sins and His call to the marginalized. How can you embrace Jesus' forgiveness in your life and extend His grace and love to those who are often overlooked or rejected?

Day 245: Tobit 12-14, Isaiah 44, Mark 2:18-28

Tobit 12-14

Reflection: Raphael reveals his true identity and the purpose of his mission, and Tobit's family gives thanks. Reflect on the revelation of God's workings and the importance of gratitude. How can you recognize God's hand in your life and cultivate a heart of gratitude for His blessings and guidance?

Isaiah 44

Reflection: God speaks of His uniqueness, promises to pour out His Spirit, and challenges idolatry. Reflect on the uniqueness and faithfulness of God. How can you affirm God's uniqueness in your life and reject any form of idolatry, fully devoting yourself to Him?

Mark 2:18-28

Reflection: Jesus teaches about fasting and the Sabbath, highlighting the spirit of the law over legalism. Reflect on the freedom and purpose found in Jesus' teachings. How can you embrace the spirit of Jesus' teachings, prioritizing relationship with God over rigid adherence to rules?

WEEK 36: God's Forgiveness and Mercy to Women

Welcome back, Faithful and Fierce women! As we keep going on this faith-filled exploration, we turn to a powerful narrative from the Gospel of John – the story of the woman caught in adultery (John 8:3-11). This seemingly simple story speaks volumes about God's boundless forgiveness and compassion, offering valuable lessons for our own lives.

A Journey of Grace:

The story unfolds with a woman accused of adultery brought before Jesus by the religious authorities. Their intentions were malicious, hoping to trap Jesus in a legal dilemma. However, Jesus responds with a surprising act of grace:

- **Shifting the Focus:** Instead of condemning the woman, Jesus redirects the attention towards her accusers, exposing their hypocrisy.

- **Extending Forgiveness:** With the simple words, "Neither do I condemn you," Jesus offers the woman forgiveness and a chance to start anew.

- **A Call for Transformation:** While offering forgiveness, Jesus encourages the woman to "Go now and leave your life of sin," suggesting a journey of personal transformation.

Beyond the Narrative: Embracing God's Forgiveness

The story of the woman caught in adultery offers a profound message about God's unconditional love and forgiveness:

- **Forgiveness for All:** This story transcends the specific sin of adultery. It signifies God's willingness to forgive any transgression, big or small, as long as we seek his mercy.

- **The Power of Grace:** Jesus' response demonstrates God's grace – his unmerited favor showered upon us despite our shortcomings.

- **A Call to Change:** While offering forgiveness, Jesus encourages the woman to choose a different path. His forgiveness empowers us to pursue self-improvement and transformation.

Self-Reflection: The Ripple Effect of Forgiveness

The message of God's forgiveness extends beyond our relationship with God. Consider this:

- Have you held onto resentment or unforgiveness towards yourself or someone else? What impact has it had on your life?

- How can you embrace God's message of forgiveness and extend similar compassion to yourself and others?

- How can you translate this forgiveness into action, creating a more peaceful and compassionate environment in your relationships?

Remember, dear sisters, God's forgiveness is a gift freely offered to all. May you embrace this gift and allow it to transform your life and your relationships.

Beyond This Book:

As we wrap up this empowering journey, remember that forgiveness is an ongoing practice:

- **Forgive Yourself:** Holding onto guilt and self-blame can be a heavy burden. Seek God's forgiveness, ask for guidance to learn from your mistakes, and forgive yourself.

- **Practice Radical Forgiveness:** Forgiving someone doesn't condone their actions, but it frees you from the burden of resentment. Practice radical forgiveness, extending compassion even in challenging situations.

- **Spread the Message of Mercy:** Let the story of the woman caught in adultery inspire you to be a beacon of God's forgiveness and mercy in the world. Offer compassion, understanding, and second chances to those around you.

BIBLE READING: Week 36

Day 246: Ezekiel 1-3, Isaiah 45, Mark 3:1-19

Ezekiel 1-3

Reflection: Ezekiel receives a vision of God's glory and is commissioned as a prophet. Reflect on the awe-inspiring vision and the weight of God's calling. How can you be attentive to God's presence in your life and respond faithfully to His calling, no matter the challenges you may face?

Isaiah 45

Reflection: God speaks through Isaiah, declaring His sovereignty and His plan for Cyrus to deliver Israel. Reflect on God's sovereignty over world events and His ability to use anyone for His purposes. How can you trust in God's sovereign plan in your life and recognize His hand in the broader events of the world?

Mark 3:1-19

Reflection: Jesus heals on the Sabbath, calls the twelve apostles, and faces opposition. Reflect on Jesus' authority, compassion, and the calling of the apostles. How can you embrace the calling God has for you and show compassion to others, even in the face of opposition?

Day 247: Ezekiel 4-5, Isaiah 46, Mark 3:20-35

Ezekiel 4-5

Reflection: Ezekiel performs symbolic acts to illustrate the coming siege and judgment of Jerusalem. Reflect on the vivid portrayal of judgment and the consequences of disobedience. How can you take seriously the call to obedience and seek to align your life with God's commands?

Isaiah 46

Reflection: God contrasts His enduring power with the impotence of idols, affirming His control over history. Reflect on the futility of idolatry and the strength of God. How can you ensure that God alone is the center of your worship and trust, rejecting all forms of modern-day idolatry?

Mark 3:20-35

Reflection: Jesus speaks about the unforgivable sin and redefines His family as those who do God's will. Reflect on the seriousness of blasphemy against the Holy Spirit and the inclusiveness of God's family. How can you prioritize doing God's will and embrace the spiritual family of believers?

Day 248: Ezekiel 6-8, Isaiah 47, Mark 4:1-25

Ezekiel 6-8

Reflection: Ezekiel prophesies against idolatry and witnesses visions of Jerusalem's abominations. Reflect on the destructive nature of idolatry and the need for true worship. How can you guard your heart against idolatry and ensure that your worship is pure and pleasing to God?

Isaiah 47

Reflection: Isaiah prophesies the humiliation of Babylon, emphasizing God's judgment on arrogance. Reflect on the consequences of pride and self-reliance. How can you cultivate humility and dependence on God, avoiding the pitfalls of pride and arrogance?

Mark 4:1-25

Reflection: Jesus teaches the parable of the sower and the lamp on a stand, emphasizing hearing and responding to God's word. Reflect on the importance of being receptive to God's word and letting it shine in your life. How can you ensure that your heart is good soil for God's word and that you let His light shine through you?

Day 249: Ezekiel 9-11, Isaiah 48, Mark 4:26-41

Ezekiel 9-11

Reflection: Ezekiel sees visions of judgment and the departure of God's glory from the temple. Reflect on the significance of God's presence and the consequences of its departure. How can you cultivate an awareness of God's presence in your life and ensure that you live in a way that honors Him?

Isaiah 48

Reflection: God calls His people to listen to His commands and promises deliverance from Babylon. Reflect on the importance of listening to God and the assurance of His deliverance. How can you practice attentive listening to God's word and trust in His promises of deliverance?

Mark 4:26-41

Reflection: Jesus teaches about the kingdom of God using parables and calms a storm, demonstrating His authority. Reflect on the nature of God's kingdom and Jesus' authority over creation. How can you trust in Jesus' authority in your life and live out the principles of His kingdom?

Day 250: Ezekiel 12-13, Isaiah 49, Mark 5:1-20

Ezekiel 12-13

Reflection: Ezekiel enacts the coming exile and speaks against false prophets. Reflect on the importance of truth and the consequences of ignoring God's warnings. How can you discern and uphold truth in your life, resisting false teachings and staying faithful to God's word?

Isaiah 49

Reflection: God speaks of His servant who will bring salvation to the ends of the earth. Reflect on the mission and faithfulness of God's servant. How can you participate in God's mission of salvation and reflect His faithfulness in your life?

Mark 5:1-20

Reflection: Jesus heals a demon-possessed man, showing His power over evil spirits. Reflect on Jesus' authority over the spiritual realm and His compassion for the afflicted. How can you trust in Jesus' power to deliver and heal, and show compassion to those who are spiritually oppressed?

Day 251: Ezekiel 14-16, Isaiah 50, Mark 5:21-43

Ezekiel 14-16

Reflection: Ezekiel condemns idolatry and unfaithfulness, using vivid imagery to describe Jerusalem's sin. Reflect on the seriousness of unfaithfulness to God and the call to repentance. How can you remain faithful to God and seek His forgiveness for any areas of unfaithfulness in your life?

Isaiah 50

Reflection: Isaiah speaks of the servant's suffering and vindication, highlighting obedience and trust in God. Reflect on the servant's example of trust and obedience amid suffering.

How can you follow this example, trusting in God's vindication and remaining obedient in difficult times?

Mark 5:21-43

Reflection: Jesus heals a bleeding woman and raises Jairus' daughter, demonstrating His power over sickness and death. Reflect on the power of faith and Jesus' compassion. How can you cultivate a deep faith in Jesus' power to heal and restore, and extend His compassion to others in need?

Day 252: Ezekiel 17-18, Isaiah 51, Mark 6:1-29

Ezekiel 17-18

Reflection: Ezekiel speaks of parables and individual responsibility, emphasizing repentance and life. Reflect on the importance of personal responsibility and the call to repentance. How can you take responsibility for your actions and seek to live a life of repentance and righteousness?

Isaiah 51

Reflection: God comforts His people and calls them to listen to Him, promising salvation and righteousness. Reflect on the comfort and promises of God. How can you find comfort in God's promises and actively listen to His guidance in your life?

Mark 6:1-29

Reflection: Jesus faces rejection in Nazareth, sends out the twelve, and John the Baptist is executed. Reflect on the themes of rejection, mission, and the cost of discipleship. How can you remain faithful to your mission despite rejection and be willing to pay the cost of following Jesus?

WEEK 37: Women and Finances: Being a Wise Steward

Welcome back, Faithful and Fierce women! As we continue this transformative journey of faith, we delve into a crucial aspect of life – finances. Throughout the Bible, we find valuable guidance on responsible stewardship, offering principles that remain relevant in today's world. This week, we'll explore how to manage your finances with wisdom and faith, becoming a wise steward of the resources God has entrusted to you.

A Journey of Financial Wisdom:

The Bible is brimming with practical wisdom on money management. Here are some key principles to guide you:

- **Living Within Your Means:** Proverbs 21:20 emphasizes the importance of avoiding debt and living frugally: "The prudent acquires wealth, but the fool squanders it." Budgeting and mindful spending are crucial for financial stability.

- **Planning for the Future:** Proverbs 6:6-8 encourages us to learn from ants and prepare for the future: "Go to the ant, you sluggard; consider its ways and be wise! It has no commander, no overseer or ruler, yet it stores its provisions in summer and gathers its food at harvest."

- **Contentment and Gratitude:** Philippians 4:11-12 reminds us that true happiness doesn't come from material possessions: "I have learned to be content whatever the circumstances. I know what it is to be in need, and I know what it is to have plenty. I have learned the secret of being content in any and every situation, whether well fed or hungry, whether living in plenty or in want." Gratitude for what you have can create a sense of abundance even with limited resources.

Beyond the Text: Putting Faith into Action

Let's translate these Biblical principles into practical steps for managing your finances wisely:

- **Create a Budget:** Track your income and expenses to identify areas where you can cut back and save more effectively.

- **Reduce Debt:** Develop a plan to pay off credit cards and other high-interest debts. There are various debt-reduction strategies available – explore resources and choose the one that aligns best with your financial situation.

- **Invest for Your Future:** Seek guidance from a financial advisor on making wise investments that secure your financial future, for example, retirement planning or saving for your children's education.

- **Practice Generosity:** While responsible financial management is vital, God also encourages generosity. Tithe (donate a portion of your income) to your church or charity and consider helping those in need.

Action Step: Empowering Your Financial Future

This week, take a concrete step towards managing your finances with wisdom:

- **Create a Budget:** Utilize online budgeting tools or a simple spreadsheet to track your income and expenses. Allocate funds for necessities, savings goals, and even some fun money.

- **Review Your Spending:** Analyze your spending habits and identify areas where you can cut back. Consider bringing a lunch instead of eating out every day or opting for cheaper alternatives for subscriptions or entertainment.

- **Develop a Savings Plan:** Whether it's an emergency fund, a down payment on a house, or retirement savings, set a goal and automate transfers from your checking account to your savings account to reach your goal consistently.

Remember, dear sisters, managing your finances wisely requires discipline, dedication, and a commitment to living within your means. Faith can play a crucial role in this journey:

- **Seek Guidance in Prayer:** Pray for wisdom and discernment as you manage your finances. Ask God to help you make wise decisions about your resources.

- **Trust in God's Provision:** While financial planning is essential, remember that God cares for your needs. Cultivate a trusting heart and believe that He will provide for you.

- **Live with Gratitude:** Be thankful for the resources you have, big or small. Gratitude can shift your focus away from material possessions and instill a sense of contentment.

Day 253: Ezekiel 19-20, Isaiah 52, Mark 6:30-56

Ezekiel 19-20

Reflection: Ezekiel laments for Israel's princes and recounts Israel's rebellion and God's mercy. Reflect on the themes of lament, rebellion, and divine mercy. How can you recognize areas of rebellion in your life and seek God's mercy and guidance for restoration?

Isaiah 52

Reflection: Isaiah calls Jerusalem to awake and speaks of the Lord's salvation and the coming servant. Reflect on the themes of awakening, redemption, and the proclamation of salvation. How can you awaken to God's call in your life and share the message of His salvation with others?

Mark 6:30-56

Reflection: Jesus feeds the five thousand, walks on water, and heals the sick in Gennesaret. Reflect on Jesus' provision, power, and compassion. How can you trust in Jesus' provision in your life and extend His compassion to those around you?

Day 254: Ezekiel 21-22, Isaiah 53, Mark 7:1-23

Ezekiel 21-22

Reflection: Ezekiel prophesies against Jerusalem and its sins, declaring God's judgment. Reflect on the themes of judgment and the call to repentance. How can you heed God's warnings and seek to live a life that honors Him, avoiding the pitfalls of sin and disobedience?

Isaiah 53

Reflection: Isaiah describes the suffering servant who bears the sins of many. Reflect on the suffering and sacrifice of the servant. How can you appreciate the depth of Jesus' sacrifice for your sins and live a life of gratitude and devotion to Him?

Mark 7:1-23

Reflection: Jesus teaches about inner purity, challenging the Pharisees' traditions. Reflect on the importance of inner purity and the dangers of external religiosity. How can you focus on cultivating a pure heart and avoid the trap of merely outward religious practices?

Day 255: Ezekiel 23-24, Isaiah 54, Mark 7:24-37

Ezekiel 23-24

Reflection: Ezekiel recounts the unfaithfulness of Oholah and Oholibah and the parable of the cooking pot, symbolizing Jerusalem's judgment. Reflect on the themes of unfaithfulness and judgment. How can you remain faithful to God and avoid the behaviors that lead to judgment?

Isaiah 54

Reflection: Isaiah speaks of the future glory of Zion, emphasizing God's everlasting covenant of peace. Reflect on the promises of restoration and peace. How can you find hope in God's promises and work towards experiencing His peace in your life?

Mark 7:24-37

Reflection: Jesus heals the Syrophoenician woman's daughter and a deaf man, showing His power and compassion. Reflect on the inclusivity and compassion of Jesus' ministry. How can you embrace and share Jesus' compassion, reaching out to those who are marginalized or in need?

Day 256: Ezekiel 25-26, Isaiah 55, Mark 8:1-26

Ezekiel 25-26

Reflection: Ezekiel prophesies against the nations surrounding Israel, declaring God's judgment. Reflect on the themes of justice and accountability. How can you understand and accept God's justice while striving to live a life that aligns with His righteous standards?

Isaiah 55

Reflection: Isaiah invites all to seek the Lord and promises an everlasting covenant. Reflect on the themes of invitation, seeking God, and the assurance of His promises. How can you actively seek God in your daily life and hold on to His promises for your future?

Mark 8:1-26

Reflection: Jesus feeds the four thousand, warns against the yeast of the Pharisees, and heals a blind man. Reflect on Jesus' provision, warnings, and healing power. How can you heed Jesus' warnings and trust in His provision and healing in your life?

Day 257: Ezekiel 27-28, Isaiah 56, Mark 8:27-38

Ezekiel 27-28

Reflection: Ezekiel laments over Tyre and prophesies against the pride of its king. Reflect on the dangers of pride and the consequences of trusting in wealth and power. How can you cultivate humility and place your trust in God rather than in worldly success?

Isaiah 56

Reflection: Isaiah speaks of salvation for foreigners and eunuchs, emphasizing inclusion in God's house. Reflect on the inclusivity of God's kingdom and His desire for righteousness and justice. How can you promote inclusivity and live out the principles of righteousness and justice?

Mark 8:27-38

Reflection: Peter confesses Jesus as the Christ, and Jesus teaches about His suffering and the cost of discipleship. Reflect on the cost of following Jesus and the importance of understanding His mission. How can you embrace the challenges of discipleship and commit to following Jesus wholeheartedly?

Day 258: Ezekiel 29-30, Isaiah 57, Mark 9:1-32

Ezekiel 29-30

Reflection: Ezekiel prophesies against Egypt, declaring its downfall and the restoration of Israel. Reflect on the themes of judgment and restoration. How can you learn from the warnings of judgment and seek God's restoration in areas of your life that need healing?

Isaiah 57

Reflection: Isaiah speaks of the righteous finding peace and the wicked facing judgment. Reflect on the contrast between the fate of the righteous and the wicked. How can you pursue righteousness and find peace in your relationship with God?

Mark 9:1-32

Reflection: Jesus is transfigured, heals a boy with an impure spirit, and predicts His death. Reflect on the glory of Jesus, His power to heal, and His path to the cross. How can you hold on to the vision of Jesus' glory and power while accepting the call to follow Him in His suffering?

Ezekiel 31-32

Reflection: Ezekiel describes the fall of Assyria and Egypt, emphasizing the consequences of pride. Reflect on the downfall of these powerful nations and the lesson on pride. How can you guard against pride in your life and remain humble before God?

Isaiah 58

Reflection: Isaiah calls out false fasting and describes true fasting that pleases God, emphasizing justice and compassion. Reflect on the difference between religious rituals and genuine devotion. How can you practice true fasting that reflects justice, compassion, and a heart devoted to God?

Mark 9:33-50

Reflection: Jesus teaches about greatness in the kingdom of God, stumbling blocks, and the seriousness of sin. Reflect on Jesus' teachings about humility, the impact of our actions, and the need to avoid sin. How can you cultivate humility, be mindful of your influence on others, and take sin seriously in your life?

WEEK 38: A Voice Heard: Hannah's Story of Persistent Prayer (Finding Strength in Faith)

Welcome back, Sisters! This week, we delve into the inspiring story of Hannah, a woman from the Old Testament whose unwavering faith and persistent prayer became a beacon of hope. Through her journey, we learn the power of prayer, the importance of trusting God's plan, and the strength found in faith.

A Barren Womb, a Yearning Heart:

The Book of 1 Samuel introduces us to Hannah, one of the wives of Elkanah. While Elkanah had another wife, Peninnah, who had children, Hannah remained childless. In those times, a childless woman faced societal pressure and a sense of incompleteness. The longing for a child filled Hannah's heart with deep sadness.

A Vow of Faith:

Year after year, Hannah endured the taunts of Peninnah and the weight of societal expectations. However, she never lost faith in God. During a pilgrimage to the temple, Hannah poured out her heart in prayer. She made a vow to God – if He blessed her with a son, she would dedicate him to serving God at the temple (1 Samuel 1:9-11).

Strength in the Face of Doubt:

Eli, the priest, initially mistook Hannah's silent, tearful prayer for drunkenness. But Hannah explained her situation and her unwavering faith. Eli blessed her, assuring her that God would hear her prayer (1 Samuel 1:12-17).

Answered Prayers and a Grateful Heart:

The Lord remembered Hannah, and she conceived a son. She named him Samuel, meaning "heard by God" (1 Samuel 1:20). True to her vow, after Samuel was weaned, Hannah brought him to the temple to serve God under Eli's guidance (1 Samuel 1:24-28).

Lessons from Hannah's Story:

Hannah's story offers valuable lessons for our own lives:

- **The Power of Persistent Prayer:** Even when faced with unanswered prayers or difficult circumstances, persistent prayer can be a source of strength and hope.

Hannah's story reminds us that God hears our prayers and answers them in his perfect timing.

- **Finding Strength in Faith:** Faith is what sustains us during challenging times. Hannah's unwavering faith in God's plan allowed her to endure hardship and find peace.

- **Letting Go and Trusting God:** Sometimes, our deepest desires don't unfold according to our expectations. Letting go and trusting God's plan, as Hannah did, can lead to unexpected blessings.

Activity: A Prayer Jar of Hope

This week, engage in an activity that reinforces the importance of prayer and trusting God's plan:

1. **Decorating the Jar:** Find a clear jar and decorate it using paint, markers, or construction paper. Consider decorating it with symbols of hope and prayer, like doves or rainbows.

2. **Writing Prayer Notes:** Throughout the week, write down your prayers, worries, and hopes on small pieces of paper. These could be personal prayers or prayers for others.

3. **Filling the Jar:** During meals or prayer time, share a prayer note from the jar and offer a short prayer.

4. **Releasing Your Worries:** The act of writing down prayers and placing them in the jar can be a symbolic way of releasing worries and trusting them to God.

Remember:

Hannah's story is a testament to the power of faith and prayer. Even when faced with seemingly insurmountable challenges, holding onto faith and trusting in God's plan can lead to answered prayers and unexpected blessings.

Bonus Activity:

Reflect on the challenges Hannah faced and how her faith in God helped her overcome them. Encourage members to share their own experiences of prayer and times when they felt God answered their prayers.

Remember, prayer is a powerful tool that connects us to God. By following Hannah's example of persistent prayer and unwavering faith, we can find strength, hope, and guidance on our own faith journeys.

BIBLE READING: Week 38

Day 260: Ezekiel 33-34, Isaiah 59, Mark 10:1-31

Ezekiel 33-34

Reflection: Ezekiel speaks of his role as a watchman and God's judgment on Israel's shepherds, promising a future shepherd, David. Reflect on the responsibilities of spiritual leaders and God's promise of a true shepherd. How can you respond to God's call to be vigilant and compassionate in your own sphere of influence?

Isaiah 59

Reflection: Isaiah highlights the separation caused by sin and God's promise to redeem. Reflect on the themes of sin, repentance, and redemption. How does recognizing your own sins draw you closer to God and inspire you to seek His redemption?

Mark 10:1-31

Reflection: Jesus teaches about marriage and divorce, blesses the children, and challenges the rich young man. Reflect on the themes of commitment, humility, and the cost of discipleship. How can you deepen your commitment to God's principles and embrace the sacrifices of following Jesus?

Day 261: Ezekiel 35-36, Isaiah 60, Mark 10:32-52

Ezekiel 35-36

Reflection: Ezekiel prophesies against Mount Seir and speaks of Israel's restoration and renewal. Reflect on the themes of judgment, renewal, and the new heart promised by God. How can you allow God to renew your heart and transform your life through His Spirit?

Isaiah 60

Reflection: Isaiah describes the future glory of Zion, emphasizing light, abundance, and God's eternal blessing. Reflect on the themes of hope, restoration, and divine glory. How does this vision of future glory inspire you to live with hope and trust in God's promises?

Mark 10:32-52

Reflection: Jesus predicts His death, teaches about servant leadership, and heals Bartimaeus. Reflect on Jesus' example of servanthood and His power to heal. How can you follow Jesus' example of serving others selflessly and seek His healing in areas of need?

Day 262: Ezekiel 37-39, Isaiah 61, Mark 11:1-14

Ezekiel 37-39

Reflection: Ezekiel's vision of the dry bones and the prophecy against Gog. Reflect on the themes of resurrection, hope, and God's victory over enemies. How can you find hope in God's power to bring life out of death and trust in His ultimate victory?

Isaiah 61

Reflection: Isaiah speaks of the Anointed One who brings good news, comfort, and freedom. Reflect on the mission of the Anointed One and the transformative impact of His work. How can you embrace and share the good news, bringing comfort and freedom to those around you?

Mark 11:1-14

Reflection: Jesus' triumphal entry into Jerusalem and the cursing of the fig tree. Reflect on the themes of expectation, fulfillment, and the fruitfulness expected by Jesus. How can you prepare your heart to receive Jesus and ensure your life bears fruit that honors Him?

Day 263: Ezekiel 40-42, Isaiah 62, Mark 11:15-33

Ezekiel 40-42

Reflection: Ezekiel's detailed vision of the new temple. Reflect on the significance of the temple as God's dwelling place and the promise of restoration. How can you honor God's presence in your life and contribute to His work of restoration and renewal?

Isaiah 62

Reflection: Isaiah speaks of Zion's new name and the Lord's delight in His people. Reflect on the themes of identity, delight, and God's faithfulness. How can you embrace your identity in God and live in a way that reflects His delight and faithfulness?

Mark 11:15-33

Reflection: Jesus cleanses the temple and teaches about faith and authority. Reflect on the importance of purity in worship and the power of faith. How can you cultivate a pure heart for worship and strengthen your faith in God's power and authority?

Day 264: Ezekiel 43-44, Isaiah 63, Mark 12:1-27

Ezekiel 43-44

Reflection: Ezekiel describes the glory of the Lord returning to the temple and the regulations for priests. Reflect on the themes of God's glory, holiness, and the role of the priesthood. How can you honor God's holiness in your life and embrace your calling to serve Him faithfully?

Isaiah 63

Reflection: Isaiah recounts God's vengeance and redemption, emphasizing His steadfast love. Reflect on the dual themes of judgment and mercy. How can you live with an awareness of God's justice and a grateful heart for His mercy and redemption?

Mark 12:1-27

Reflection: Jesus teaches the parable of the tenants, answers questions about paying taxes, and speaks on the resurrection. Reflect on Jesus' wisdom and authority. How can you submit to Jesus' authority in your life and live out His teachings with integrity?

Day 265: Ezekiel 45-46, Isaiah 64, Mark 12:28-44

Ezekiel 45-46

Reflection: Ezekiel outlines the division of the land and the regulations for worship. Reflect on the themes of order, worship, and community. How can you contribute to a community that honors God's order and worships Him with sincerity and devotion?

Isaiah 64

Reflection: Isaiah prays for God's intervention and acknowledges human sinfulness. Reflect on the themes of prayer, repentance, and God's intervention. How can you cultivate a heart of repentance and seek God's intervention in your life and community?

Mark 12:28-44

Reflection: Jesus teaches the greatest commandments and commends the widow's offering. Reflect on the themes of love, devotion, and sacrificial giving. How can you prioritize love for God and others, and practice sacrificial giving in your daily life?

Day 266: Ezekiel 47-48, Isaiah 65, Mark 13:1-23

Ezekiel 47-48

Reflection: Ezekiel's vision of the river from the temple and the division of the land. Reflect on the themes of life, healing, and inheritance. How can you experience and share the life-giving and healing presence of God, and embrace your inheritance in His kingdom?

Isaiah 65

Reflection: Isaiah speaks of the new heavens and new earth, and God's promise of joy and blessing. Reflect on the themes of renewal, joy, and God's faithfulness. How can you live with hope and anticipation of God's promise of a new creation and His eternal blessings?

Mark 13:1-23

Reflection: Jesus speaks of the signs of the end times and warns of coming tribulations. Reflect on the themes of vigilance, faithfulness, and readiness. How can you remain vigilant and faithful in your walk with God, prepared for His return and the fulfillment of His promises?

WEEK 39: Women and Technology: Using Technology for Faith and Connection

Welcome back, Faithful and Fierce women! As we continue this enriching exploration of faith, we delve into the ever-present influence of technology in our lives. This week, we explore the role technology can play in a Catholic woman's life, focusing on its potential to enhance your faith journey and connection with your community.

A Journey of Connection:

Technology has become an undeniable force in our world, impacting how we connect, learn, and even practice our faith. For Catholic women, technology offers a unique opportunity to:

- **Deepen Your Faith:** Numerous Catholic apps, websites, and online resources offer access to daily prayers, scripture readings, and inspirational content to strengthen your faith.

- **Connect with Your Community:** Online platforms like Catholic forums, social media groups, and virtual bible studies allow you to connect with fellow Catholic women, share experiences, and offer support to one another.

- **Spread the Faith:** Social media and other online platforms can be powerful tools for sharing your faith journey and inspiring others. You can create faith-based content, participate in online discussions, and invite others to explore the Catholic faith.

Beyond the Convenience: Balancing Technology with Faith

While technology offers numerous benefits, it's important to be mindful of its potential drawbacks:

- **Distraction and Information Overload:** The constant barrage of notifications and online stimuli can be distracting and make it difficult to focus on prayer, reflection, or attending mass.

- **Isolation and Loneliness:** Overreliance on online interactions can lead to a sense of isolation and disconnect from the real world, including your local faith community.

- **Misinformation and Unreliable Sources:** The internet is saturated with information, not all of it accurate. Be discerning about the online resources you use for religious knowledge and inspiration.

Discussion Starter: Navigating the Digital Landscape

Technology presents a double-edged sword. Let's explore it together:

- Share some ways you've used technology to enhance your faith journey.

- How can we strike a healthy balance between utilizing technology for our faith and maintaining a strong connection with our local Catholic community?

- Have you encountered any challenges related to technology use and your faith? If so, how did you address them?

Remember, dear sisters, finding a balance is key. Technology can be a powerful tool for strengthening your faith, but it should never replace your personal connection with God, prayer, and participation in your local church community.

Beyond This Book:

As we wrap up this week's empowering journey, remember that technology is a tool, and like any tool, it's up to you to use it wisely for your spiritual growth:

- **Be Mindful of Your Time:** Set boundaries for technology use. Create sacred spaces for prayer and reflection free from distractions.

- **Seek Quality Content:** Seek out reliable and trustworthy Catholic resources online that align with your beliefs.

- **Stay Connected:** Use technology to enhance your connection with your local church community, but prioritize attending mass, participating in church activities, and fostering real-life relationships with your fellow parishioners.

BIBLE READING: Week 39

Day 267: 1 Peter 1-2, Isaiah 66, Mark 13:24-37

1 Peter 1-2

Reflection: Peter encourages believers to live holy lives and describes them as a chosen people. Reflect on the themes of holiness, identity, and spiritual growth. How can you pursue holiness in your daily life and embrace your identity as God's chosen people?

Isaiah 66

Reflection: Isaiah concludes with a vision of God's judgment and the new creation. Reflect on the themes of judgment, hope, and God's sovereignty. How does this vision of the future inspire you to live faithfully and anticipate God's ultimate restoration?

Mark 13:24-37

Reflection: Jesus speaks about His return and urges watchfulness. Reflect on the themes of vigilance, preparedness, and faithfulness. How can you stay spiritually alert and live in a way that reflects readiness for Christ's return?

Day 268: 1 Peter 3-5, Daniel 1, Mark 14:1-21

1 Peter 3-5

Reflection: Peter gives instructions for Christian living, suffering, and leadership. Reflect on the themes of suffering, humility, and leadership. How can you apply Peter's teachings to endure suffering faithfully and lead with humility?

Daniel 1

Reflection: Daniel and his friends remain faithful to God in Babylon. Reflect on the themes of faithfulness, integrity, and God's favor. How can you remain faithful to God's principles even in challenging circumstances?

Mark 14:1-21

Reflection: The plot to arrest Jesus and the Last Supper. Reflect on the themes of betrayal, sacrifice, and communion. How does understanding Jesus' sacrifice deepen your appreciation for the Lord's Supper and commitment to Him?

Day 269: Haggai, Zechariah 1-2, Daniel 2, Mark 14:22-52

Haggai

Reflection: Haggai encourages the rebuilding of the temple and promises God's presence and blessing. Reflect on the themes of priorities, obedience, and God's presence. How can you prioritize God's work in your life and trust in His promises?

Zechariah 1-2

Reflection: Zechariah's visions of encouragement and the promise of God's protection. Reflect on the themes of divine protection, restoration, and hope. How do these visions encourage you to trust in God's protection and His plans for restoration?

Daniel 2

Reflection: Daniel interprets Nebuchadnezzar's dream about the kingdoms. Reflect on the themes of God's sovereignty and wisdom. How does Daniel's confidence in God's wisdom inspire you to seek and trust God's guidance in your life?

Mark 14:22-52

Reflection: The institution of the Lord's Supper and Jesus' arrest. Reflect on the themes of covenant, sacrifice, and faithfulness. How can you honor Jesus' sacrifice through your commitment to Him and faithfulness in times of trial?

Day 270: Zechariah 3-6, Daniel 3:1-45, Mark 14:53-72

Zechariah 3-6

Reflection: Zechariah's visions of Joshua the high priest, the golden lampstand, and flying scroll. Reflect on the themes of cleansing, empowerment, and justice. How can you seek God's cleansing, rely on His Spirit, and uphold His standards of justice?

Daniel 3:1-45

Reflection: The story of Shadrach, Meshach, and Abednego in the fiery furnace. Reflect on the themes of faith, deliverance, and God's power. How does their unwavering faith in God's power encourage you to stand firm in your beliefs?

Mark 14:53-72

Reflection: Jesus' trial before the Sanhedrin and Peter's denial. Reflect on the themes of courage, weakness, and redemption. How can you find strength in Jesus' example and seek His forgiveness and restoration in moments of weakness?

Day 271: Zechariah 7-9, Daniel 3:46-100, Mark 15:1-15

Zechariah 7-9

Reflection: Zechariah calls for true justice and prophesies the coming King. Reflect on the themes of justice, repentance, and messianic hope. How can you practice true justice and live with the hope of Christ's return?

Daniel 3:46-100

Reflection: Continuation of the deliverance of Shadrach, Meshach, and Abednego. Reflect on the themes of faithfulness and God's miraculous intervention. How does their story inspire you to trust in God's ability to deliver you from trials?

Mark 15:1-15

Reflection: Jesus before Pilate and the crowd choosing Barabbas. Reflect on the themes of injustice, sacrifice, and public opinion. How can you stand up for truth and righteousness, even when it is unpopular or comes with a cost?

Day 272: Zechariah 10-11, Daniel 4, Mark 15:16-47

Zechariah 10-11

Reflection: Zechariah speaks of God's care for His flock and the rejection of the shepherd. Reflect on the themes of God's care, leadership, and rejection. How can you respond to God's care and leadership, and how do you handle rejection in light of God's sovereignty?

Daniel 4

Reflection: Nebuchadnezzar's dream of the tree and his subsequent humbling. Reflect on the themes of pride, humility, and God's sovereignty. How can you cultivate humility in your life and recognize God's sovereignty over your circumstances?

Mark 15:16-47

Reflection: Jesus' crucifixion and burial. Reflect on the themes of suffering, sacrifice, and redemption. How does the reality of Jesus' sacrifice affect your understanding of redemption and your commitment to live for Him?

Day 273: Zechariah 12-14, Daniel 5, Mark 16

Zechariah 12-14

Reflection: Zechariah's prophecies of Jerusalem's deliverance and the coming day of the Lord. Reflect on the themes of deliverance, repentance, and future hope. How do these prophecies shape your understanding of God's plans for the future and your role in His story?

Daniel 5

Reflection: The writing on the wall and the fall of Babylon. Reflect on the themes of judgment, divine intervention, and humility. How does the story of Belshazzar's downfall remind you of the importance of humility and recognizing God's authority?

Mark 16

Reflection: The resurrection of Jesus. Reflect on the themes of victory, new life, and mission. How does the resurrection of Jesus empower you to live a life of victory and engage in the mission of spreading the good news?

WEEK 40: Leaving a Godly Legacy: Mentoring Younger Women

Welcome back, Faithful and Fierce women! As we continue this transformative journey of faith exploration, we turn our hearts towards a beautiful concept – leaving a godly legacy. This week, we delve into the importance of mentoring younger women, fostering their faith, and empowering them to live fulfilling Christian lives. By sharing your wisdom and experiences, you can become a beacon of guidance and inspiration for the next generation.

A Journey of Generational Impact:

As Christian women, we have a responsibility to nurture the faith of future generations. Here's why mentoring younger women is crucial:

- **Passing the Torch of Faith:** Mentorship allows you to share your knowledge of the Bible, Christian traditions, and personal faith journey with younger women. This knowledge becomes the foundation for their own spiritual growth.

- **Empowering the Next Generation:** Mentorship provides younger women with a role model, someone they can look up to for guidance and support as they navigate their faith journey.

- **Building a Strong Christian Community:** By mentoring younger women, you contribute to a vibrant and thriving Christian community where each generation uplifts and empowers the next.

Beyond Inspiration: The Art of Mentorship

Mentoring is more than simply offering advice. Here are ways to become an effective mentor:

- **Create a Safe Space:** Foster a trusting and open environment where younger women feel comfortable asking questions, expressing doubts, and sharing their experiences.

- **Active Listening:** Be a patient and attentive listener. Pay attention to the younger woman's needs, concerns, and aspirations related to faith.

- **Offer Guidance and Support:** Draw upon your own experiences to offer guidance, encouragement, and support on topics like prayer, scripture study, navigating life challenges with faith, and finding a place in the church community.

- **Lead by Example:** Live your faith authentically. Let your actions and values reflect your Christian beliefs and inspire the younger woman on her own journey.

Action Step: Lighting the Way for Others

This week, I challenge you to take a concrete step towards leaving a godly legacy:

- **Become a Mentor:** Reach out to your church leadership or a local Christian organization to inquire about formal mentoring opportunities for young women.

- **Share Your Faith Journey:** Is there a younger female family member or friend who might benefit from hearing your story of faith? Schedule a time to connect and share your experiences openly.

- **Offer a Listening Ear:** Be present for younger women in your life who might be struggling with their faith. Listen without judgment and offer your support.

Dear sisters, leaving a godly legacy isn't about grand gestures; it's about making a positive impact on a younger woman's faith journey. Your willingness to share your wisdom and experiences can have a profound ripple effect for generations to come.

Beyond This Book:

Remember that mentoring is a continuous act of love and service:

- **Continue Learning:** Always strive to learn more about your faith. This ongoing exploration fuels your ability to guide younger women effectively.

- **Be a Positive Role Model:** Let your Christian values shine through in every aspect of your life. Inspire others through your actions and words.

- **Celebrate Each Other:** Mentorship is a two-way street. Learn from the younger woman you mentor and celebrate her growth and achievements in faith.

BIBLE READING: Week 40

Day 274: Esther A-2, Daniel 6, Luke 1:1-38

Esther A-2

Reflection: The story of Esther begins with her rise to queen and Mordecai uncovering a plot. Reflect on the themes of divine providence, courage, and destiny. How can you see God's hand at work in your life, guiding you to fulfill your unique purpose?

Daniel 6

Reflection: Daniel in the lion's den. Reflect on the themes of faithfulness, divine protection, and courage. How does Daniel's unwavering faith in the face of danger inspire you to trust in God's protection and remain steadfast in your faith?

Luke 1:1-38

Reflection: The announcements of John the Baptist's and Jesus' births. Reflect on the themes of divine intervention, miraculous birth, and faith. How do the responses of Zechariah and Mary challenge you to trust in God's promises and His power to accomplish the impossible?

Day 275: Esther 3, Daniel 7, Luke 1:39-80

Esther 3

Reflection: Haman's plot against the Jews and Mordecai's response. Reflect on the themes of evil plots, courage, and advocacy. How can you stand up against injustice and advocate for others, trusting in God's ultimate justice?

Daniel 7

Reflection: Daniel's vision of the four beasts and the Ancient of Days. Reflect on the themes of divine sovereignty, judgment, and eternal kingdom. How does this vision encourage you to trust in God's control over history and His ultimate victory over evil?

Luke 1:39-80

Reflection: Mary's visit to Elizabeth and Zechariah's prophecy. Reflect on the themes of joy, prophecy, and fulfillment. How do the expressions of joy and prophetic declarations in this passage inspire you to celebrate God's work and proclaim His promises?

Day 276: Esther 5, Daniel 8, Luke 2:1-21

Esther 5

Reflection: Esther's bravery in approaching the king and the unfolding plan to save her people. Reflect on the themes of courage, advocacy, and divine timing. How does Esther's courage inspire you to take bold steps of faith and advocate for others?

Daniel 8

Reflection: Daniel's vision of the ram and the goat. Reflect on the themes of prophetic vision, conflict, and divine interpretation. How does understanding God's foreknowledge of future events encourage you to trust in His plans and seek His wisdom?

Luke 2:1-21

Reflection: The birth of Jesus and the visit of the shepherds. Reflect on the themes of incarnation, divine revelation, and worship. How does the humble birth of Jesus and the response of the shepherds challenge you to recognize and celebrate God's presence in unexpected places?

Day 277: Esther 6, Daniel 9, Luke 2:22-52

Esther 6

Reflection: The honor given to Mordecai and Haman's downfall. Reflect on the themes of justice, reversal of fortune, and divine intervention. How does this story encourage you to trust in God's justice and His ability to turn situations around for His glory?

Daniel 9

Reflection: Daniel's prayer and the prophecy of the seventy weeks. Reflect on the themes of repentance, divine mercy, and prophetic fulfillment. How can you incorporate heartfelt prayer and repentance into your life, trusting in God's mercy and faithfulness to His promises?

Luke 2:22-52

Reflection: Jesus' presentation at the temple and His visit at age twelve. Reflect on the themes of dedication, revelation, and spiritual growth. How does Jesus' early life inspire you to dedicate yourself to God's service and seek growth in wisdom and understanding?

Day 278: Esther 8, Daniel 10, Luke 3:1-22

Esther 8

Reflection: The Jews' deliverance and the institution of Purim. Reflect on the themes of deliverance, celebration, and remembrance. How can you celebrate and remember God's deliverance in your life, and how does this story inspire you to trust in His faithfulness?

Daniel 10

Reflection: Daniel's vision of a man and the spiritual battle revealed. Reflect on the themes of spiritual warfare, divine strength, and perseverance. How does this vision encourage you to be aware of the spiritual battles around you and rely on God's strength?

Luke 3:1-22

Reflection: John the Baptist's ministry and Jesus' baptism. Reflect on the themes of repentance, preparation, and divine approval. How can you prepare your heart for Jesus' coming and live a life that reflects true repentance and dedication to God?

Day 279: Ezra 1-2, Daniel 11, Luke 3:23-38

Ezra 1-2

Reflection: The return of the exiles and the rebuilding of the temple. Reflect on the themes of restoration, worship, and community. How can you participate in God's work of restoration in your community and contribute to rebuilding what has been broken?

Daniel 11

Reflection: The detailed prophecy of future kings and conflicts. Reflect on the themes of prophecy, conflict, and divine sovereignty. How does understanding God's control over future events strengthen your faith and commitment to His plans?

Luke 3:23-38

Reflection: The genealogy of Jesus. Reflect on the themes of heritage, divine plan, and fulfillment. How does tracing Jesus' lineage back to Adam reinforce your understanding of God's overarching plan for humanity and your place within it?

Day 280: Ezra 3:1-4:23, Daniel 12, Luke 4:1-13

Ezra 3:1-4:23

Reflection: The rebuilding of the altar and temple, and the opposition faced. Reflect on the themes of worship, perseverance, and opposition. How can you remain steadfast in your efforts to honor God and build His kingdom, despite opposition?

Daniel 12

Reflection: The prophecy of the end times and the promise of resurrection. Reflect on the themes of hope, resurrection, and eternal life. How does the promise of resurrection and eternal life give you hope and motivate you to live faithfully for God?

Luke 4:1-13

Reflection: Jesus' temptation in the wilderness. Reflect on the themes of temptation, scripture, and victory. How can you use God's Word to overcome temptations and follow Jesus' example of resisting the devil's schemes?

Part 3: Deepening Your Faith

(Weeks 41-52)

Theme: A Lifelong Journey with God

WEEK 41: Lectio Divina: A Deeper Dive into Scripture

Welcome back, Faithful and Fierce women! As we continue our exploration of faith beyond the Book, this week, we delve deeper into a powerful practice – Lectio Divina, a form of prayerful Bible reading. Lectio Divina goes beyond mere intellectual understanding; it's a transformative journey into the heart of God's Word, fostering intimacy and personal transformation.

A Journey of Encounter:

Lectio Divina, meaning "divine reading" in Latin, is an ancient Christian practice with profound benefits:

- **Encountering God:** Through Lectio Divina, you actively engage with scripture, allowing God's word to speak directly to your heart. It becomes a conversation, not a monologue.

- **Deeper Understanding:** Lectio Divina fosters a deeper understanding of scripture beyond the literal meaning. It invites reflection and contemplation, revealing deeper truths and hidden meanings.

- **Personal Transformation:** As you engage with scripture in this way, God's word can transform your thoughts, feelings, and actions. It becomes a catalyst for personal growth and a closer relationship with God.

Lectio Divina: A Four-Step Journey

Lectio Divina is a four-stage process that allows you to savor the richness of scripture:

1. **Lectio (Reading):** Begin by slowly and attentively reading a chosen passage. Focus on each word and phrase, allowing the words to sink in.

2. **Meditatio (Meditation):** Reflect on what you've read. What words or phrases stand out to you? What emotions do they evoke? Journaling can be a helpful tool for meditation.

3. **Oratio (Prayer):** Respond to God's message in prayer. Thank Him for the insights you received, express your struggles and concerns, and offer yourself to Him in service.

4. **Contemplatio (Contemplation):** Rest in God's presence. Allow the scripture to settle within you, transforming your heart and mind. This may involve silence, reflection, or even imagery.

Action Step: Embarking on a Sacred Journey

This week, I challenge you to embark on a personal Lectio Divina experience:

- **Choose a Scripture Passage:** Select a scripture passage that resonates with you at this moment in your life. Perhaps a specific verse has been on your mind lately, or maybe you're drawn to a particular book of the Bible.

- **Create a Sacred Space:** Find a quiet place where you can be free from distractions. Light a candle, play calming music, or simply create an environment conducive to prayer and reflection.

- **Practice Lectio Divina:** Follow the four stages outlined above – reading, meditation, prayer, and contemplation. Allow yourself ample time for each stage, letting the Holy Spirit guide your journey.

- **Journaling:** After completing Lectio Divina, take some time to journal about your experience. What insights did you gain? How did the scripture passage touch your heart?

Remember, dear sisters, Lectio Divina is a practice, not a performance. There's no right or wrong way to do it. Approach it with an open heart and allow God to speak to you through His Word.

Beyond This Week:

As you integrate Lectio Divina into your faith journey, remember:

- **Consistency is Key:** While a daily practice is ideal, even a few minutes dedicated to Lectio Divina each week can have a profound impact.

- **Seek Guidance:** If you're new to Lectio Divina, consider joining a Lectio Divina group or seeking guidance from a spiritual leader. They can offer support and insights on your journey.

- **Open Yourself to Transformation:** Lectio Divina can be a transformative practice. Be open to the ways God's Word is shaping your thoughts, actions, and relationship with Him.

Day 281: Ezra 4:24-6:22, Daniel 13, Luke 4:14-44

Ezra 4:24-6:22

Reflection: The continuation of the temple rebuilding and the decree of Darius. Reflect on the themes of perseverance, divine intervention, and celebration. How does this passage encourage you to persist in God's work despite opposition and to celebrate His faithfulness?

Daniel 13

Reflection: The story of Susanna and Daniel's intervention. Reflect on the themes of justice, integrity, and divine wisdom. How does Susanna's faith and Daniel's wisdom inspire you to stand firm in righteousness and trust in God's deliverance?

Luke 4:14-44

Reflection: Jesus' ministry in Galilee, including His teaching, healings, and exorcisms. Reflect on the themes of authority, compassion, and the fulfillment of prophecy. How does Jesus' authoritative ministry challenge you to recognize His power and respond to His call?

Day 282: Ezra 7-8, Daniel 14, Luke 5:1-26

Ezra 7-8

Reflection: Ezra's return to Jerusalem and the gathering of exiles. Reflect on the themes of leadership, provision, and God's guidance. How does Ezra's example inspire you to seek God's guidance in your journey and to lead others with integrity and faithfulness?

Daniel 14

Reflection: The stories of Bel and the dragon. Reflect on the themes of idolatry, divine power, and faithfulness. How do these stories challenge you to confront false beliefs and trust in God's supreme power?

Luke 5:1-26

Reflection: Jesus calls His first disciples and heals a paralytic. Reflect on the themes of calling, faith, and forgiveness. How can you respond to Jesus' call in your life and bring others to Him for healing and forgiveness?

Day 283: Ezra 9-10, Wisdom 1, Luke 5:27-39

Ezra 9-10

Reflection: Ezra's prayer and the people's repentance for intermarriage. Reflect on the themes of confession, repentance, and purity. How does Ezra's heartfelt prayer and the community's response encourage you to seek purity and repent from anything that separates you from God?

Wisdom 1

Reflection: The love of righteousness and the avoidance of wickedness. Reflect on the themes of wisdom, righteousness, and divine protection. How does this passage motivate you to pursue wisdom and righteousness, trusting in God's protection?

Luke 5:27-39

Reflection: The calling of Levi and the parables of the new patch and wineskins. Reflect on the themes of transformation, inclusion, and renewal. How does Jesus' call to Levi and His teaching about new life challenge you to embrace change and renewal in your spiritual walk?

Day 284: Nehemiah 1-3, Wisdom 2, Luke 6:1-26

Nehemiah 1-3

Reflection: Nehemiah's prayer, inspection of Jerusalem's walls, and the rebuilding effort. Reflect on the themes of leadership, prayer, and community effort. How does Nehemiah's dedication to prayer and action inspire you to lead and work together with others in God's mission?

Wisdom 2

Reflection: The wicked plot against the righteous. Reflect on the themes of persecution, divine justice, and hope. How does this passage encourage you to remain steadfast in righteousness despite opposition, trusting in God's ultimate justice?

Luke 6:1-26

Reflection: Jesus' teachings on the Sabbath and the Beatitudes. Reflect on the themes of mercy, blessing, and true discipleship. How do Jesus' radical teachings challenge your understanding of blessing and call you to a deeper commitment to living out His values?

Day 285: Nehemiah 4-5, Wisdom 3, Luke 6:27-49

Nehemiah 4-5

Reflection: The opposition to rebuilding and Nehemiah's reforms. Reflect on the themes of perseverance, justice, and leadership. How can Nehemiah's example of addressing opposition and implementing reforms inspire you to pursue justice and lead with integrity?

Wisdom 3

Reflection: The destiny of the righteous and the hope of immortality. Reflect on the themes of eternal life, hope, and God's faithfulness. How does this passage give you hope for the future and encourage you to live righteously in light of God's promises?

Luke 6:27-49

Reflection: Jesus' teachings on love for enemies, judgment, and building on a firm foundation. Reflect on the themes of love, forgiveness, and obedience. How can you apply Jesus' radical teachings on love and forgiveness in your daily life, building your life on His solid foundation?

Day 286: Nehemiah 6-7, Wisdom 4, Luke 7:1-28

Nehemiah 6-7

Reflection: The completion of the wall and the listing of exiles. Reflect on the themes of accomplishment, community, and dedication. How does the completion of Jerusalem's wall inspire you to persevere in your endeavors and celebrate communal achievements?

Wisdom 4

Reflection: The short life of the righteous and the futility of wickedness. Reflect on the themes of legacy, righteousness, and divine favor. How does this passage challenge you to consider the lasting impact of your life and to prioritize righteousness over worldly success?

Luke 7:1-28

Reflection: Jesus heals the centurion's servant and raises the widow's son, and John the Baptist's inquiry. Reflect on the themes of faith, compassion, and divine authority. How do these miracles and Jesus' response to John's disciples strengthen your faith in His power and compassion?

Day 287: Nehemiah 8-9, Wisdom 5, Luke 7:29-50

Nehemiah 8-9

Reflection: The reading of the Law and the confession of sins. Reflect on the themes of revival, confession, and covenant renewal. How does the public reading of Scripture and the people's confession inspire you to seek personal and communal revival in your faith?

Wisdom 5

Reflection: The triumph of the righteous and the judgment of the wicked. Reflect on the themes of vindication, divine judgment, and hope. How does this passage encourage you to remain faithful to God, trusting in His ultimate justice and the vindication of the righteous?

Luke 7:29-50

Reflection: Jesus' commendation of John the Baptist and the forgiveness of the sinful woman. Reflect on the themes of repentance, forgiveness, and love. How do the stories of John the Baptist and the sinful woman inspire you to seek God's forgiveness and respond with love and gratitude?

WEEK 42: Catholic Bible Resources: Expanding Your Knowledge

Welcome back, Faithful and Fierce women! As we reach the 42nd week of our enriching exploration of faith, let's celebrate the transformative power of scripture. The Bible is a living document, brimming with wisdom and guidance. This week, we delve into a treasure trove of Catholic Bible resources designed to deepen your understanding and ignite your passion for God's Word.

A Journey of Exploration:

The Bible is a vast and multifaceted book. These Catholic resources offer diverse ways to engage with scripture:

- **Catholic Bible Studies:** Numerous Catholic Bible study programs, available online or in physical books, provide structured learning with insightful commentary, discussion questions, and historical context.

- **Websites and Online Resources:** Websites like the United States Conference of Catholic Bishops (USCCB) website, Catholic News Agency (CNA), and Bible Gateway offer scripture readings, commentaries, and articles written from a Catholic perspective.

- **Catholic Podcasts and Audio Dramas:** Podcasts like "The Bible for Normal People" or "The Catholic Bible Project" offer engaging and informative discussions on scripture. Additionally, audio Bible dramas can bring scripture to life in a captivating way.

- **Books by Catholic Scholars:** Renowned Catholic scholars have written countless books offering in-depth analysis and commentary on various biblical texts. Popular choices include Dr. Scott Hahn, Ignatius of Loyola, and Brant Pitre.

Beyond the Text: A World of Resources

Choosing the right resources depends on your learning style and interests. Here's how to navigate the abundant options:

- **Consider Your Learning Style:** Do you prefer structured study programs, interactive online resources, or in-depth scholarly works?

- **Identify Your Interests:** Are you drawn to a specific book of the Bible, or are you looking for a broader overview of scripture?

- **Seek Recommendations:** Talk to your priest, spiritual director, or fellow parishioners about Catholic Bible resources they recommend.

Challenge: Embracing Ongoing Learning

This week, I challenge you to expand your knowledge of scripture with a new resource:

- **Explore a Catholic Bible Study Program:** Research online options or inquire at your local church about group Bible studies.

- **Delve into Websites and Podcasts:** Choose a website or podcast that caters to your interests and delve into its content. Consider subscribing for ongoing learning.

- **Read a Book by a Catholic Scholar:** Visit your local Catholic bookstore or online retailer and choose a book that aligns with your current scripture study goals.

Remember, dear sisters, the journey of exploring God's Word is a lifelong adventure. Be open to new resources, embrace diverse perspectives, and allow the richness of scripture to transform your life.

Beyond This Book:

As you conclude this faith-filled exploration, remember:

- **Create a Bible Study Routine:** Dedicate time daily or weekly to studying scripture. Consistency is key to reaping the benefits of God's Word.

- **Join a Faith-Sharing Community:** Consider joining a Bible study group or online forum to discuss scripture with other Catholic women. Sharing your insights and learning from others can deepen your understanding.

- **Let Scripture Guide Your Life:** Don't let scripture remain on the page. Reflect on how God's Word applies to your daily life, relationships, and challenges.

Day 288: Nehemiah 10-11, Wisdom 6, Luke 8:1-25

Nehemiah 10-11

Reflection: The covenant renewal and the settlement of Jerusalem. Reflect on the themes of commitment, community, and dedication to God's commandments. How does the community's dedication to uphold the covenant inspire you to renew your commitment to God's word and actively participate in your faith community?

Wisdom 6

Reflection: The call to seek wisdom and the responsibilities of rulers. Reflect on the themes of wisdom, leadership, and justice. How does this passage encourage you to seek wisdom in your decisions and to lead others with justice and integrity?

Luke 8:1-25

Reflection: The parables of the sower and the lamp, and the calming of the storm. Reflect on the themes of faith, receptiveness, and trust in Jesus. How can you ensure that your heart is like good soil, ready to receive God's word and bear fruit? How does Jesus calming the storm reassure you in times of fear and uncertainty?

Day 289: Nehemiah 12-13, Wisdom 7, Luke 8:26-56

Nehemiah 12-13

Reflection: The dedication of the wall and Nehemiah's reforms. Reflect on the themes of celebration, dedication, and purification. How does the dedication of Jerusalem's wall inspire you to celebrate God's work in your life? What steps can you take to purify and dedicate your life more fully to God?

Wisdom 7

Reflection: Solomon's pursuit of wisdom. Reflect on the themes of wisdom, understanding, and divine revelation. How does Solomon's quest for wisdom encourage you to value and seek wisdom in your own life? How can you apply this divine wisdom in your daily decisions?

Luke 8:26-56

Reflection: The healing of the demon-possessed man, the woman with the issue of blood, and the raising of Jairus's daughter. Reflect on the themes of faith, healing, and Jesus' power over life and death. How do these miracles strengthen your faith in Jesus' power to heal and restore? How can you reach out in faith for His touch in your life?

Day 290: Judith 1-3, Wisdom 8, Luke 9:1-27

Judith 1-3

Reflection: The threat against Israel and the initial responses. Reflect on the themes of threat, preparation, and God's protection. How do the people's reactions to the threat inspire you to prepare and trust in God during times of danger and uncertainty?

Wisdom 8

Reflection: The virtues of wisdom and her role in life. Reflect on the themes of wisdom, virtue, and guidance. How does the description of wisdom's virtues motivate you to seek and cherish wisdom in your own life? How can wisdom guide you in your daily actions and decisions?

Luke 9:1-27

Reflection: Jesus sends out the twelve, feeds the five thousand, and Peter's confession of Christ. Reflect on the themes of mission, provision, and recognition of Jesus' identity. How does Jesus' provision and the disciples' mission encourage you to trust in His provision and to boldly proclaim His identity?

Day 291: Judith 4-5, Wisdom 9, Luke 9:28-50

Judith 4-5

Reflection: The prayer of the people and the counsel of Achior. Reflect on the themes of prayer, reliance on God, and wisdom from unexpected sources. How does the community's prayer life inspire you to deepen your own prayer practices? How can you remain open to wisdom and guidance from unexpected places?

Wisdom 9

Reflection: Solomon's prayer for wisdom. Reflect on the themes of divine guidance, humility, and reliance on God. How does Solomon's humble request for wisdom inspire you to seek God's guidance in all aspects of your life?

Luke 9:28-50

Reflection: The Transfiguration, the healing of the demon-possessed boy, and teachings on greatness. Reflect on the themes of divine revelation, faith, and humility. How does the Transfiguration strengthen your understanding of Jesus' divine nature? How can you practice humility and faith in your daily interactions?

Day 292: Judith 6-7, Wisdom 10, Luke 9:51-62

Judith 6-7

Reflection: The siege of Bethulia and the people's despair. Reflect on the themes of endurance, faith under pressure, and God's deliverance. How can the people's struggle during the siege encourage you to maintain faith and endurance in difficult times?

Wisdom 10

Reflection: Wisdom's protection and guidance throughout history. Reflect on the themes of protection, guidance, and God's providence. How does this passage encourage you to trust in God's wisdom and guidance in your own life?

Luke 9:51-62

Reflection: The cost of following Jesus. Reflect on the themes of commitment, sacrifice, and discipleship. How does Jesus' teaching about the cost of discipleship challenge you to evaluate your own commitment to following Him?

Day 293: Judith 8-9, Wisdom 11, Luke 10:1-24

Judith 8-9

Reflection: Judith's prayer and preparation. Reflect on the themes of courage, faith, and divine assistance. How does Judith's faith and courage inspire you to take bold actions for God, relying on His strength and guidance?

Wisdom 11

Reflection: God's providence and mercy in creation. Reflect on the themes of divine mercy, creation, and providence. How does this passage deepen your appreciation for God's care and mercy in your life and the world around you?

Luke 10:1-24

Reflection: The sending of the seventy-two and their return. Reflect on the themes of mission, joy, and spiritual authority. How does Jesus' commission to the seventy-two inspire you to participate in His mission? How can you rejoice in the spiritual victories God grants you?

Day 294: Judith 10-11, Wisdom 12, Luke 10:25-42

Judith 10-11

Reflection: Judith's encounter with Holofernes. Reflect on the themes of bravery, strategy, and God's guidance. How does Judith's boldness and reliance on God inspire you to face challenges with faith and wisdom?

Wisdom 12

Reflection: God's patience and purpose in dealing with sinners. Reflect on the themes of divine patience, justice, and mercy. How does this passage shape your understanding of God's patience and the purpose behind His actions?

Luke 10:25-42

Reflection: The parable of the Good Samaritan and Jesus' visit with Mary and Martha. Reflect on the themes of compassion, service, and devotion. How can you practice the compassion of the Good Samaritan in your daily life? How do you balance service with the need to sit at Jesus' feet and learn from Him?

WEEK 43: Catholic Women and Apologetics: Defending Your Faith with Confidence

Welcome back, Faithful and Fierce women! As we continue this empowering exploration of faith, we turn to a crucial skill – apologetics. Apologetics is the art of defending your faith in a respectful and reasoned way. This week, we explore how Catholic women can confidently articulate their beliefs, navigate challenging conversations, and become strong advocates for their faith.

A Journey of Reason and Faith:

The Catholic faith is rich in tradition and supported by reason and logic. Here's why apologetics is essential for Catholic women:

- **Equipping Yourself:** Knowing your faith allows you to answer questions with confidence and clarity. Apologetics empowers you to articulate your beliefs in a clear and compelling manner.

- **Engaging in Meaningful Dialogue:** In today's world, conversations about faith often arise. Apologetics equips you to engage in respectful discussions about Catholicism with friends, family, and even strangers.

- **Combating Misconceptions:** The Catholic faith is often misunderstood. Apologetics allows you to address these misconceptions and present a clear picture of Catholic beliefs and practices.

Beyond Inspiration: Embracing Apologetics

Apologetics isn't about aggressive debate; it's about presenting a reasoned defense of your faith. Here's how you can start:

- **Know the Basics:** Solidify your understanding of core Catholic doctrines like the Trinity, the Eucharist, the role of the Virgin Mary, and the Sacraments.

- **Seek Reliable Resources:** Utilize Catholic apologetics websites, books by reputable Catholic scholars, and resources from reputable Catholic organizations like the Catholic Answers website (Catholic Answers) to deepen your knowledge.

- **Practice Respectful Dialogue:** Focus on understanding another person's perspective before presenting your own. Listen actively, and engage in respectful conversation.

Discussion Starter: Navigating Challenging Conversations

Here's where we delve deeper together:

- Share some common challenges you've encountered regarding the Catholic faith.

- How can we effectively address these challenges in a respectful and informative way?

- What resources have you found helpful for learning more about Catholic apologetics?

Remember, dear sisters, apologetics requires courage and confidence. However, it's ultimately a journey of love. Your goal is to share the richness of your faith with others in a way that fosters understanding and respect.

Beyond This Book:

As you embark on your own apologetics journey, remember:

- **Start Small:** Don't feel pressured to engage in complex theological debates. Begin with simple conversations about faith with those closest to you.

- **Lead by Example:** Live your faith authentically. Your actions and Christ-like values will speak volumes and make your words even more impactful.

- **Never Stop Learning:** The field of apologetics is constantly evolving. Stay up-to-date on current issues and continue to deepen your knowledge of the faith.

BIBLE READING: Week 43

Day 295: Judith 12:1-14:10, Wisdom 13, Luke 11:1-28

Judith 12:1-14:10

Reflection: Judith's cunning plan to save her people. Reflect on the themes of courage, strategy, and God's deliverance. How does Judith's bravery and reliance on God's guidance inspire you to trust in His provision and wisdom in your own life?

Wisdom 13

Reflection: The folly of idolatry and the revelation of God's existence through creation. Reflect on the themes of idolatry, creation, and divine revelation. How does this passage challenge you to examine the idols in your life and recognize God's presence in the world around you?

Luke 11:1-28

Reflection: Jesus teaches His disciples to pray, warns against hypocrisy, and affirms His authority. Reflect on the themes of prayer, sincerity, and the kingdom of God. How does Jesus' model of prayer inspire you to deepen your own prayer life? How can you align your desires and priorities with God's kingdom?

Day 296: Judith 14:11-16:25, Wisdom 14, Luke 11:29-54

Judith 14:11-16:25

Reflection: Judith's triumph over Holofernes and her return to Bethulia. Reflect on the themes of victory, courage, and divine intervention. How does Judith's story remind you of God's faithfulness and His power to deliver His people from their enemies?

Wisdom 14

Reflection: The folly of idolatry and the contrast with true wisdom. Reflect on the themes of idolatry, wisdom, and divine judgment. How does this passage challenge you to discern between true wisdom and the false promises of idolatry in your own life?

Luke 11:29-54

Reflection: Jesus rebukes the Pharisees and warns against hypocrisy. Reflect on the themes of hypocrisy, repentance, and the rejection of God's messengers. How does Jesus' warning against hypocrisy challenge you to examine your own heart and motives? How can you cultivate sincerity and humility in your relationship with God?

Day 297: Malachi, Obadiah, Wisdom 15, Luke 12:1-34

Malachi

Reflection: Malachi's prophecy about the coming judgment and the messenger of the Lord. Reflect on the themes of repentance, obedience, and God's faithfulness. How does Malachi's message encourage you to turn back to God and trust in His promises?

Obadiah

Reflection: Obadiah's prophecy against Edom and the assurance of God's judgment. Reflect on the themes of pride, justice, and divine retribution. How does Obadiah's message remind you of the consequences of pride and the assurance of God's justice?

Wisdom 15

Reflection: The contrast between idols and the living God. Reflect on the themes of idolatry, creation, and divine sovereignty. How does this passage inspire you to worship the true God and recognize His sovereignty over all creation?

Luke 12:1-34

Reflection: Jesus warns against hypocrisy, encourages trust in God's provision, and teaches about the kingdom. Reflect on the themes of sincerity, faith, and the kingdom of God. How can you guard against hypocrisy and trust in God's provision for your needs? How does Jesus' teaching on the kingdom shape your priorities and perspective on life?

Day 298: Joel, Wisdom 16, Luke 12:35-59

Joel

Reflection: Joel's prophecy about the day of the Lord and the call to repentance. Reflect on the themes of repentance, restoration, and God's mercy. How does Joel's message challenge you to turn back to God and seek His forgiveness?

Wisdom 16

Reflection: God's mercy and provision during the exodus. Reflect on the themes of mercy, deliverance, and divine providence. How does this passage deepen your appreciation for God's faithfulness and His care for His people?

Luke 12:35-59

Reflection: Jesus teaches about readiness, faithfulness, and interpreting the times. Reflect on the themes of preparedness, stewardship, and discernment. How does Jesus' teaching on readiness and faithfulness challenge you to live with a sense of urgency and anticipation for His return? How can you cultivate a heart that is prepared to meet the Lord?

Day 299: Jonah 1-2, Wisdom 17, Luke 13:1-17

Jonah 1-2

Reflection: Jonah's disobedience, the storm, and his prayer from the belly of the fish. Reflect on the themes of obedience, repentance, and God's sovereignty. How does Jonah's experience remind you of the consequences of disobedience and the importance of turning back to God in repentance?

Wisdom 17

Reflection: God's protection of His people and the darkness of Egypt. Reflect on the themes of divine protection, judgment, and deliverance. How does this passage deepen your appreciation for God's faithfulness in protecting His people and His power to overcome darkness?

Luke 13:1-17

Reflection: Jesus warns against hypocrisy and calls for repentance, heals a crippled woman on the Sabbath. Reflect on the themes of repentance and how you can show mercy to others as Jesus showed to the crippled woman.

Day 300: Jonah 3-4, Wisdom 18, Luke 13:18-35

Jonah 3-4

Reflection: Jonah's preaching to Nineveh and his displeasure at God's mercy towards them. Reflect on the themes of obedience, mercy, and God's compassion for all people. How does Jonah's reaction challenge you to examine your own attitudes towards those you may consider undeserving of God's grace?

Wisdom 18

Reflection: God's protection of His people during the Exodus and the Passover. Reflect on the themes of deliverance, faithfulness, and divine intervention. How does this passage deepen your understanding of God's faithfulness in fulfilling His promises and His power to save His people?

Luke 13:18-35

Reflection: Jesus teaches about the kingdom of God through the parables of the mustard seed and the yeast, and laments over Jerusalem. Reflect on the themes of growth, judgment, and the urgency of repentance. How does Jesus' teaching prompt you to consider the condition of your heart and the need for ongoing repentance and spiritual growth?

Day 301: Job 1-3, Wisdom 19, Luke 14

Job 1-3

Reflection: The story of Job's suffering and his initial response. Reflect on the themes of suffering, faithfulness, and the mystery of God's providence. How does Job's example challenge you to trust in God's goodness even in the midst of adversity?

Wisdom 19

Reflection: The book of Wisdom recounts the events of the Exodus and highlights God's protection and provision for His people. Reflect on the themes of divine justice, mercy, and the consequences of disobedience. How does this passage deepen your appreciation for God's guidance and provision in your life?

Luke 14

Reflection: Jesus teaches about humility, hospitality, and the cost of discipleship. Reflect on the themes of humility, sacrifice, and the call to follow Jesus wholeheartedly. How does Jesus' teaching challenge you to examine your priorities and commitments in following Him?

WEEK 44: Women's Bible Study Groups: Continuing the Journey

Welcome back, Faithful and Fierce women! As we continue this transformative exploration of faith, let's celebrate the power of community. This week, we delve into the enriching world of Catholic women's Bible study groups. These groups offer a supportive environment for ongoing learning, fellowship, and spiritual growth.

A Journey of Shared Exploration:

Women's Bible study groups provide a unique space for Catholic women to:

- **Deepen Their Understanding:** Engaging with scripture alongside other women fosters diverse perspectives and a richer understanding of God's Word.

- **Find Support and Encouragement:** Sharing your faith journey with other women creates a sense of belonging and provides a safe space to ask questions and express doubts.

- **Develop Lasting Friendships:** Connecting with women who share your faith can lead to meaningful friendships that enrich your life beyond Bible study.

Beyond Inspiration: Finding Your Ideal Group

The perfect Bible study group will depend on your specific needs and preferences. Here's how to find the right fit:

- **Consider Your Schedule:** Are you looking for a weekday evening group, a weekend morning study session, or perhaps an online option?

- **Explore Your Interests:** Do you prefer a structured study program or a more open-ended discussion format? Are there specific books of the Bible you'd like to focus on?

- **Seek Recommendations:** Talk to your priest, family, or friends who participate in Bible study groups. They may have recommendations based on your location and interests.

Action Step: Joining the Sisterhood of Scripture

This week, I challenge you to take a step towards finding your ideal Bible study group:

- **Research Local Groups:** Contact your local Catholic church or search online for Catholic women's Bible study groups in your area. Many parishes offer Bible studies, and online directories can connect you with groups in your region.

- **Consider Starting a Group:** If you can't find a group that aligns with your needs, consider starting your own! Invite fellow parishioners or friends who are interested in forming a study group together.

- **Embrace Virtual Options:** Explore online Catholic communities or platforms offering virtual Bible studies. This is a convenient option for women with busy schedules or those who live in areas without local groups.

Remember, dear sisters, a Bible study group is a journey, not a destination. Be open to the unique gifts and perspectives each woman brings to the table.

Beyond This Book:

As you embark on this enriching experience, remember:

- **Be an Active Participant:** Come prepared to discuss the assigned readings, share your insights, and actively engage with the group.

- **Respect Different Viewpoints:** Remember that everyone is at a different stage in their faith journey. Approach discussions with openness and respect for diverse perspectives.

- **Nurture Your New Connections:** Invest time and energy in building relationships with the women in your Bible study group. These friendships can be a source of continuous support and inspiration.

Day 302: Jb 4-7, Sirach 1, Lk 15:1-10

Jb 4-7

Reflection: Job's friends speak to him, offering various perspectives on suffering and divine justice. Reflect on the themes of suffering, friendship, and the limits of human understanding. How do Job's friends' responses challenge you to think about the nature of suffering and God's role in it?

Sirach 1

Reflection: The book of Sirach begins with an exhortation to seek wisdom. Reflect on the importance of wisdom in life and its practical applications. How does this passage encourage you to pursue wisdom and live wisely in your daily life?

Lk 15:1-10

Reflection: Jesus teaches about the joy of finding the lost sheep and the lost coin. Reflect on the themes of repentance, forgiveness, and God's relentless pursuit of sinners. How does this passage inspire you to seek reconciliation with God and others, and to rejoice in the redemption of the lost?

Day 303: Job 8-10, Sirach 2, Luke 15:11-32

Job 8-10

Reflection: Job's friend Bildad responds to Job's suffering with his perspective on God's justice. Reflect on the themes of suffering, friendship, and understanding God's ways. How does Bildad's counsel prompt you to contemplate God's sovereignty in the midst of trials?

Sirach 2

Reflection: Sirach offers wisdom on enduring trials and trusting in God's mercy. Reflect on the themes of perseverance, humility, and the rewards of righteousness. How does Sirach's wisdom encourage you to remain faithful in the face of adversity?

Luke 15:11-32

Reflection: Jesus teaches the parable of the prodigal son, revealing God's unconditional love and forgiveness. Reflect on the themes of repentance, forgiveness, and reconciliation. How does this parable challenge you to embrace God's grace and extend forgiveness to others?

Day 304: Job 11-14, Sirach 3, Luke 16:1-15

Job 11-14

Reflection: Job continues to wrestle with his suffering and search for meaning. Reflect on the themes of despair, faith, and the mystery of suffering. How does Job's struggle resonate with your own experiences of adversity and questioning God's ways?

Sirach 3

Reflection: Sirach emphasizes the importance of honoring parents and seeking wisdom. Reflect on the themes of family, respect, and the pursuit of wisdom. How does Sirach's wisdom guide you in your relationships and decision-making?

Luke 16:1-15

Reflection: Jesus teaches about stewardship and the proper use of wealth through the parable of the shrewd manager. Reflect on the themes of accountability, integrity, and the true value of possessions. How does this parable challenge you to use your resources wisely for God's kingdom?

Day 305: Job 15-17, Sirach 4, Luke 16:16-31

Job 15-17

Reflection: Job's friend Eliphaz accuses him of sin and offers counsel on God's justice. Reflect on the themes of judgment, righteousness, and the limits of human understanding. How does Eliphaz's perspective on suffering prompt you to examine your own views on God's justice?

Sirach 4

Reflection: Sirach encourages seeking wisdom and avoiding the path of wickedness. Reflect on the themes of wisdom, virtue, and the consequences of sin. How does Sirach's wisdom inspire you to pursue righteousness and avoid temptation?

Luke 16:16-31

Reflection: Jesus teaches about the rich man and Lazarus, illustrating the consequences of greed and neglecting the poor. Reflect on the themes of wealth, compassion, and the reality of life after death. How does this parable challenge you to prioritize eternal values and show compassion to those in need?

Day 306: Job 18-19, Sirach 5, Luke 17:1-19

Job 18-19

Reflection: Job responds to Bildad's accusations and expresses his longing for a mediator. Reflect on the themes of suffering, longing, and the search for understanding. How does Job's lament resonate with your own experiences of pain and seeking answers from God?

Sirach 5

Reflection: Sirach offers wisdom on trusting in God's providence and avoiding overconfidence. Reflect on the themes of trust, humility, and the uncertainty of life. How does Sirach's wisdom encourage you to cultivate a humble reliance on God in all circumstances?

Luke 17:1-19

Reflection: Jesus teaches about forgiveness, faith, and gratitude through various encounters. Reflect on the themes of forgiveness, faithfulness, and gratitude. How do these stories challenge you to cultivate a spirit of forgiveness, deepen your faith, and express gratitude in your daily life?

Day 307: Job 20-21, Sirach 6, Luke 17:20-37

Job 20-21

Reflection: Job's friend Zophar responds to Job's lament with his perspective on the fate of the wicked. Reflect on the themes of justice, judgment, and the consequences of sin. How does Zophar's counsel prompt you to reflect on the consequences of your actions before God?

Sirach 6

Reflection: Sirach emphasizes the value of true friendship and the importance of choosing companions wisely. Reflect on the themes of friendship, loyalty, and discernment. How does Sirach's wisdom guide you in cultivating healthy relationships and avoiding harmful influences?

Luke 17:20-37

Reflection: Jesus teaches about the kingdom of God and the signs of its coming. Reflect on the themes of the kingdom, readiness, and faithfulness. How does Jesus' teaching challenge you to live in anticipation of His return and to prioritize the values of His kingdom in your life?

Day 308: Job 22-24, Sirach 7, Luke 18:1-14

Job 22-24

Reflection: Job's friend Eliphaz continues his counsel, accusing Job of various sins. Reflect on the themes of judgment, integrity, and the limits of human understanding. How does Eliphaz's perspective prompt you to consider the importance of maintaining integrity in the face of adversity?

Sirach 7

Reflection: Sirach offers practical wisdom on various aspects of life, including wealth, speech, and humility. Reflect on the themes of wisdom, humility, and the importance of right speech. How does Sirach's advice challenge you to live wisely and speak with kindness and humility?

Luke 18:1-14

Reflection: Jesus teaches about persistence in prayer and the importance of humility through the parable of the persistent widow and the Pharisee and the tax collector. Reflect on the themes of prayer, humility, and God's grace. How do these parables encourage you to cultivate a humble and persistent prayer life before God?

WEEK 45: Women and Catholic Social Teaching: Living Out Your Faith in Action

Welcome back, Faithful and Fierce women! As we continue this empowering exploration of faith, let's turn our hearts towards action. Catholic Social Teaching (CST) is a vibrant Journey of principles that guide us towards building a more just and compassionate world. This week, we delve into the power of CST and explore how Catholic women can actively participate in creating positive social change.

A Journey of Justice and Compassion

Catholic Social Teaching is rooted in the Gospel message of love, justice, and the inherent dignity of every human person. Here's how CST calls us to action:

- **Option for the Poor:** CST prioritizes the needs of the most vulnerable in society, urging us to advocate for the poor, marginalized, and oppressed.

- **The Common Good:** We are called to work towards a society that prioritizes the well-being of all its members, not just the privileged few.

- **Solidarity:** CST emphasizes our interconnectedness as human beings. We are called to stand in solidarity with those facing injustice, fighting for their rights and dignity.

Beyond Inspiration: Embracing Your Role

Catholic women have a vital role to play in embodying CST principles:

- **Identifying Your Passion:** What social issues move your heart? Is it poverty, human trafficking, educational inequality, or environmental stewardship? Identifying a cause you're passionate about will fuel your commitment.

- **Finding Your Niche:** There are countless ways to contribute to social change. Consider volunteering your time at a local organization aligned with your chosen cause. You can also advocate for policy changes, donate resources, or raise awareness through social media platforms.

- **Living by Example:** Beyond specific actions, let your daily life reflect CST principles. Be a compassionate neighbor, a fair employer, and a voice for social justice in your community.

Challenge: Putting Faith into Action

This week, I challenge you to take a concrete step towards living out CST principles:

- **Volunteer Your Time:** Research local organizations working on issues aligned with your passion. Offer your time and skills at a soup kitchen, homeless shelter, or organization advocating for educational equity.

- **Advocate and Raise Awareness:** Contact your local representatives about policies that impact the most vulnerable in your community. Use social media to raise awareness about social justice issues and encourage others to get involved.

- **Support Catholic Charities:** Numerous Catholic charities are dedicated to alleviating poverty, providing healthcare, and fighting social injustice. Consider donating resources or volunteering your time with a Catholic organization aligned with your interests.

Remember, dear sisters, even small acts of compassion can create a ripple effect. Your willingness to serve and advocate for justice makes a difference.

Beyond This Book:

As you embark on your own CST journey, remember:

- **Stay Informed:** Educate yourself on current social justice issues and Catholic teachings related to those issues. Numerous Catholic organizations provide resources and educational materials.

- **Empower Others:** Share your passion for CST with other Catholic women. Encourage them to get involved in social change efforts and create a network of support.

- **Live with Purpose:** Integrate CST principles into every aspect of your life. Let your faith be a catalyst for positive change in yourself and the world around you.

BIBLE READING: Week 45

Day 309: Job 25-28, Sirach 8, Luke 18:15-43

Job 25-28

Reflection: Job reflects on the power and wisdom of God, culminating in a profound declaration of God's sovereignty. Reflect on the themes of divine wisdom, human frailty, and the fear of the Lord. How does Job's meditation on God's greatness inspire you to seek wisdom and reverence in your own life?

Sirach 8

Reflection: Sirach advises on how to interact with various types of people and situations. Reflect on the themes of prudence, respect, and wisdom in relationships. How can Sirach's guidance help you navigate your relationships with greater wisdom and integrity?

Luke 18:15-43

Reflection: Jesus welcomes children, speaks to the rich young ruler, and heals a blind beggar. Reflect on the themes of humility, sacrifice, and faith. How do these encounters with Jesus challenge you to approach Him with childlike faith, prioritize eternal treasures, and trust in His healing power?

Day 310: Job 29-31, Sirach 9, Luke 19:1-27

Job 29-31

Reflection: Job reminisces about his past blessings, laments his current suffering, and defends his integrity. Reflect on the themes of memory, integrity, and self-examination. How does Job's reflection on his life encourage you to examine your own integrity and faithfulness to God?

Sirach 9

Reflection: Sirach warns against various temptations and advises on maintaining purity and wisdom. Reflect on the themes of self-control, wisdom, and purity. How can Sirach's warnings help you to avoid temptation and live a life of purity and wisdom?

Luke 19:1-27

Reflection: Jesus interacts with Zacchaeus, tells the parable of the ten minas, and emphasizes faithful stewardship. Reflect on the themes of repentance, stewardship, and accountability.

How do Jesus' teachings encourage you to seek repentance and faithfully steward the resources God has entrusted to you?

Day 311: Job 32-34, Sirach 10, Luke 19:28-48

Job 32-34

Reflection: Elihu speaks, offering his perspective on Job's suffering and God's justice. Reflect on the themes of youth, wisdom, and divine justice. How does Elihu's speech challenge you to consider different perspectives on suffering and to seek God's wisdom in understanding His justice?

Sirach 10

Reflection: Sirach discusses the role of leadership, pride, and humility. Reflect on the themes of leadership, pride, and humility. How can Sirach's wisdom help you to cultivate humility and recognize the importance of just leadership in your community?

Luke 19:28-48

Reflection: Jesus' triumphant entry into Jerusalem and His cleansing of the temple. Reflect on the themes of kingship, worship, and righteous indignation. How do these events challenge you to honor Jesus as King in your life and to pursue righteousness in your actions and worship?

Day 312: Job 35-37, Sirach 11, Luke 20:1-19

Job 35-37

Reflection: Elihu continues to speak, emphasizing God's greatness and justice. Reflect on the themes of divine justice, power, and the awe of God. How does Elihu's speech deepen your understanding of God's majesty and inspire you to trust in His justice?

Sirach 11

Reflection: Sirach offers insights on success, humility, and the unpredictability of life. Reflect on the themes of humility, wisdom, and trust in God. How can Sirach's advice help you to navigate life's uncertainties with humility and trust in God's providence?

Luke 20:1-19

Reflection: Jesus faces questions about His authority and tells the parable of the wicked tenants. Reflect on the themes of authority, rejection, and accountability. How does Jesus' teaching challenge you to acknowledge His authority and to consider your own accountability to God?

Day 313: Job 38-39, Sirach 12, Luke 20:20-47

Job 38-39

Reflection: God responds to Job, questioning him about the mysteries of creation. Reflect on the themes of divine wisdom, power, and human limitation. How does God's response to Job inspire you to trust in His wisdom and to recognize the limits of human understanding?

Sirach 12

Reflection: Sirach advises on generosity, trust, and dealing with enemies. Reflect on the themes of discernment, generosity, and caution. How can Sirach's wisdom guide you in showing generosity while being discerning in your relationships?

Luke 20:20-47

Reflection: Jesus answers questions about paying taxes, the resurrection, and the greatest commandment. Reflect on the themes of wisdom, authority, and love. How do Jesus' answers challenge you to live with wisdom, respect for authority, and a love for God and others?

Day 314: Job 40-42, Sirach 13, Luke 21:1-19

Job 40-42

Reflection: Job responds to God's challenge, repents, and is restored. Reflect on the themes of humility, repentance, and restoration. How does Job's encounter with God and his subsequent restoration inspire you to seek humility and trust in God's redemptive power?

Sirach 13

Reflection: Sirach offers insights on wealth, status, and friendship. Reflect on the themes of wealth, humility, and true friendship. How can Sirach's wisdom help you to navigate relationships and possessions with humility and discernment?

Luke 21:1-19

Reflection: Jesus speaks about the widow's offering, the signs of the end times, and perseverance. Reflect on the themes of generosity, faithfulness, and endurance. How do Jesus' teachings encourage you to live with generosity and to remain faithful through trials?

Day 315: 2 Peter, Sirach 14, Luke 21:20-38

2 Peter

Reflection: Peter writes about the importance of growing in faith, the certainty of Christ's return, and the call to holy living. Reflect on the themes of spiritual growth, hope, and holiness. How does Peter's message inspire you to grow in your faith and to live in anticipation of Christ's return?

Sirach 14

Reflection: Sirach offers reflections on the pursuit of wisdom, wealth, and contentment. Reflect on the themes of wisdom, contentment, and the pursuit of true riches. How can Sirach's wisdom guide you in seeking contentment and valuing the true riches found in wisdom and godliness?

Luke 21:20-38

Reflection: Jesus speaks about the destruction of Jerusalem, the coming of the Son of Man, and the need for watchfulness. Reflect on the themes of prophecy, vigilance, and hope. How do Jesus' teachings encourage you to live with vigilance and hope, trusting in His promises and looking forward to His return?

WEEK 46: Women on a Mission: Sharing Your Faith with Others

Welcome back, Faithful and Fierce women! As we reach the 46th week of this faith-filled exploration, let's turn our hearts outwards. Sharing your faith isn't about forceful conversion; it's about sharing the love and light of Christ with the world around you. This week, we delve into various ways Catholic women can confidently and authentically spread the Good News.

A Journey of Sharing:

Spreading the faith doesn't require grand gestures. Here's how you can share your faith in powerful ways:

- **Be a Living Example:** Let your actions speak louder than words. Live out your Christian values through kindness, compassion, and service to others. Your authentic faith will naturally draw people in.

- **Embrace Everyday Opportunities:** Simple conversations about your faith with friends, family, or even strangers can plant seeds of hope and curiosity. Speak with confidence about your beliefs, but always approach these conversations with respect for others' viewpoints.

- **Offer Invitations:** Invite friends or family to join you for Mass, a church event, or a Bible study group. Sharing your faith experiences can spark their interest in learning more.

- **Utilize Social Media Platforms:** Use social media responsibly to share inspirational quotes, faith-based content, or reflections on your own faith journey. Remember, kindness and positivity resonate most in the online world.

Beyond Inspiration: Finding Your Voice

Sharing your faith can feel daunting, but it doesn't have to be. Here's how to overcome hesitation and find your voice:

- **Identify Your Strengths:** Do you feel comfortable speaking one-on-one, or are you more inclined to share your faith through writing or social media? Identifying your strengths helps you choose effective ways to share the Gospel message.

- **Start Small:** Don't feel pressured to deliver intricate theological lectures. Begin with simple conversations or sharing short, inspirational messages.

- **Lead by Example:** Share your faith journey openly and honestly. Talk about the challenges and triumphs of your faith life. Your vulnerability can inspire others.

- **Focus on Love:** Remember, the core of Christianity is love. Let your passion for God and His message of love be the driving force behind your desire to share your faith.

Self-Reflection: Discovering Your Sharing Style

Take a moment to reflect on your unique way of sharing the faith:

- **Consider situations where you already feel comfortable talking about your faith.** Is it with close friends, family, or during online discussions?

- **Imagine inviting someone to church or a Bible study group. What approach would make you feel most comfortable?** Would you extend a casual invitation or offer a brief explanation of why you find your faith community meaningful?

- **Do you feel drawn to sharing inspirational content online?** If so, what types of messages resonate with you, and how can you use social media platforms to spread the Good News authentically?

Remember, dear sisters, sharing your faith is a journey, not a destination. There's no one-size-fits-all approach. Embrace your unique voice and let your love for God shine through in all you do.

Beyond This Book:

As you embark on your mission of sharing your faith, remember:

- **Live with Purpose:** Integrate your faith into every aspect of your life. Let your actions and words reflect your Christian values.

- **Seek Guidance:** Talk to your priest, spiritual director, or other Catholic mentors about your desire to share your faith. They can offer support and guidance.

- **Celebrate Small Victories:** Sharing your faith can be a humbling experience. Celebrate even small victories, like a meaningful conversation or someone expressing interest in learning more about your faith.

Day 316: Ecclesiastes 1-3, Sirach 15, Luke 22:1-38

Ecclesiastes 1-3

Reflection: The author of Ecclesiastes reflects on the vanity of life, the pursuit of pleasure, and the seasons of life. Reflect on the themes of meaning, purpose, and the cycles of life. How do these reflections challenge you to seek lasting meaning and purpose in your life?

Sirach 15

Reflection: Sirach speaks about free will, the love of wisdom, and the consequences of choices. Reflect on the themes of wisdom, responsibility, and the fear of the Lord. How does Sirach's teaching encourage you to make wise choices and to seek wisdom in your daily life?

Luke 22:1-38

Reflection: Jesus prepares for the Passover, institutes the Lord's Supper, and speaks of His betrayal and denial. Reflect on the themes of sacrifice, covenant, and betrayal. How does Jesus' example and teachings inspire you to live a life of sacrifice and faithfulness?

Day 317: Ecclesiastes 4-6, Sirach 16, Luke 22:39-71

Ecclesiastes 4-6

Reflection: The author of Ecclesiastes discusses the oppression of the poor, the futility of wealth, and the limitations of human effort. Reflect on the themes of justice, contentment, and the pursuit of true fulfillment. How do these reflections challenge you to seek justice and find contentment beyond material possessions?

Sirach 16

Reflection: Sirach reflects on God's judgment and the consequences of sin. Reflect on the themes of justice, repentance, and divine retribution. How does Sirach's teaching encourage you to live righteously and to seek God's forgiveness?

Luke 22:39-71

Reflection: Jesus prays in Gethsemane, is betrayed by Judas, and denied by Peter. Reflect on the themes of prayer, betrayal, and faithfulness. How do Jesus' actions and experiences in these passages inspire you to remain faithful in times of trial and to seek strength through prayer?

Day 318: Ecclesiastes 7-8, Sirach 17, Luke 23:1-32

Ecclesiastes 7-8

Reflection: The author of Ecclesiastes offers various proverbs and reflections on wisdom, folly, and righteousness. Reflect on the themes of wisdom, humility, and the fear of the Lord. How do these reflections guide you to live a life of wisdom and humility?

Sirach 17

Reflection: Sirach speaks about God's creation of humanity and the call to repentance. Reflect on the themes of creation, repentance, and God's mercy. How does Sirach's teaching encourage you to recognize God's creative power and to seek His mercy through repentance?

Luke 23:1-32

Reflection: Jesus stands trial before Pilate and Herod and is led to the crucifixion. Reflect on the themes of suffering, innocence, and redemption. How does Jesus' journey to the cross inspire you to endure suffering and to trust in God's redemptive plan?

Day 319: Ecclesiastes 9-12, Sirach 18, Luke 23:33-43

Ecclesiastes 9-12

Reflection: The author of Ecclesiastes reflects on the inevitability of death, the unpredictability of life, and the importance of fearing God. Reflect on the themes of mortality, purpose, and the fear of the Lord. How do these reflections challenge you to live with purpose and to fear God in all things?

Sirach 18

Reflection: Sirach speaks about God's mercy and the call to humility and repentance. Reflect on the themes of mercy, humility, and repentance. How does Sirach's teaching encourage you to embrace God's mercy and to live a life of humility and repentance?

Luke 23:33-43

Reflection: Jesus is crucified and promises paradise to the repentant thief. Reflect on the themes of forgiveness, redemption, and hope. How does Jesus' response to the thief on the cross inspire you to seek forgiveness and to offer hope to others?

Day 320: Song of Songs 1-4, Sirach 19, Luke 23:44-56

Song of Songs 1-4

Reflection: The Song of Songs celebrates love and affection between lovers. Reflect on the themes of love, beauty, and intimacy. How does the portrayal of love in these passages inspire you to appreciate the beauty and depth of love in your relationships?

Sirach 19

Reflection: Sirach discusses the dangers of gossip, the importance of discretion, and the pursuit of wisdom. Reflect on the themes of speech, discretion, and wisdom. How does Sirach's teaching guide you to use your words wisely and to seek wisdom in your interactions?

Luke 23:44-56

Reflection: Jesus dies on the cross and is buried. Reflect on the themes of sacrifice, redemption, and hope. How does Jesus' sacrifice on the cross inspire you to live a life of gratitude and hope in the promise of resurrection?

Day 321: Song of Songs 5-8, Sirach 20, Luke 24:1-35

Song of Songs 5-8

Reflection: The Song of Songs continues to celebrate the beauty and depth of love between lovers. Reflect on the themes of love, commitment, and intimacy. How does this celebration of love inspire you to cultivate deep and meaningful relationships?

Sirach 20

Reflection: Sirach offers wisdom on speech, silence, and the consequences of actions. Reflect on the themes of wisdom, prudence, and accountability. How does Sirach's teaching encourage you to be mindful of your words and actions?

Luke 24:1-35

Reflection: The resurrection of Jesus and His appearance to the disciples on the road to Emmaus. Reflect on the themes of resurrection, revelation, and hope. How does the resurrection of Jesus inspire you to live with hope and to seek His presence in your life?

Day 322: 1 Maccabees 1-2, Sirach 21, Luke 24:36-53

1 Maccabees 1-2

Reflection: The beginning of the Maccabean revolt and the fight for religious freedom. Reflect on the themes of courage, faith, and resistance. How does the story of the Maccabean revolt inspire you to stand firm in your faith and to resist compromise?

Sirach 21

Reflection: Sirach offers wisdom on sin, repentance, and the pursuit of righteousness. Reflect on the themes of sin, repentance, and righteousness. How does Sirach's teaching encourage you to turn away from sin and to seek a life of righteousness?

Luke 24:36-53

Reflection: The risen Jesus appears to His disciples, commissions them, and ascends to heaven. Reflect on the themes of resurrection, mission, and ascension. How does Jesus' resurrection and commission inspire you to live out your faith and to share the good news with others?

WEEK 47: The Spiritual Gifts of Women: Using Your Talents for God's Glory

Welcome back, Faithful and Fierce women! As we continue this empowering exploration of faith, let's celebrate the unique gifts bestowed upon each of us by the Holy Spirit. These gifts are not mere talents; they are divine tools for building up the Church and spreading the Gospel message. This week, we delve into the beautiful Journey of spiritual gifts possessed by Catholic women and explore ways to use them for God's glory.

A Journey of Divine Empowerment:

The Holy Spirit equips every believer with unique spiritual gifts (1 Corinthians 12:7-11). These gifts are not meant to be hidden; they are meant to be used for the benefit of the Church community. Here's how Catholic women can identify and utilize their spiritual gifts:

- **Understanding Spiritual Gifts:** Spiritual gifts are different from natural talents. While talents are our abilities, spiritual gifts are empowerments by the Holy Spirit to serve the Church. Common spiritual gifts for women include teaching, hospitality, administration, encouragement, and prophecy (Romans 12:6-8).

- **Identifying Your Gifts:** Reflect on your passions, skills, and experiences. What activities energize you? What tasks do you excel at? Conversations with trusted friends, mentors, or spiritual directors can help you identify your unique gifts.

Beyond Inspiration: Embracing Your Calling

Identifying your spiritual gifts is only the first step. Here's how to utilize them for the benefit of your parish and the wider Church:

- **Seek Opportunities to Serve:** Most parishes offer a variety of ministries catering to diverse skills and interests. Explore opportunities in areas that align with your spiritual gifts.

- **Volunteer Your Time and Talents:** Is your gift for teaching? Consider volunteering for a children's catechesis program. Do you possess strong organizational skills? Offer to assist with parish events or administrative tasks.

- **Step Outside Your Comfort Zone:** Don't be afraid to try something new! The Holy Spirit might be prompting you to explore an unfamiliar ministry that aligns perfectly with your spiritual gifts.

Action Step: Unleashing Your Divine Spark

This week, I challenge you to take a concrete step towards using your spiritual gifts for service:

- **Identify Your Gifts:** Reflect on your strengths, skills, and experiences. What are you naturally drawn to? What activities energize you? Consider taking a spiritual gifts assessment found online or in Catholic resources.

- **Brainstorm Opportunities:** Research ministries offered by your parish or local Catholic organizations. Talk to parishioners involved in various ministries to gain insights into their roles.

- **Commit to Service:** Choose a ministry that aligns with your gifts and interests. Contact the ministry leader and express your desire to serve.

Remember, dear sisters, God has equipped you with unique gifts for a reason. Using them for His glory brings fulfillment to your own life and strengthens the Church community.

Beyond This Book:

As you embark on this journey of service, remember:

- **Pray for Guidance:** Ask the Holy Spirit to reveal your spiritual gifts and guide you towards opportunities where you can use them effectively.

- **Seek Guidance and Mentorship:** Talk to your priest, spiritual director, or experienced parishioners who actively use their gifts in ministry. Their insights and encouragement can be invaluable.

- **Be Open to Growth:** Ministry work can be a learning experience. Embrace challenges and setbacks as opportunities for growth in your faith and service.

Day 323: 1 Maccabees 3-4, Sirach 22, John 1:1-18

1 Maccabees 3-4

Reflection: The battles led by Judas Maccabeus to reclaim and purify the temple. Reflect on the themes of bravery, faith, and restoration. How does the courage of Judas Maccabeus inspire you to fight for what is right and to seek spiritual renewal?

Sirach 22

Reflection: Sirach discusses the sluggard, the fool, and the value of friendship. Reflect on the themes of diligence, wisdom, and relationships. How do Sirach's teachings encourage you to cultivate wisdom and to value true friendship?

John 1:1-18

Reflection: The Prologue of John's Gospel introduces Jesus as the Word made flesh. Reflect on the themes of incarnation, light, and grace. How does the incarnation of Jesus deepen your understanding of God's love and presence in the world?

Day 324: 1 Maccabees 5-6, Sirach 23, John 1:19-51

1 Maccabees 5-6

Reflection: The continued struggles and leadership of Judas Maccabeus and his brothers. Reflect on the themes of leadership, perseverance, and divine guidance. How do the efforts of Judas and his brothers inspire you to lead with courage and to persevere in difficult times?

Sirach 23

Reflection: Sirach speaks on the control of speech, lust, and the fear of the Lord. Reflect on the themes of self-control, purity, and reverence. How do Sirach's teachings guide you in living a life that honors God in word and deed?

John 1:19-51

Reflection: John the Baptist's testimony about Jesus and the calling of the first disciples. Reflect on the themes of witness, calling, and discipleship. How does the example of John the Baptist and the first disciples inspire you to bear witness to Jesus and to follow Him wholeheartedly?

Day 325: 1 Maccabees 7-8, Sirach 24, John 2:1-12

1 Maccabees 7-8

Reflection: The political alliances and conflicts during the time of the Maccabees. Reflect on the themes of loyalty, diplomacy, and faithfulness. How do the political maneuvers of the Maccabees inspire you to navigate challenges with wisdom and integrity?

Sirach 24

Reflection: Sirach extols the praise of wisdom, likening it to a tree and a river. Reflect on the themes of wisdom, nourishment, and divine presence. How does Sirach's celebration of wisdom inspire you to seek and cherish godly wisdom in your life?

John 2:1-12

Reflection: The miracle at the wedding at Cana, where Jesus turns water into wine. Reflect on the themes of transformation, joy, and divine power. How does this miracle encourage you to trust in Jesus' ability to bring about transformation and to celebrate His provision in your life?

Day 326: 1 Maccabees 9-10, Sirach 25, John 2:13-25

1 Maccabees 9-10

Reflection: The ongoing battles and political strategies of Jonathan and Simon Maccabeus. Reflect on the themes of perseverance, leadership, and divine favor. How do the actions of Jonathan and Simon inspire you to lead with perseverance and to seek God's guidance in your endeavors?

Sirach 25

Reflection: Sirach discusses the joys of a good life and the troubles of a bad one. Reflect on the themes of contentment, relationships, and wisdom. How do Sirach's teachings guide you in pursuing a life that is pleasing to God and fulfilling in relationships?

John 2:13-25

Reflection: Jesus cleanses the temple and speaks of His resurrection. Reflect on the themes of purity, zeal, and resurrection. How does Jesus' cleansing of the temple challenge you to pursue holiness and to trust in His promise of new life?

Day 327: 1 Maccabees 11-12, Sirach 26, John 3:1-21

1 Maccabees 11-12

Reflection: The diplomatic efforts and battles of Jonathan and Simon Maccabeus. Reflect on the themes of diplomacy, faith, and perseverance. How do the efforts of Jonathan and Simon encourage you to engage in diplomacy and to persevere in faith?

Sirach 26

Reflection: Sirach praises the virtues of a good wife and warns against the wickedness of others. Reflect on the themes of virtue, relationships, and integrity. How do Sirach's teachings inspire you to value and cultivate virtuous relationships?

John 3:1-21

Reflection: Jesus' conversation with Nicodemus about being born again and God's love for the world. Reflect on the themes of new birth, salvation, and divine love. How does Jesus' teaching about being born again challenge you to embrace a transformative relationship with God?

Day 328: 1 Maccabees 13-14, Sirach 27, John 3:22-36

1 Maccabees 13-14

Reflection: The leadership of Simon Maccabeus and the peace he brings to Israel. Reflect on the themes of leadership, peace, and divine blessing. How does Simon's leadership inspire you to seek peace and to lead others with wisdom and integrity?

Sirach 27

Reflection: Sirach discusses honesty, speech, and the consequences of actions. Reflect on the themes of truthfulness, integrity, and accountability. How do Sirach's teachings guide you to live a life of honesty and integrity?

John 3:22-36

Reflection: John the Baptist exalts Jesus and speaks of eternal life. Reflect on the themes of humility, testimony, and eternal life. How does John the Baptist's testimony inspire you to exalt Jesus in your life and to share the promise of eternal life with others?

Day 329: 1 Maccabees 15-16, Sirach 28, John 4:1-42

1 Maccabees 15-16

Reflection: The reign of Simon Maccabeus and the final battles of the Maccabees. Reflect on the themes of legacy, faithfulness, and divine protection. How does the story of Simon and the Maccabees inspire you to leave a legacy of faithfulness and to trust in God's protection?

Sirach 28

Reflection: Sirach speaks on forgiveness, anger, and the power of speech. Reflect on the themes of forgiveness, reconciliation, and the impact of words. How do Sirach's teachings challenge you to practice forgiveness and to be mindful of your words?

John 4:1-42

Reflection: Jesus' encounter with the Samaritan woman at the well and the revelation of living water. Reflect on the themes of acceptance, revelation, and transformation. How does Jesus' interaction with the Samaritan woman inspire you to seek and share the living water He offers?

WEEK 48: Leaning on the Everlasting Arms: Trusting God Like Sarah

Welcome back, sisters! This week, we delve into the beautiful story of Sarah, the wife of Abraham, and explore the power of trusting in God's promises, even when they seem impossible. Sarah's journey teaches us valuable lessons about faith, patience, and the unwavering love of God.

A Promise Planted:

The Book of Genesis introduces us to Sarah, a woman known for her beauty and strength. God makes a covenant with her husband, Abraham, promising him a land and descendants as numerous as the stars (Genesis 12:1-3). However, there's a catch – Sarah is barren.

The Seeds of Doubt:

Years pass, and Sarah, well beyond childbearing age, begins to doubt God's promise. Cultural expectations and the longing for a child weigh heavily on her. In an attempt to fulfill God's promise on her own terms, she offers her handmaid, Hagar, to Abraham (Genesis 16:1-3). This decision leads to complications and family tension.

Laughter in the Face of Faith:

Decades later, God reiterates his promise to Abraham, specifically mentioning Sarah would conceive (Genesis 17:15-19). At this point, Sarah laughs in disbelief. The idea of her, an elderly woman, bearing a child seems absurd (Genesis 18:12). But God assures them, "Is anything too hard for the Lord?" (Genesis 18:14).

A Miracle Unfolds:

True to his word, God blesses Sarah, and miraculously, she becomes pregnant at an age when childbearing is considered impossible (Genesis 21:1-2). Sarah gives birth to Isaac, the son of promise, fulfilling God's covenant.

Lessons from Sarah's Story:

Sarah's journey offers valuable lessons for our own lives:

- **Trusting God's Timing:** God's plans often unfold on his own time frame, not ours. Learning to trust his timing and wait patiently is crucial.

- **Faith in the Face of Doubt:** Even the most faithful people experience moments of doubt. Sarah's story reminds us that faith isn't about the absence of doubt; it's about trusting God even when we don't understand his plan.

- **The Power of Surrender:** Letting go of control and surrendering to God's will can lead to unexpected blessings. When Sarah finally releases her own desires and trusts in God, a miracle unfolds.

Activity: Planting Seeds of Faith

This week, engage in an interactive activity that reinforces the theme of trust and God's promises:

1. **Planting the Seed:** Gather some potting soil, seeds (beans or peas work well), and small cups or containers. Plant a seed in each container.

2. **Nurturing the Seed:** Place the containers in a sunny location and water them regularly. Discuss the importance of patience and care as the seeds germinate and grow.

3. **God's Promises:** As the seeds sprout and grow, talk about God's promises in your lives. Discuss how, like the seeds, God's promises may take time to unfold, but with faith and trust, they will come to fruition.

Remember:

Sarah's story is a testament to God's faithfulness. Even when faced with seemingly impossible situations, we can hold onto the promise that God's plans are always good and his timing is perfect.

Bonus Activity:

Discuss the challenges Sarah faced and how her faith ultimately led to a miracle. Encourage each member to share their own experiences of trusting God's promises in their lives.

Remember, God's love and faithfulness are everlasting. By learning from Sarah's story and nurturing our own faith, we can find strength and trust in the face of life's challenges. May your faith journey be filled with hope and the unwavering belief in God's promises!

BIBLE READING: Week 48

Day 330: Jude, Sirach 29, John 4:43-54

Jude

Reflection: Jude's letter addresses false teachers and urges believers to contend for the faith. Reflect on the themes of vigilance, faithfulness, and divine protection. How does Jude's message encourage you to stay true to your faith and to be vigilant against false teachings?

Sirach 29

Reflection: Sirach discusses lending, borrowing, and the importance of being trustworthy. Reflect on the themes of generosity, responsibility, and trust. How do Sirach's teachings guide you in being responsible and trustworthy in your relationships and dealings with others?

John 4:43-54

Reflection: Jesus heals the official's son through the power of His word. Reflect on the themes of faith, healing, and divine authority. How does this miracle encourage you to trust in Jesus' word and to believe in His power to heal and restore?

Day 331: 2 Maccabees 1-2, Sirach 30, John 5:1-30

2 Maccabees 1-2

Reflection: The letters urging the Jews in Egypt to celebrate the Feast of Dedication and the restoration of the temple. Reflect on the themes of celebration, restoration, and faithfulness. How do these letters inspire you to remember and celebrate God's faithfulness and acts of restoration in your life?

Sirach 30

Reflection: Sirach speaks about the care of children and the importance of discipline. Reflect on the themes of parenting, discipline, and well-being. How do Sirach's teachings encourage you to cultivate a nurturing and disciplined environment for growth and well-being?

John 5:1-30

Reflection: Jesus heals the man at the pool of Bethesda and speaks about His relationship with the Father. Reflect on the themes of healing, authority, and divine sonship. How does

Jesus' authority and His relationship with the Father deepen your understanding of His divine mission and power?

Day 332: 2 Maccabees 3-4, Sirach 31, John 5:31-47

2 Maccabees 3-4

Reflection: The desecration of the temple and the subsequent events leading to conflict. Reflect on the themes of sacredness, conflict, and divine justice. How do the events in these chapters remind you of the importance of reverence for the sacred and the assurance of God's justice?

Sirach 31

Reflection: Sirach offers guidance on wealth, generosity, and moderation. Reflect on the themes of stewardship, generosity, and contentment. How do Sirach's teachings inspire you to manage your resources wisely and to live a life of generosity and contentment?

John 5:31-47

Reflection: Jesus speaks about the witnesses to His identity and mission. Reflect on the themes of testimony, belief, and divine revelation. How does Jesus' teaching about the witnesses challenge you to deepen your belief in Him and to recognize the various ways God reveals Himself?

Day 333: 2 Maccabees 5-6, Sirach 32, John 6:1-24

2 Maccabees 5-6

Reflection: The suffering and martyrdom of the Jews under Antiochus Epiphanes. Reflect on the themes of persecution, faith, and martyrdom. How does the faithfulness of the martyrs inspire you to stand firm in your faith, even in the face of persecution?

Sirach 32

Reflection: Sirach gives advice on conduct at banquets and in daily life. Reflect on the themes of wisdom, self-control, and proper conduct. How do Sirach's teachings guide you to live a life marked by wisdom and self-control in all areas of your life?

John 6:1-24

Reflection: Jesus feeds the five thousand and walks on water. Reflect on the themes of provision, power, and divine presence. How do these miracles of Jesus encourage you to trust in His provision and to recognize His presence and power in your life?

Day 334: 2 Maccabees 7-8, Sirach 33, John 6:25-59

2 Maccabees 7-8

Reflection: The story of the seven brothers and their mother who are martyred for their faith. Reflect on the themes of faith, courage, and eternal hope. How does their unwavering faith and hope in eternal life challenge you to live with boldness and conviction?

Sirach 33

Reflection: Sirach speaks about the order of creation and the wisdom of God's governance. Reflect on the themes of order, wisdom, and divine sovereignty. How does Sirach's view of creation inspire you to trust in God's wisdom and governance over all things?

John 6:25-59

Reflection: Jesus teaches about the bread of life and the necessity of believing in Him. Reflect on the themes of spiritual nourishment, belief, and eternal life. How does Jesus' teaching about the bread of life deepen your understanding of the importance of faith and spiritual sustenance?

Day 335: 2 Maccabees 9-10, Sirach 34, John 6:60-71

2 Maccabees 9-10

Reflection: The illness and death of Antiochus Epiphanes and the purification of the temple. Reflect on the themes of repentance, divine judgment, and purification. How does the story of Antiochus' demise and the rededication of the temple encourage you to seek repentance and spiritual renewal?

Sirach 34

Reflection: Sirach discusses dreams, false hopes, and the fear of the Lord. Reflect on the themes of discernment, hope, and reverence. How do Sirach's teachings guide you to seek true hope and to live a life marked by reverence for God?

John 6:60-71

Reflection: Many disciples turn away from Jesus after His teaching about the bread of life. Reflect on the themes of commitment, faith, and loyalty. How does the reaction of the disciples challenge you to stay committed to Jesus, even when His teachings are difficult to understand?

Day 336: 2 Maccabees 11-12, Sirach 35, John 7:1-13

2 Maccabees 11-12

Reflection: The continued struggles and victories of Judas Maccabeus and his brothers. Reflect on the themes of perseverance, faith, and divine assistance. How do the victories and challenges faced by Judas inspire you to persevere in your faith and to trust in God's help?

Sirach 35

Reflection: Sirach speaks about offerings, justice, and the fear of the Lord. Reflect on the themes of worship, justice, and reverence. How do Sirach's teachings encourage you to offer your best to God and to live a life marked by justice and reverence?

John 7:1-13

Reflection: Jesus goes to the Feast of Tabernacles in secret and faces opposition. Reflect on the themes of timing, courage, and divine mission. How does Jesus' approach to His mission encourage you to trust in God's timing and to be courageous in fulfilling your calling?

WEEK 49: Standing Strong: Miriam, the Courageous Prophetess

Welcome back, Sisters! This week, we meet Miriam, a remarkable woman from the Bible. Sister to Moses and Aaron, Miriam plays a pivotal role in the Israelites' exodus from Egypt and their journey towards the Promised Land. Her story highlights the importance of faith, and courage in the face of adversity.

A Family on the Nile:

The Book of Exodus introduces us to Miriam at a critical time in Israelite history. Pharaoh, fearing the growing Israelite population, has ordered the killing of all Hebrew baby boys. Miriam's mother, Jochebed, defies this decree by placing her baby brother, Moses, in a basket on the Nile River (Exodus 1:22-23).

A Watchful Eye:

Miriam, though just a young girl, bravely positions herself near the riverbank to watch over her brother. When Pharaoh's daughter discovers Moses, Miriam sees an opportunity. She cleverly suggests fetching a Hebrew woman to nurse the baby, and reunites Moses with his own mother (Exodus 2:4-8). This act of courage and quick thinking ensures Moses' survival and sets the stage for his future role as liberator.

Leading the Way:

Years later, Moses leads the Israelites out of Egypt, a monumental feat requiring courage and unwavering faith. Miriam emerges as a leader in her own right. The Bible describes her as a "prophetess" (Exodus 15:20) – a woman chosen by God to speak messages of inspiration and guidance.

A Song of Triumph:

After the Israelites miraculously cross the Red Sea, escaping Pharaoh's army, Miriam leads the women in a joyous song of praise to God. This powerful song, known as the "Song of the Sea," celebrates God's deliverance and the Israelites' newfound freedom (Exodus 15:20-21).

Challenges and Resilience:

The journey through the wilderness is fraught with challenges. At one point, both Miriam and Aaron question Moses' leadership, causing God's displeasure. However, Miriam's faith and unwavering commitment to her family and her people remain strong (Numbers 12:1-15).

A Legacy of Faith:

Miriam, though she doesn't reach the Promised Land, leaves an enduring legacy. Her courage, leadership, and unwavering faith inspire generations of Israelites. She serves as a reminder of the vital role women play in God's plan and the importance of family in our faith journeys.

Lessons from Miriam's Story:

Miriam's story offers valuable lessons for our own lives as women:

- **The Importance of Family:** Miriam's unwavering love and support for her brother are a testament to the strength of family bonds. Her actions remind us to cherish our families and support one another through thick and thin.

- **Courage in the Face of Fear:** Miriam demonstrates incredible courage, risking her own safety to watch over Moses and taking initiative to reunite him with his mother. Her story reminds us to face our fears and stand up for what we believe in.

- **Faith as a Guiding Light:** Throughout her life, Miriam's faith guides her actions. Her story reminds us that faith provides strength and resilience during difficult times.

Activity: A Song of Gratitude

This week, engage in a musical activity that faith and family:

1. **Creating a Song of Thanks:** Reflect on things you're grateful for. Write down keywords or phrases on a piece of paper.

2. **Compose Your Melody:** Using a simple melody or a familiar tune, create a short song, expressing your gratitude to God.

3. **Performance Time:** Practice your song and then perform it. This can be a fun way to express your faith and celebrate.

Remember:

Miriam's story reminds us of the power of faith, and courage. Just like Miriam stood by her brother, we can find strength and support in our own families. By nurturing our faith and facing challenges with courage, we can overcome obstacles and create our own journeys of hope and resilience.

Group Activity:

Discuss the challenges they faced and how Miriam's courage and quick thinking helped ensure Moses' survival. Later in the week, read the story of the "Song of the Sea" (Exodus 15:20-21). Sing or recite the song together, celebrating God's power and the Israelites' freedom.

BIBLE READING: Week 49

Day 337: 2 Maccabees 13-14, Sirach 36, John 7:14-36

2 Maccabees 13-14

Reflection: The continued warfare and struggles of the Maccabees. Reflect on the themes of perseverance, faith, and divine intervention. How do the Maccabees' resilience and reliance on God inspire you to remain steadfast in your faith during trials?

Sirach 36

Reflection: A prayer for God's mercy and the restoration of Israel. Reflect on the themes of mercy, restoration, and God's faithfulness. How does this prayer encourage you to seek God's mercy and trust in His power to restore and renew?

John 7:14-36

Reflection: Jesus teaches at the Feast of Tabernacles, revealing His divine mission and facing opposition. Reflect on the themes of divine teaching, revelation, and opposition. How does Jesus' teaching challenge you to seek deeper understanding and stand firm in your faith despite opposition?

Day 338: 2 Maccabees 15, Sirach 37, John 7:37-52

2 Maccabees 15

Reflection: The final victory of Judas Maccabeus over Nicanor. Reflect on the themes of faith, victory, and divine assistance. How does Judas' trust in God and subsequent victory encourage you to place your trust in God during battles in your life?

Sirach 37

Reflection: Advice on choosing friends and counselors. Reflect on the themes of wisdom, friendship, and discernment. How do Sirach's teachings guide you in forming wise and trustworthy relationships?

John 7:37-52

Reflection: Jesus speaks about living water and causes division among the people. Reflect on the themes of spiritual thirst, belief, and division. How does Jesus' promise of living water inspire you to seek Him for your spiritual needs?

Day 339: Acts 1:1-2:13, Sirach 38, John 7:53-8:11

Acts 1:1-2:13

Reflection: The ascension of Jesus and the coming of the Holy Spirit at Pentecost. Reflect on the themes of promise, empowerment, and witness. How does the coming of the Holy Spirit equip you to be a witness for Christ?

Sirach 38

Reflection: The importance of physicians and healing. Reflect on the themes of health, healing, and God's provision. How do Sirach's teachings encourage you to value and seek proper medical care while trusting in God's healing power?

John 7:53-8:11

Reflection: The story of the woman caught in adultery and Jesus' response. Reflect on the themes of mercy, judgment, and forgiveness. How does Jesus' response challenge you to show mercy and forgiveness to others?

Day 340: Acts 2:14-3:26, Sirach 39, John 8:12-30

Acts 2:14-3:26

Reflection: Peter's sermon at Pentecost and the healing of the lame man. Reflect on the themes of proclamation, repentance, and healing. How does Peter's bold proclamation inspire you to share the gospel and believe in God's power to heal?

Sirach 39

Reflection: The wisdom and blessings of the scribe. Reflect on the themes of wisdom, study, and divine blessing. How do Sirach's teachings encourage you to seek wisdom and understanding through diligent study and reverence for God?

John 8:12-30

Reflection: Jesus declares Himself the light of the world and speaks of His relationship with the Father. Reflect on the themes of light, truth, and divine identity. How does Jesus being the light of the world impact your understanding of truth and guidance in your life?

Day 341: Acts 4-5, Sirach 40, John 8:31-59

Acts 4-5

Reflection: The early church's growth, persecution, and Ananias and Sapphira. Reflect on the themes of boldness, integrity, and community. How do the actions of the early church inspire you to live boldly and with integrity within your faith community?

Sirach 40

Reflection: Reflections on human hardship and the fear of the Lord. Reflect on the themes of suffering, hope, and divine justice. How do Sirach's insights encourage you to find hope in God despite life's hardships?

John 8:31-59

Reflection: Jesus speaks about truth, freedom, and His identity. Reflect on the themes of freedom, truth, and divine sonship. How does Jesus' teaching on truth and freedom challenge you to embrace His identity and message fully?

Day 342: Acts 6:1-8:3, Sirach 41, John 9

Acts 6:1-8:3

Reflection: The appointment of the seven deacons and Stephen's martyrdom. Reflect on the themes of service, faithfulness, and sacrifice. How does the example of Stephen inspire you to serve faithfully and stand firm in your faith even unto death?

Sirach 41

Reflection: The inevitability of death and the importance of a good name. Reflect on the themes of mortality, legacy, and righteousness. How do Sirach's teachings encourage you to live a life that leaves a lasting, positive legacy?

John 9

Reflection: Jesus heals a man born blind and the ensuing controversy. Reflect on the themes of spiritual sight, faith, and opposition. How does this miracle challenge you to see with eyes of faith and to trust Jesus amid opposition?

Day 343: Acts 8:4-9:43, Sirach 42, John 10:1-21

Acts 8:4-9:43

Reflection: The spread of the gospel in Samaria and the conversion of Saul. Reflect on the themes of evangelism, transformation, and divine calling. How do the stories of Philip and Saul inspire you to share the gospel and to believe in God's power to transform lives?

Sirach 42

Reflection: Warnings against shameful behavior and reflections on God's creation. Reflect on the themes of conduct, wisdom, and divine creation. How do Sirach's warnings and reflections guide you to live wisely and appreciate God's creation?

John 10:1-21

Reflection: Jesus as the Good Shepherd who lays down His life for the sheep. Reflect on the themes of guidance, sacrifice, and relationship. How does Jesus' role as the Good Shepherd comfort and guide you in your walk with Him?

WEEK 50: Spiritual Direction: Seeking Guidance on Your Faith Journey

Welcome back, Faithful and Fierce women! As we continue this transformative exploration of faith, let's delve into a powerful tool for ongoing growth - spiritual direction. Spiritual direction is a sacred practice where you receive personalized guidance and support on your faith journey. This week, we explore the concept of spiritual direction, its benefits, and how Catholic women can embark on this enriching experience.

A Journey of Support and Growth:

Imagine having a trusted mentor who walks alongside you on your faith journey, offering guidance, encouragement, and a safe space for reflection. That's the essence of spiritual direction. Here's why it's valuable for Catholic women:

- **Deepened Self-Awareness:** A spiritual director helps you explore your faith experiences, motivations, and challenges. This introspection fosters a deeper understanding of yourself and your relationship with God.

- **Discernment and Decision-Making:** Life throws curveballs, and sometimes faith-based decisions can feel complex. A spiritual director can help you discern God's will in your life and navigate challenges with clarity.

- **Personalized Growth:** Spiritual direction isn't a one-size-fits-all approach. Your director tailors their guidance to your unique needs and goals, fostering your personal growth in faith.

Beyond Inspiration: Embracing Spiritual Direction

Spiritual direction isn't about judgment or coercion; it's about offering support and fostering deeper reflection. Here's how Catholic women can embrace this practice:

- **Understanding Spiritual Direction:** Spiritual direction differs from confession or therapy. It's a dedicated time for focused conversation about your faith journey.

- **Finding a Spiritual Director:** Many priests, religious sisters, and lay people serve as spiritual directors. Talk to your priest, trusted friends, or faith mentors for recommendations.

- **Setting Expectations:** Discuss your goals with your spiritual director and establish ground rules around frequency and structure of your meetings.

Challenge: Embarking on Your Guided Journey

This week, I challenge you to take a concrete step towards spiritual direction:

- **Research Spiritual Direction:** Explore online resources, books, or articles about spiritual direction. Gain a clear understanding of the practice and its benefits.

- **Consider Seeking a Spiritual Director:** Reflect on whether seeking a spiritual director feels like a right fit for you at this stage in your faith journey.

- **Start Your Search:** If seeking a spiritual director feels right, talk to your priest, religious communities in your area, or Catholic organizations for recommendations.

Remember, dear sisters, spiritual direction is a powerful tool for growth. Embrace it as an opportunity to deepen your faith, gain clarity on your path, and experience the joy of a guided journey towards a more fulfilling relationship with God.

Beyond This Book:

As you conclude this faith-enriching journey, remember:

- **Be Patient:** Finding the right spiritual director may take time. Approach the search with an open mind and trust in God's guidance.

- **Embrace the Process:** Spiritual direction is a journey, not a destination. Be open to the insights and challenges your director offers, and be prepared to invest time and effort into your own growth.

- **Maintain Open Communication:** Honest and open communication is crucial for a successful spiritual direction relationship. Don't hesitate to voice your concerns or ask questions.

BIBLE READING: Week 50

Day 344: Acts 10-11, Sirach 43, John 10:22-42

Acts 10-11

Reflection: The conversion of Cornelius and Peter's vision. Reflect on the themes of divine guidance, inclusivity, and the work of the Holy Spirit. How do Peter's experiences challenge you to embrace God's vision for reaching all people?

Sirach 43

Reflection: Praise of God's creation and majesty. Reflect on the themes of awe, creation, and divine power. How does Sirach's depiction of creation inspire you to worship God and appreciate the beauty of the world around you?

John 10:22-42

Reflection: Jesus at the Feast of Dedication, declaring His divinity. Reflect on the themes of belief, identity, and opposition. How does Jesus' declaration of being one with the Father strengthen your faith and understanding of His divine nature?

Day 345: Acts 12-13, Sirach 44, John 11:1-54

Acts 12-13

Reflection: The miraculous rescue of Peter and the missionary journeys of Paul and Barnabas. Reflect on the themes of deliverance, mission, and the spread of the gospel. How do the stories of Peter's rescue and Paul's mission inspire you to trust in God's deliverance and share the gospel boldly?

Sirach 44

Reflection: Praise of famous men and their virtues. Reflect on the themes of legacy, virtue, and remembrance. How does Sirach's praise of these figures inspire you to live a life worthy of remembrance and honor?

John 11:1-54

Reflection: The raising of Lazarus and the reaction of the Jewish leaders. Reflect on the themes of resurrection, belief, and opposition. How does Jesus' miracle of raising Lazarus strengthen your belief in His power over life and death?

Day 346: Acts 14:1-15:35, Sirach 45, John 11:55-12:19

Acts 14:1-15:35

Reflection: Paul and Barnabas' missionary journey and the Council at Jerusalem. Reflect on the themes of unity, mission, and resolving conflict. How do the efforts of Paul and Barnabas and the decisions of the Council encourage you to pursue unity and mission in your faith community?

Sirach 45

Reflection: Praise of Moses, Aaron, and Phinehas. Reflect on the themes of leadership, faithfulness, and divine favor. How do the examples of Moses, Aaron, and Phinehas inspire you to lead with faithfulness and seek God's favor?

John 11:55-12:19

Reflection: The plot to kill Jesus and His anointing at Bethany. Reflect on the themes of sacrifice, devotion, and opposition. How does Mary's act of anointing Jesus and the plot against Him deepen your understanding of sacrificial love and devotion?

Day 347: Acts 15:36-16:40, Sirach 46, John 12:20-36

Acts 15:36-16:40

Reflection: The missionary journeys of Paul and Silas, and the conversion of Lydia and the jailer. Reflect on the themes of evangelism, conversion, and divine guidance. How do the conversions of Lydia and the jailer inspire you to share the gospel and trust in God's guidance?

Sirach 46

Reflection: Praise of Joshua and Caleb. Reflect on the themes of courage, faith, and divine reward. How do the stories of Joshua and Caleb encourage you to be courageous and faithful in your walk with God?

John 12:20-36

Reflection: Jesus speaks about His death and the purpose of His coming. Reflect on the themes of sacrifice, glorification, and following Jesus. How does Jesus' teaching about His impending death challenge you to follow Him and understand the purpose of His sacrifice?

Day 348: Acts 17-18, Sirach 47, John 12:37-50

Acts 17-18

Reflection: Paul's missionary work in Thessalonica, Berea, Athens, and Corinth. Reflect on the themes of proclamation, perseverance, and cultural engagement. How does Paul's approach to preaching in different cities inspire you to share the gospel with perseverance and cultural sensitivity?

Sirach 47

Reflection: Praise of David and Solomon. Reflect on the themes of leadership, wisdom, and divine favor. How do the lives of David and Solomon inspire you to seek wisdom and lead with integrity?

John 12:37-50

Reflection: Jesus speaks about unbelief and judgment. Reflect on the themes of belief, light, and divine mission. How does Jesus' teaching on unbelief challenge you to remain steadfast in your faith and share the light of Christ with others?

Day 349: Acts 19-20, Sirach 48, John 13:1-20

Acts 19-20

Reflection: Paul's ministry in Ephesus and his farewell to the Ephesian elders. Reflect on the themes of discipleship, perseverance, and leadership. How does Paul's ministry in Ephesus and his farewell speech inspire you to persevere in discipleship and lead with dedication?

Sirach 48

Reflection: Praise of Elijah and Elisha. Reflect on the themes of prophetic ministry, miracles, and divine power. How do the lives of Elijah and Elisha inspire you to believe in God's power and seek His intervention in your life?

John 13:1-20

Reflection: Jesus washes the disciples' feet and teaches about servanthood. Reflect on the themes of humility, service, and love. How does Jesus' act of washing the disciples' feet challenge you to serve others with humility and love?

Acts 21:1-22:29

Reflection: Paul's journey to Jerusalem, his arrest, and defense before the crowd. Reflect on the themes of courage, testimony, and divine purpose. How does Paul's courage and testimony in the face of arrest inspire you to stand firm in your faith and share your testimony?

Sirach 49

Reflection: Praise of the great men of Israel's history. Reflect on the themes of legacy, faithfulness, and divine favor. How do the examples of these great men inspire you to live a life of faithfulness and seek God's favor?

John 13:21-38

Reflection: Jesus predicts His betrayal and commands the disciples to love one another. Reflect on the themes of betrayal, love, and discipleship. How does Jesus' command to love one another challenge you to show genuine love and commitment to others?

WEEK 51: Women and Contemplative Prayer: Finding Quiet Time with God

Welcome back, Faithful and Fierce women! As we continue this remarkable exploration of faith, let's turn our hearts inward and explore the transformative power of contemplative prayer. In a world filled with noise and distraction, contemplative prayer offers a sacred space for quiet reflection, allowing us to encounter the divine presence within ourselves. This week, we delve into various methods of contemplative prayer, empowering you to cultivate a deeper connection with God through stillness.

A Journey of Quiet Communion:

Contemplative prayer is not about bombarding God with requests; it's about cultivating a space of quiet attentiveness, allowing yourself to simply be present in God's presence. Here's how contemplative prayer can enrich the lives of Catholic women:

- **Stress Reduction:** In our fast-paced lives, contemplative prayer offers a much-needed respite. By quieting the mind, we can alleviate stress and anxiety, allowing ourselves to experience inner peace and tranquility.

- **Deeper Self-Awareness:** Contemplative prayer fosters introspection. By quieting the external noise, we gain a clearer understanding of our thoughts, emotions, and desires, allowing us to connect with our authentic selves and deepen our relationship with God.

- **Enhanced Discernment:** The quietude of contemplative prayer can create an environment conducive to discernment. By quieting our minds, we can become more receptive to God's will and guidance in our lives.

Beyond Inspiration: Exploring Methods of Contemplative Prayer

Contemplative prayer isn't a rigid formula; it's a personalized journey towards encountering the divine. Here are some common methods to explore:

- **Centering Prayer:** This method involves silently repeating a chosen sacred word or phrase as a way to focus the mind and quiet distractions.

- **Lectio Divina (Divine Reading):** This practice involves meditative reading of scripture, followed by reflection and prayerful response.

- **Ignatian Contemplation:** Developed by St. Ignatius of Loyola, this method uses scripture or an image to spark guided reflection and prayer.

- **Breath Prayer:** Connecting your breath to a simple prayer phrase fosters focus and allows you to enter a state of peaceful contemplation.

Action Step: Embracing Quiet Reflection

This week, I challenge you to dedicate time to contemplative prayer using a chosen method:

- **Choose a Method:** Research the various methods described above or explore other forms of contemplative prayer that resonate with you.

- **Find a Quiet Space:** Create a dedicated space for prayer, free from distractions. This could be a simple corner of your home, a church pew, or a peaceful outdoor setting.

- **Set a Timer:** Begin with short sessions, gradually increasing the time as you become more comfortable with contemplative prayer.

- **Embrace the Journey:** Contemplative prayer can be challenging at first. Don't get discouraged by wandering thoughts. Gently guide your focus back to your chosen method and trust that even brief moments of quiet stillness hold immense value.

Remember, dear sisters, contemplative prayer is a gift. Be patient with yourself and trust that through dedicated practice, you will cultivate a deeper connection with God and experience the profound peace that comes from encountering the divine within.

Beyond This Book:

As you conclude this empowering journey, remember:

- **Consistency is Key:** Regular practice is crucial for reaping the benefits of contemplative prayer. Commit to setting aside dedicated time for quiet reflection, even if it's just a few minutes each day.

- **Join a Community:** Consider joining a contemplative prayer group or online community for support and encouragement. Sharing your experiences with others can enrich your practice.

- **Embrace the Mystery:** Contemplative prayer is not about achieving a specific outcome; it's about surrendering to the mystery of God's presence. Be open to the unforeseen ways in which God will touch your heart through stillness.

BIBLE READING: Week 51

Day 351: Acts 22:30-24:27, Sirach 50, John 14

Acts 22:30-24:27

Reflection: Paul before the Sanhedrin and his trial before Felix. Reflect on the themes of perseverance, testimony, and divine protection. How does Paul's unwavering commitment to his mission inspire you to stand firm in your faith and trust in God's protection?

Sirach 50

Reflection: The praise of Simon the high priest. Reflect on the themes of leadership, worship, and divine blessing. How does the example of Simon's leadership and devotion to worship inspire you to seek excellence in your own spiritual leadership and worship practices?

John 14

Reflection: Jesus comforts His disciples and promises the Holy Spirit. Reflect on the themes of peace, the Holy Spirit, and abiding in Jesus. How do Jesus' promises and teachings in this chapter encourage you to rely on the Holy Spirit and find peace in His presence?

Day 352: Acts 25-26, Sirach 51, John 15:1-10

Acts 25-26

Reflection: Paul's defense before Festus and King Agrippa. Reflect on the themes of courage, witness, and divine calling. How does Paul's bold witness before high officials inspire you to share your faith courageously and trust in God's calling for your life?

Sirach 51

Reflection: A prayer of thanksgiving. Reflect on the themes of gratitude, deliverance, and praise. How does this prayer of thanksgiving encourage you to cultivate a heart of gratitude and praise for God's deliverance in your life?

John 15:1-10

Reflection: Jesus teaches about the vine and the branches. Reflect on the themes of abiding, fruitfulness, and love. How does Jesus' analogy of the vine and branches challenge you to remain deeply connected to Him and bear fruit through His love?

Day 353: Acts 27-28, Hebrews 1, John 15:11-17

Acts 27-28

Reflection: Paul's journey to Rome and his ministry there. Reflect on the themes of faith, perseverance, and divine providence. How does Paul's unwavering faith and perseverance during his journey to Rome encourage you to trust in God's providence in difficult circumstances?

Hebrews 1

Reflection: The supremacy of God's Son. Reflect on the themes of divinity, revelation, and authority. How does the portrayal of Jesus' supremacy in this chapter deepen your understanding of His divine nature and authority?

John 15:11-17

Reflection: Jesus commands His disciples to love one another. Reflect on the themes of joy, love, and friendship. How does Jesus' command to love one another challenge you to cultivate deeper, sacrificial love in your relationships?

Day 354: Revelation 1, Hebrews 2, John 15:18-16:4a

Revelation 1

Reflection: The vision of the Son of Man. Reflect on the themes of revelation, majesty, and divine presence. How does John's vision of the glorified Christ inspire you to live with a sense of awe and reverence for His majesty and authority?

Hebrews 2

Reflection: Jesus made fully human. Reflect on the themes of incarnation, salvation, and solidarity. How does the understanding of Jesus sharing in our humanity deepen your appreciation for His work of salvation and His solidarity with us in our struggles?

John 15:18-16:4a

Reflection: Jesus warns about the world's hatred. Reflect on the themes of persecution, witness, and perseverance. How does Jesus' warning prepare you to face opposition and encourage you to remain steadfast in your witness for Him?

Day 355: Revelation 2, Hebrews 3, John 16:4b-15

Revelation 2

Reflection: Letters to the seven churches. Reflect on the themes of faithfulness, repentance, and reward. How do the messages to the seven churches challenge you to examine your own spiritual condition and heed Jesus' call to faithfulness and repentance?

Hebrews 3

Reflection: Jesus greater than Moses. Reflect on the themes of faithfulness, rest, and obedience. How does the comparison of Jesus to Moses inspire you to trust in Jesus' superior leadership and strive for the rest promised to the faithful?

John 16:4b-15

Reflection: The work of the Holy Spirit. Reflect on the themes of guidance, truth, and conviction. How does Jesus' teaching on the Holy Spirit's work encourage you to seek the Spirit's guidance and rely on His truth and conviction in your life?

Day 356: Revelation 3, Hebrews 4, John 16:16-33

Revelation 3

Reflection: Messages to the remaining churches. Reflect on the themes of vigilance, repentance, and reward. How do the messages to the churches challenge you to stay vigilant in your faith, repent where needed, and seek the rewards promised to the faithful?

Hebrews 4

Reflection: The promise of rest. Reflect on the themes of Sabbath rest, faith, and God's word. How does the promise of rest encourage you to trust in God's promises and find peace and rest through faith in Him?

John 16:16-33

Reflection: Jesus speaks about His departure and the disciples' grief turning to joy. Reflect on the themes of sorrow, joy, and peace. How does Jesus' assurance of joy and peace amidst trials encourage you to find hope and strength in Him?

Day 357: Revelation 4-5, Hebrews 5, John 17

Revelation 4-5

Reflection: The throne room of heaven and the Lamb who is worthy. Reflect on the themes of worship, sovereignty, and redemption. How do the visions of the heavenly throne and the Lamb inspire you to worship God's sovereignty and celebrate the redemption He provides?

Hebrews 5

Reflection: Jesus the high priest. Reflect on the themes of priesthood, obedience, and spiritual maturity. How does understanding Jesus as our high priest encourage you to grow in spiritual maturity and follow His example of obedience?

John 17

Reflection: Jesus' high priestly prayer. Reflect on the themes of unity, sanctification, and mission. How does Jesus' prayer for His disciples challenge you to seek unity, holiness, and a commitment to His mission in the world?

WEEK 52: Women and Eucharistic Adoration: Encountering Christ in the Blessed Sacrament

Welcome back, Faithful and Fierce women! As we reach the final week of this faith-enriching exploration, let's delve into a profoundly intimate practice – Eucharistic Adoration. In the quiet presence of the Blessed Sacrament, we encounter Christ not through a book or a sermon, but in a real and tangible way. This week, we explore the power of Eucharistic Adoration, its significance for Catholic women, and how it can transform your relationship with God.

A Journey of Divine Intimacy:

The Eucharist is not merely a symbol; it is the real presence of Jesus Christ, body, blood, soul, and divinity. Eucharistic Adoration offers a sacred space to encounter this presence in a profoundly intimate way. Here's why it holds immense value for Catholic women:

- **Deepened Relationship with Christ:** Adoration allows us to spend uninterrupted time with Jesus, pouring out our hearts, expressing gratitude, or simply basking in His loving presence.

- **Quiet Reflection and Discernment:** The stillness of Adoration fosters introspection and allows us to discern God's will for our lives. This quiet space can be a wellspring of clarity and direction.

- **Spiritual Renewal and Peace:** In the presence of Jesus, we find solace and strength. The anxieties and burdens of daily life can melt away as we experience the peace and comfort radiating from the Blessed Sacrament.

Beyond Inspiration: Unveiling the Power of Adoration

Eucharistic Adoration isn't about elaborate rituals; it's about a sincere encounter with Christ. Here's how you can embrace the transformative power of Adoration:

- **Understanding Adoration:** Explore the theology of the Real Presence and learn about the practice of Eucharistic Adoration. This understanding will deepen your reverence and appreciation for this sacred practice.

- **Finding Adoration Opportunities:** Many churches offer Adoration chapels open for quiet prayer throughout the day or week. Research Adoration schedules in your area.

- **Approaching the Blessed Sacrament:** There's no right or wrong way to pray during Adoration. Come with an open heart, express gratitude, share your burdens, or simply sit in peaceful silence.

Challenge: A Rendezvous with the Divine

This week, I challenge you to embark on a transformative experience:

- **Visit a Church:** Find a church with a dedicated Adoration chapel or a time designated for Eucharistic Adoration.

- **Prepare for the Encounter:** Dedicate some time before your visit to quiet reflection. Consider what you might like to express to Jesus or what areas of your life you might want to lay before Him.

- **Spend Time in Adoration:** There's no prescribed duration. Allow yourself to be guided by the Holy Spirit. Even a brief encounter can be profoundly impactful.

- **Reflect on the Experience:** After your prayer time, take some moments to reflect on what transpired within you. Did you experience a sense of peace? Did any insights or feelings emerge during your time in Adoration?

Remember, dear sisters, Eucharistic Adoration is a gift, a sacred space to encounter the Divine Love in its purest form. Embrace it as a source of strength, renewal, and a transformative experience that deepens your relationship with Jesus Christ.

Beyond This Book:

As you conclude this faith-enriching journey, remember:

- **Make Adoration a Habit:** Integrate Adoration into your spiritual routine. Regular visits will deepen your connection with Christ and become a source of ongoing strength and peace.

- **Share the Experience:** Talk to other women about your experiences with Adoration. Encourage them to discover the transformative power of this sacred practice.

- **Live a Life Reflecting His Love:** Let the love and peace you experience during Adoration radiate outwards, influencing your interactions and actions in the world.

BIBLE READING: Week 52

Day 358: Revelation 6-7, Hebrews 6, John 18:1-27

Revelation 6-7

Reflection: The opening of the seven seals and the sealing of the 144,000. Reflect on the themes of judgment, protection, and salvation. How does the imagery of the seals and the sealing of God's people encourage you to trust in His protection and look forward to His ultimate salvation?

Hebrews 6

Reflection: A call to maturity and the certainty of God's promise. Reflect on the themes of spiritual growth, perseverance, and hope. How does this chapter challenge you to pursue spiritual maturity and hold firmly to the hope set before you?

John 18:1-27

Reflection: Jesus' arrest and Peter's denial. Reflect on the themes of betrayal, fear, and faithfulness. How does Peter's denial and Jesus' response to His arrest inspire you to remain faithful and courageous in your walk with Christ?

Day 359: Revelation 8-9, Hebrews 7, John 18:28-40

Revelation 8-9

Reflection: The sounding of the seven trumpets. Reflect on the themes of judgment, repentance, and God's sovereignty. How do the trumpet judgments call you to examine your life and respond with repentance and trust in God's sovereignty?

Hebrews 7

Reflection: The priesthood of Melchizedek and Jesus. Reflect on the themes of intercession, eternal priesthood, and salvation. How does understanding Jesus as our eternal high priest encourage you to rely on His intercession and the salvation He provides?

John 18:28-40

Reflection: Jesus before Pilate. Reflect on the themes of truth, kingship, and sacrifice. How does Jesus' interaction with Pilate challenge you to bear witness to the truth and acknowledge Jesus as your King?

Day 360: Revelation 10-11, Hebrews 8, John 19:1-30

Revelation 10-11

Reflection: The mighty angel and the two witnesses. Reflect on the themes of prophecy, witness, and God's sovereignty. How do the messages and actions of the angel and the two witnesses inspire you to faithfully proclaim God's truth and trust in His sovereign plan?

Hebrews 8

Reflection: The new covenant. Reflect on the themes of covenant, forgiveness, and transformation. How does the promise of the new covenant encourage you to embrace the forgiveness and transformation offered through Jesus?

John 19:1-30

Reflection: The crucifixion of Jesus. Reflect on the themes of sacrifice, love, and redemption. How does Jesus' sacrificial death on the cross deepen your understanding of God's love and the redemption He provides?

Day 361: Revelation 12-13, Hebrews 9, John 19:31-42

Revelation 12-13

Reflection: The woman, the dragon, and the two beasts. Reflect on the themes of spiritual warfare, perseverance, and faith. How do these visions of conflict and victory encourage you to persevere in your faith amidst spiritual battles?

Hebrews 9

Reflection: The earthly and heavenly sanctuaries. Reflect on the themes of atonement, purification, and Christ's sacrifice. How does the contrast between the old and new covenants deepen your appreciation for Christ's once-for-all sacrifice and the purification He offers?

John 19:31-42

Reflection: Jesus' burial. Reflect on the themes of death, fulfillment, and hope. How does the account of Jesus' burial fulfill prophecy and provide hope for the resurrection and new life in Him?

Day 362: Revelation 14-16, Hebrews 10, John 20:1-18

Revelation 14-16

Reflection: The Lamb and the 144,000, the harvest of the earth, and the seven bowls of God's wrath. Reflect on the themes of judgment, righteousness, and God's wrath. How do these chapters challenge you to live righteously and prepare for God's final judgment?

Hebrews 10

Reflection: A call to persevere in faith. Reflect on the themes of sacrifice, perseverance, and community. How does the call to persevere in faith and encourage one another inspire you to remain steadfast in your walk with God and support your faith community?

John 20:1-18

Reflection: The resurrection of Jesus. Reflect on the themes of resurrection, hope, and transformation. How does the resurrection of Jesus provide hope and inspire you to live a transformed life in the power of His resurrection?

Day 363: Revelation 17-18, Hebrews 11, John 20:19-31

Revelation 17-18

Reflection: The fall of Babylon. Reflect on the themes of judgment, corruption, and God's sovereignty. How do the judgments on Babylon challenge you to evaluate the influences in your life and trust in God's ultimate victory over evil?

Hebrews 11

Reflection: Faith in action. Reflect on the themes of faith, obedience, and endurance. How do the examples of faith in Hebrews 11 inspire you to live out your faith with obedience and endurance, even in challenging circumstances?

John 20:19-31

Reflection: Jesus appears to His disciples and to Thomas. Reflect on the themes of belief, peace, and mission. How does Jesus' post-resurrection appearance strengthen your faith, bring you peace, and challenge you to embrace the mission He gives?

Day 364: Revelation 19-20, Hebrews 12, John 21:1-14

Revelation 19-20

Reflection: The return of Christ and the final judgment. Reflect on the themes of victory, judgment, and eternal life. How do the visions of Christ's return and the final judgment inspire you to live with hope and prepare for His coming?

Hebrews 12

Reflection: Running the race of faith. Reflect on the themes of discipline, endurance, and holiness. How does the call to run the race with endurance and pursue holiness encourage you to remain steadfast in your faith journey?

John 21:1-14

Reflection: Jesus appears to His disciples by the Sea of Galilee. Reflect on the themes of restoration, provision, and commissioning. How does Jesus' interaction with His disciples after the resurrection encourage you to seek restoration, trust in His provision, and embrace His commission?

Day 365: Revelation 21-22, Hebrews 13, John 21:15-25

Revelation 21-22

Reflection: The new heaven and new earth. Reflect on the themes of renewal, hope, and eternal life. How do the visions of the new heaven and new earth inspire you to live with hope and anticipation for the fulfillment of God's promises?

Hebrews 13

Reflection: Concluding exhortations. Reflect on the themes of love, hospitality, and faithfulness. How do the final exhortations in Hebrews encourage you to live a life of love, hospitality, and faithfulness to God?

John 21:15-25

Reflection: Jesus reinstates Peter. Reflect on the themes of forgiveness, restoration, and discipleship. How does Jesus' reinstatement of Peter inspire you to embrace His forgiveness, seek restoration, and follow Him wholeheartedly?

Bonus Features: Deepen Your Faith Journey

Appendix 1: Glossary of Bible Terms

- **Covenant:** A binding agreement between God and His people.

- **Discernment:** The process of seeking God's will for your life.

- **Eucharist:** The sacrament of bread and wine, believed by Catholics to be the real presence of Jesus Christ.

- **Faith:** Trust and belief in God, even in the absence of complete understanding.

- **Grace:** God's undeserved love and favor bestowed upon humanity.

- **Incarnation:** The belief that God became flesh and dwelt among us in the person of Jesus Christ.

- **Kingdom of God:** The reign and rule of God, both present and future, in the hearts of believers and ultimately in the transformed world.

- **Sacrament:** A visible sign instituted by Jesus Christ to convey invisible grace.

- **Saint:** A person recognized by the Church for their exemplary life of holiness.

- **Scripture:** The inspired word of God, contained in the Old and New Testaments.

- **Sin:** Disobedience to God's will.

- **Spiritual Gift:** A unique talent or ability bestowed by the Holy Spirit to serve the Church.

- **Stewardship:** The responsibility to manage God's creation wisely.

Appendix 2: Women's Prayer Resources

- **A Prayer for Strength:** "Dear Lord, grant me the strength to face whatever challenges come my way. Empower me to overcome obstacles and persevere through difficult times. Guide me with your wisdom and fill me with your courage. Amen."

- **A Prayer for Guidance:** "Heavenly Father, as I navigate life's uncertainties, I seek your guidance. Help me discern your will for my life and open my heart to receive your wisdom. Lead me on the path you have designed for me. Amen."

- **A Prayer for Motherhood:** "Dear God, I thank you for the gift of motherhood. Bless my children and guide them on their journeys. Grant me the patience, wisdom, and strength to nurture and love them unconditionally. May I be a reflection of your love in their lives. Amen."

- **A Prayer for Peace:** "God of peace, I come to you amidst life's storms. Calm my anxieties and fill me with your serenity. Grant me the strength to face challenges with a peaceful heart. May your peace reign within me and radiate outwards to those around me. Amen."

Explore additional prayers specifically tailored to various life situations by visiting these resources:

- **The National Catholic Women's Conference:** https://www.nccw.org/

- **Catholic Relief Services Women's Prayer Corner:** https://www.crs.org/get-involved/prayer-resources

- **Magnificat Magazine:** https://bookstore.magnificat.net/booklets.html

Appendix 3: Recommended Reading List

- **The Bible:** The foundation of our faith. Start with the Gospels (Matthew, Mark, Luke, and John) to gain a deeper understanding of Jesus' life and teachings.

- **"The Story of a Soul" by St. Therese of Lisieux:** A captivating autobiography detailing the "Little Way" of spiritual perfection.

- **"Mere Christianity" by C.S. Lewis:** A clear and engaging explanation of core Christian beliefs.

- **"Forgotten God" by Francis Chan:** A thought-provoking exploration of living a life centered on God's will.

- **"The Reed of God" by Caryll Houselander:** A profound and poetic reflection on the spiritual life.

- **"Catholic Women Saints" by Barbara Calamari & Sandra Miesel:** Inspiring stories of remarkable women who shaped the Catholic Church.

- **"Theology of the Body" by Pope John Paul II:** A groundbreaking exploration of human sexuality and relationships from a Catholic perspective.

Websites and Online Resources:

- **Catholic Online:** https://www.catholic.org/

- **Aleteia:** https://aleteia.org/category/inspiring-stories/

- **Busted Halo:** https://bustedhalo.com/

- **Formed.org:** https://formed.org/ (Subscription-based platform with Catholic movies, studies, and talks)

May God Bless You Abundantly!

Made in the USA
Coppell, TX
03 January 2025

43829217R00195